Classrooms
of
WONDER
and
WISDOM

DATE DUE

JAN 04 2015			

JAN 26 2011

Demco, Inc. 38-293

Dedicated to
Greg,
Molly, &
Julia,
three remarkably unique
and
wonderful
people.

Classrooms
of
WONDER
and
WISDOM

Reading, Writing, and Critical Thinking for the 21st Century

Kurtis S. Meredith
Jeannie L. Steele

CORWIN
A SAGE Company

For information:

Corwin
A SAGE Company
2455 Teller Road
Thousand Oaks,
    California 91320
(800) 233-9936
Fax: (800) 417-2466
www.corwin.com

SAGE Ltd.
1 Oliver's Yard
55 City Road
London EC1Y 1SP
United Kingdom

SAGE India Pvt. Ltd.
B 1/I 1 Mohan Cooperative
    Industrial Area
Mathura Road, New Delhi 110 044
India

SAGE Asia-Pacific Pte. Ltd.
33 Pekin Street #02-01
Far East Square
Singapore 048763

Printed in the United States of America.

Library of Congress Cataloging-in-Publication Data

Meredith, Kurtis S.
Classrooms of wonder and wisdom : reading, writing, and critical thinking for the 21st century /
Kurtis S. Meredith, Jeannie L. Steele.
    p. cm.
Includes bibliographical references and index.
ISBN 978-1-4129-1815-2 (pbk.)

1. Language arts. 2. Critical thinking—Study and teaching. 3. Effective teaching. I. Steele,
Jeannie L. II. Title.

LB1576.M453 2011
428.0071—dc22   2010031220

This book is printed on acid-free paper.

10 11 12 13 14 10 9 8 7 6 5 4 3 2 1

Acquisitions Editor:	Cathy Hernandez
Editorial Assistant:	Allison Scott
Production Editor:	Cassandra Margaret Seibel
Copy Editor:	Jeannette K. McCoy
Typesetter:	C&M Digitals (P) Ltd.
Proofreader:	Caryne Brown
Indexer:	Sheila Bodell
Cover Designer:	Michael Dubowe

Contents

Preface

PREPARING STUDENTS FOR THE 21ST CENTURY

Today, we are witness to an information explosion of unprecedented proportions. The volumes of new information gathered every hour dwarfs even the most outrageous predictions from only 10 years ago. The February 27, 2010, *Economist* special report on the "data deluge" provides some startling examples. "Everywhere you look," the article reported, "the quantity of information in the world is soaring. According to one estimate, mankind created 150 exabytes (billion gigabytes or two to the 60th power bytes) of data in 2005. This year, it will create 1,200 exabytes" (Cukier, 2010, p. 11). Mind-bending evidence is offered from all corners of the human experience. For instance, consider the following:

- Facebook is home to 40 billion photos.
- Wal-Mart processes one million customer transactions every hour, entering data into a 2.5 petabyte (two to the 50th power) database, which is 167 times larger than all the books in the Library of Congress.
- In 2000, the Sloan Digital Sky Survey collected in a few weeks more data than had been collected previously in human history. By 2016, the next generation telescope will collect that much information every five days.

At the present rate, the amount of information available increases tenfold every five years. As the article in the *Economist* (Cukier, 2010) concludes, this surge of information " . . . is already starting to transform business, government, science and everyday life." (p. 11)

The extraordinary production of information coupled with unprecedented information access for most makes it impossible to conclude that enough content can be taught in schools to make a sizable dent in available knowledge. Direct content instruction will constitute only a small fraction of any content-area information base and represent only a fraction of the information students will need to know throughout their lifetime.

As more and more societies wrestle with the transition to and the fallout from a global economy, the central question educators must ask is "How can we best prepare students for life in the 21st century?" While learning content is essential, understanding learning processes is equally important. It is imperative that students acquire the skills for learning, take responsibility for their own learning, and recognize that learning is only fully accomplished when their knowledge level is sufficient to foster critical thought and informed actions (Meredith, 2002). Students must be prepared to successfully engage with and manipulate new information while seeking, through deliberate inquiry, answers to their own questions. Their own independence will rely on their capacity to consider information and ideas irrespective of others and act in accordance with their own informed judgments, making information not only useful but life sustaining. Their prosperity and their contribution to society will depend on their ability to examine new ideas from multiple perspectives and make judgments about the veracity and value of various ideas based on their individual and community needs and purposes. In short, if we are to prepare our students to manage and benefit from the incredibly exciting flow of information and ideas that populate their universe and, at the same time, protect them from the harm that can come from being unable to sort information into the useful or the useless—or as the *Economist* suggests, "pluck the diamonds from the waste"—then they will need experiences interacting and managing complex ideas and information. Responding to these 21st-century demands requires introducing into classrooms alternative constructs for teaching and learning. This text offers an alternative instructional approach founded upon what teachers already do well while leading students through the kinds of learning experiences that prepare them to cope with 21st-century demands.

The instructional model offered here is offered knowing, in fact counting on, practicing teachers and other participants being a protective and careful lot. Each year, teachers are challenged by a disparate cohort of students who inhabit their classrooms and who are entrusted to their care. Each class presents its own set of demands, needs, eccentricities, and each must travel from an array of starting points toward a somewhat uniform destination. The tasks and skills required to get everyone from here to there are numerous and complex. We are distant from the time when we thought the old-fashioned cattle drive model might accomplish the job. Today, when teachers gain skills and employ strategies that successfully guide students toward some of the myriad goals set for them, they are not likely to easily discard them. Thoughtful instructors engage a dynamic instructional model intended to move students seamlessly through a series of strategies to achieve a particular learning outcome. Often, there are strategies that work well but that may coexist with others that are less successful. How do we separate those successful practices from those others we know serve our students less well? How do we add new skills and strategies to an already existing instructional construct so we can take advantage of new understandings about teaching and learning without abandoning what is already working? How do we know why a strategy works in one situation but is not right in another? Upon what basis does a teacher select an instructional approach for the content at any given point in the learning process? Knowing when, why, and how to employ a particular strategy is critical to effective instruction and student learning but is not always easily determined. This text will disclose a model for instructional decision making that informs teachers about where students are in their learning process. Equipped with this information and a model for understanding how, when, and why specific instructional strategies work, teachers are able to successfully guide learners through the learning process to reach achievement goals.

SYSTEMATIC AND SUPPORTIVE CHANGE EXPERIENCE

Accommodating to a new model involves change, and sometimes change is uncomfortable. This text is structured to lead readers through a change experience that is systematic and supportive. It is organized so participants may work independently, in book groups or in larger district professional development settings.

Responding to new demands and new realities requires changes not only in how we teach but also in how we organize and think about teaching and how we think about ourselves as teachers. Successfully navigating a change process demands careful planning and delivery and must respond to adult learning needs. We believe there are two key characteristics of the change process that must be present from the beginning for practicing educators to engage in an agreeable and lasting change process.

The first is that the process must build and sustain teacher confidence. Confidence can be compromised as we engage in change. Change engenders uncertainty and confusion for some. We ask ourselves if what we were doing before was wrong or perhaps inadequate. This is invariably not the case yet is a common concern as we approach professional development experiences. There are two important ways in which confidence is sustained through this change experience. Participants must be invited into the process with the confidence that what they are already doing well will be respected and protected. We begin here by acknowledging the exceptional instruction already being delivered in classrooms everywhere. As a participant, be assured you are engaging in a learning experience from a position of equality with your peers and with the authors. To support this contention, this text is presented as a conversation among educators rather than something delivered to educators. It is framed as a shared professional experience anticipating collective growth and will rely on the insights of participants to make the experience whole.

Another type of confidence we address is the confidence teachers demand before implementing something new for their students. Teachers must believe in the potential for success of any new approaches and must have confidence that they are adequately prepared for implementation. We strive to build confidence by sharing the voices of teachers engaged in instructional practice change all over the world. The professional development sequence offered here has not simply incubated in a laboratory. It has been implemented in literally thousands of classrooms and at all levels of instruction in countries around the world. From classrooms in the United States to those in Europe, Asia, and Central America, teachers have been engaged with this professional development model. These many extraordinary teachers have not been passive participants. Indeed, that has not been permitted. Participants have been partners in the development of this experience, giving their voice to content and process. They have implemented the model and strategies contained here and have done so successfully but not without making the practices their own and fashioning them, in collaboration with their peers, to meet the needs of *their* students. They participated in a series of integrated learning experiences drawn together by a powerful model for teaching and learning that classroom teachers have employed in their instruction with great success. Confidence also comes from and is sustained by providing authentic learning opportunities where strategies are modeled within the context of content-specific instruction.

The second key characteristic of successful, lasting change is derived from this latter source of confidence and relates to time and opportunity. Teachers must be given adequate time and opportunity to develop mastery of models and strategies before engaging their students. The professional development sequence that unfolds here allows you opportunities to learn through direct experience and then through practice with your own curriculum to become comfortable with just how to implement new approaches in your own classroom. This enables you to proceed, knowing you have the necessary skills and understanding to be successful.

The audiences for this text include, among others

- inservice and preservice teachers,
- district professional development specialists,
- curriculum development specialists,
- school administrators,
- university teacher preparation faculty, and
- interested educators.

The text is presented so an individual reader can follow the sequence, applying the content to his or her instructional practice. However, we encourage readers to come together in book groups or other forms of learning communities where questions can be raised, experiences shared. Importantly, throughout the process, dedicated inservice and preservice teachers can find support for an instructional approach that promises to lead to both enhanced student learning and enhanced student capacity to be effective lifelong learners.

PROFESSIONAL DEVELOPMENT SEQUENCE STRUCTURE

This course of study is designed for immediate implementation. It blends theory with practice to provide implementers with substantiation for their teaching while detailing instructional approaches for classroom implementation across grades and content areas. Being practice oriented, it leads to immediate changes in classroom practice. Because changes occur immediately, school administrators must be informed as to what changes are taking place so they will recognize positive growth in professional practice. Administrators can inhibit positive change when uninformed. Their involvement in the change process not only provides sanction, it also allows them to make informed judgments about implementation process and success, enabling them to provide an ongoing, positive contribution to professional development outcomes.

At this point, it is probably clear that here you will encounter a teaching-learning model experientially. The text is organized so you will first experience the various strategies within a lesson embedded within a model framework. This first encounter is followed by a careful deconstruction of the lesson to make the underlying functions of the applied strategies and the learning experience whole and transparent. Then, you will be asked to consider how the methods or strategies might be implemented in your classroom within your curriculum. If working within a cohort or book group, foundational to success is creation of a positive learning community. You are encouraged to enter into your learning community with an open, positive frame of mind. This does not suggest you enter without a fair degree of skepticism. Open and positive merely imply a willingness to hear, understand, consider thoughtfully, and try out in practice what is being shared. As we emphasized from the beginning, good teachers weigh carefully new instructional approaches before incorporating them permanently into their instructional retinue. Care and caution are warranted. What is asked here is simply that, as a participant, you commit to implementation in good faith in your own practice using your own content. After several implementations and appropriate modifications, if best judgment and student responses indicate implementation of a strategy is ineffective for you, then it should be discussed honestly in your learning community and, if other modifications are not offered, discontinued.

The three-phase instructional model that underscores this text is well supported, reflecting research on how people learn best. Models approximating the thinking and learning processes have been presented in numerous forms by numerous authors and researchers; some of whom include Temple and Gillet (1996); Vaughn and Estes (1986); Ogle (1986); Tierney, Readence, and Dishner (1985) and Herber (1970). The model here elaborates a means by which teachers can think about, organize, and guide students through the cognitive process in which learners must engage so that they might truly benefit from that learning experience.

In the first portion of this Professional Development Sequence (PDS), one activity is modeled at each stage of the framework for illustrative purposes. It is important to realize that the strategies and activities modeled at each stage of the framework are not limited to those presented in these model lessons. There exists a host of strategies that can be used effectively at each stage. Throughout the text, more strategies are added to each framework phase with the goal of building a large repertoire of strategies by phase. The number of strategies for each phase is, however, limited only by the imagination and creativity of teachers and students to design and implement more strategies.

CHAPTER BY CHAPTER

Chapter 1 provides a clear picture of how this professional development sequence unfolds. It will describe a linear process, conceptualized within a framework for teaching and learning that is cyclical in nature and intended to pattern more closely how people actually learn. From the outset, participants are expected to take an active role in the professional development process by engaging with the text and the tasks outlined. The authors' assumptions about teaching and learning and the philosophical perspectives underlying conceptual framework of the PDS are also described. Each chapter will build on the previous chapters with respect to applications of the framework for thinking and learning to the classroom instruction. Each chapter begins and ends with clear expectations for learning along with the development of plans for immediate implementation. Finally, each chapter provides opportunities for participants to work together and reflect on the content and its impact on their teaching.

Chapter 2 presents the first experiential lesson through which the basic framework for teaching and learning is presented. Participants will experience a content lesson as students of that content and then debrief the experience as pedagogs. As participants do so, the framework is exposed within a genuine learning environment. Participants are then asked to begin developing plans for application of the framework to their own teaching. This sets the pattern for the remainder of the PDS of genuine learning experience followed by analysis, planning, and practice.

In **Chapter 3,** the framework is applied to a narrative text experience. Readers are engaged in a multitiered application of the framework with questioning at the heart of the guided reading lesson. The critical role of questioning and engaging students at multiple levels through self-interest is addressed in practical ways. A variety of instructional strategies are modeled within the framework application, making transparent when and why particular strategies are employed.

Chapter 4 details how critical thought is best incorporated within classroom instruction and why. Critical thinking is presented as a complex, multilayered event that must be planned for rather than hoped for. Readers will experience an enhanced lecture on critical thought proffered within the framework, modeling strategies for student engagement.

Chapter 5 focuses on writing for thinking and models three writing for thinking strategies. Additional strategies are also presented within the three phases of the framework. A discussion of the importance of using writing as a tool for thinking in content-area studies is presented.

Cooperative learning and additional emphasis on fostering critical thought underscore the work in **Chapter 6**. Along with practical strategies, some discussion is offered regarding what is implied when a classroom becomes an environment for thinking and how cooperative-learning strategies can contribute to such an environment.

Chapter 7 introduces a way of thinking about literacy (reading, writing, speaking listening, and thinking) as a tool for critical thought rather than as a subject of study. Readers' workshop is used as the format for experiencing how the tool of literacy can be used to enhance learning across content and grade levels. In this chapter, a science lesson is modeled along with the now familiar debriefing. Explicit rules for engaging in a readers' workshop type experience are provided to guide planning.

Chapter 8 further explores writing for thinking approaches for content-area learning and guides learners through several framework-based strategies for content-area study. The writing process is discussed in greater detail here to make more evident the power of writing for thinking. And in **Chapter 9,** participants reflect on the PDS experience, develop specific plans for further implementation, and identify additional needs for continuing professional development. Participants are asked to reflect on the personal goals they identified from Chapter 1 and consider whether they have attained these goals and objectives and if not, what is needed to reach them.

Acknowledgments

Corwin gratefully acknowledges the contributions of the following reviewers:

Eric Combs
History and Social Studies Teacher
Fairborn High School
Bellbrook, OH

Victoria Ridgeway Gillis
Associate Professor of Reading
    Education
Clemson University
Clemson, SC

Connie Harris
Gifted Language Arts Teacher
Three Oaks Middle School
Fort Myers School
Fort Myers, FL

Meredith Lewis
Co-Director
Center for Early Childhood
    Professionals
Division of Continuing Education
Bank Street College of Education
New York, NY

Sarah L. Morris
English Teacher
Berkeley Springs High School
Berkeley Springs, WV

Tamara Rhone
History Teacher
Denver East High School
Denver, CO

David B. Root
Principal
Rocky River Middle School
Rocky River, OH

About the Authors

 **Kurtis S. Meredith** is presently serving as Interim Assistant Provost for International Programs at the University of Northern Iowa. He is also an Associate Professor in Literacy Education. He has taught and consulted with educators for over 30 years and is internationally known for his work in school restructuring and democratic educational practices. Along with Jeannie Steele, Kurt cofounded the Orava Association for Democratic Education, an organization dedicated to the professional development of teachers and the largest self-governing non-governmental organization in the Republic of Slovakia. While living in Slovakia, he received the Order of St. Gorazd, the highest civilian award for meritorious service to Slovak education. He also received UNESCO (United Nations Educational, Scientific, and Cultural Organization) recognition as coauthor of the Reading and Writing for Critical Thinking (RWCT) program, one of 25 practices recommended worldwide for crisis prevention and peace building. Closer to home, he has received the Iowa Board of Regents Award for Faculty Excellence and the University of Northern Iowa Ross A. Nielson Distinguished Service Award.

 **Jeannie L. Steele** is a professor of literacy education at the University of Northern Iowa, where she was awarded the Iowa Board of Regents Award for Faculty Excellence. Formerly a classroom teacher for over 20 years, she also served as consultant for educational reform for school districts in the United States and is Past President of the Virginia State Reading Association. She received a PhD from The University of Virginia in 1985. In more recent years, Jeannie has worked on international educational reform and is internationally respected for her work in teacher professional development. Along with Kurt Meredith, she cofounded the Orava Association for Democratic Education, an organization dedicated to the professional development of teachers and the largest self-governing nongovernmental organization in the Republic of Slovakia. While living in Slovakia, she received the Order of St. Gorazd, the highest civilian award for meritorious service to Slovak education. She also received UNESCO recognition as coauthor of the Reading and Writing for Critical Thinking (RWCT) program, one of 25 practices recommended worldwide for crisis prevention and peace building.

Introduction

To become a better teacher, I must nurture a sense of self that both does and does not depend on the responses of others.

—Parker J. Palmer

SOME HISTORY

We owe an enormous debt of gratitude to the thousands of educators with whom we have worked over the decades. These opportunities to share teaching experiences and learn from one another have been incredibly enriching. We believe it is important to share part of this background so you will have some insight into how our thinking about teaching and learning evolved. During the 1980s, we were privileged to be working with teachers across the United States in school restructuring efforts. We worked collaboratively with teachers of all grades to try to reshape instructional practice to better meet students' learning needs and improve achievement. As is always the case when we engage in professional development activities, these experiences are all at once intense, complicated, hilarious, moving, inspiring, and daunting. Each day is full of tough questions, cautious acceptance, outright rejection, creative adoption, wonderful stories, and enormous care. In the end, the push and pull of these efforts always comes down to what is best for students and, for us, what we learned from our partners in the professional development process that makes us better at what we do.

Through this work, we met thousands of educators across the country. We shared stories, spoke of hardships and successes, lamented the state of things, celebrated the resiliency of teachers and students no matter the "state of things," and spoke with hope and optimism about the future. It was also through this work that we were invited to engage in something we never imagined. We were invited to the Republic of Slovakia (originally the state of Slovakia in the Czechoslovak Federation) to assist the Ministry of Education with the transformation of the education system from a communist to post-communist one that nurtured democratic thought and behavior. The whole story of this humbling and exhilarating experience is for another time. What is significant here is that through this work, we met thousands of Slovak educators and subsequently we had the great fortune to work with many thousands more over the next decade or so, as our work there expanded to another 30 nations.

As you might imagine, we had more to learn than to teach as we shared teaching experiences with educators in countries from Lithuania and Estonia to Bosnia-Herzegovina and Azerbaijan and Mongolia, and from the Burmese refugee camp schools in Thailand. In each setting, the school culture reflected the unique character of the national culture, creating fascinating ways to think about and organize learning experiences. In school after school, we would encounter ways of teaching that informed us about how versatile we are as people, how able we are to open ourselves to opportunities, and how many wonderful means there are for accomplishing great and small things.

Of course, along with the myriad differences, we discovered how easy it was to find common ground. A discussion of teaching always begins with an abiding sense of responsibility for the personal and educational well-being of students. Discussions of teaching rarely dwell in the abstract. Teaching is grounded by the realities of the faces of students, whether eager or anxious, cautious or expectant, engaged or disenfranchised and what these expressions demand, if our teaching mission is to truly be accomplished. In tandem with the strong commitment to students is an equally dogged commitment to the content of learning, to the subject matter to be taught. Universally, teachers believe in their work and are committed to bringing knowledge to students that will enhance their capacity to live fruitful and fulfilled lives.

We have been on an extraordinary journey, one wholly unanticipated as it took us from our local school district to faraway places we never imagined. We met educators working to meet the needs of their students while dealing with staggering obstacles. We worked with teachers who had not been paid in seven months yet were enthusiastic to learn how they might better serve their students. What has always been most inspiring has been the ingenuity, the sheer cleverness of teachers to find ways to make instruction better. As you work through the pages of this text, it is our hope that you will work with other inspired educators, and together, we can continue to make instruction better.

COLLABORATION

Over the many years partnering with teachers, we have constantly been amazed by the remarkable conversations teachers hold about teaching when given the opportunity and time to discuss their profession in an atmosphere of trust and mutual respect. Teachers from across cultural, economic, and political divides easily identify with one another and enter into deeply resonant discussions about how best to practice their craft. One remarkable example unfolded before us as we had occasion to work with multiple teams of teachers in a weeklong intensive seminar. The timing for the seminar was just after the war between Armenia and Azerbaijan. We were meeting in Budapest, Hungary, to work with a number of teams. Due to visa problems for several teams attempting to enter Hungary, the two groups who made it to the seminar were from Armenia and Azerbaijan. As you might expect, the atmosphere in the room on day one was extremely tense. Undaunted, we moved forward, holding fast to our conviction, buoyed by years of experience working with teachers, that the universality of teaching and the unequivocal care and commitment to the well-being of young people ever present in dedicated teachers would overcome these tensions. It was not easy to overcome the powerful sentiments held by our participants, but we plowed forward, and in the end, we were right. By day three, teachers were meeting in mixed groups to discuss the anguish for both groups for not being able to meet student needs in the aftermath of conflict. Better still, they were speaking about what to do to solve the situation in their respective classrooms.

By day four, they were working together in the evenings to develop grade-level plans that worked across their two distinct cultures. By day five, they were determined to work together to bring about something better for both peoples. One year later, our teachers from Armenia were the first Armenians in the aftermath of hostilities allowed to drive across the border separating Armenia from Azerbaijan. There, they were met by their Azerbaijani colleagues to continue the collaboration begun in Budapest. This experience and so many others have convinced us that instructional change is not only possible but also welcome and that teachers working together accomplish whatever they set about to accomplish.

We have witnessed over and over how effectively teachers work collaboratively to bring about change. School culture as a manifestation of the status quo is deeply ingrained and often appears as an immovable object. Great force is required to impact something so intractable, great force applied not merely to the institution but as well to our own inclinations to do as we have always done. Collaboration offers a context for change that allows for differences to exist while still insisting that all participants are responsible for ushering through their classroom doors the core instructional changes needed to effect real growth in student achievement. There is more than anecdotal evidence that a collaborative model serves change process best. In an investigation of which teacher change models best result in student achievement growth, Goddard, Goddard, and Tschannen-Moran (2007) summarized their results: "The more teachers collaborate, the more they are able to converse knowledgeably about theories, methods, and processes of teaching and learning, and thus improve instruction" (p. 2).

As you progress through the text, you will form numerous partnerships. The text is structured to support individual learning experiences, book groups, or large groups. As you proceed, you might be working in partnership with grade-level peers, building peers, or district partners. Whichever approach you take, we look forward to being your first partner in this process and to partnering with you throughout your experience.

INTERESTEDNESS

Our experience taught us something else educators have in common around the world. It seems all of us recognize that students come to us, come to school, full of wonder. Early on, this presents as unbridled interest in discovery. We understand that it is one of our essential tasks to sustain such interest. Yet we hold common the recognition that while sustaining interest is one of our most important tasks, it is also one of our greatest challenges and one that we too often fail. We all have watched as interest dims in the bright eyes of our students. The exuberance young learners naturally bring to school too often succumbs to other pressures, to misplaced priorities, to misunderstandings about what truly matters. There is tragedy in the loss of interest, as it is a powerful force for learning. The desire to know coupled with the exquisitely elegant feeling that comes from a sense of knowing propels human learning and exploration better than any other means we have and sustains learners long after they have left us and formal instruction. As powerful a force as interest is, it is remarkable how easily we can miss it altogether and how disappointed those in our charge can be when we do miss it. This experience of, at first missing a child's interest, is caught beautifully in the delightful poem "Coconut" by Paul Hostovsky.[1]

---

1. Reprinted with permission from Paul Hostovsky.

Coconut

Bear with me I
want to tell you
something about
happiness
it's hard to get at
but the thing is
I wasn't looking
I was looking
somewhere else
when my son found it
in the fruit section
and came running
holding it out
in his small hands
asking me what
it was and could we
keep it it only
cost 99 cents
hairy and brown
hard as a rock
and something swishing
around inside
and what on earth
and this was happiness
this little ball
of interest beating
inside his chest
this interestedness
beaming out
from his face pleading
happiness
and because I wasn't
happy I said
to put it back
because I didn't want it
because we didn't need it
and because he was happy
he started to cry
right there in aisle
five so when we
got it home we
put it in the middle
of the kitchen table
and sat on either
side of it and began
to consider how
to get inside of it.

You will see as you enter this PDS that considerable energy is committed to either uncovering or creating interest. From the beginning of Chapter 1, you will be called upon to think about your purposes for learning: what questions you have, what big issues you want to address, what direction you want to go, what possibilities you want to consider, what moves you to explore, what inspires you, and just what catches your fancy. We should confess though that our notion of interest might be agreeable in some ways but less so in others. We believe in exploring the inner secrets of coconuts when and where we find them. Not tomorrow, not in science class, but *right now!* There are a couple of kinds of ways of thinking about interest. One way of thinking about interest is that it is something that is under our control. That is to say, it comes from within us as something we have determined through reason or reflection that we are interested in learning about. We then make plans to pursue that interest, follow our plans, and explore the topic in some orderly, perhaps well-mapped-out strategy or procedure. This requires sustained (on task) and attenuated attention. The kind of attention we typically associate with self-control and discipline. This kind of interest is, of course, quite useful and is the "stuff" of discipline studies.

There is a second kind of interest or interestedness that we also encourage. We see enormous value in spontaneous interest that is immediate and pressing, a kind of interest that may not be affiliated with any long-term purpose such as a good job or a better grade. This kind of interest is not an interest carefully considered from within but results from encounters with the world. We believe in the strength of these spontaneous sparks of intrigue as also defining who we are and as the means by which we remain intimately linked to our world.

You will see as we progress through the text that we explore a number of seemingly dichotomous psychological or pedagogical constructs. We examine how these can be joined together in real instructional experiences that exploit both, seemingly opposite, ends of a continuum. We do this because we believe we are all of one mind with multiple interconnected realities and that learning best occurs across these realities rather than in spite of them or with deference to one over another. We consider many of these apparently dichotomous relationships are more aptly understood as compatible co-contributors to more complete understandings. For example, David Wong (2007) suggested, with respect to our discussion of interest, that while it appears we have one interest that is self-driven and one that is environmentally driven, we are better to think about the "... 'interface' between person and situation" (p. 5) and what each kind of interest brings to us. We will seek as well to address what Rosenblatt referred to as the efferent and the aesthetic—the rational and the emotional, what Steven Pinker referred to as the creative versus reality-testing, and what John Dewey called the doing and reflective undergoing and how they might matter in our teaching practice.

1

Beginning a Professional Development Journey

The first word, "ah" blossoms into all others.

—Kuhai

EVOCATION 1

In his *New York Times* review of Steven Pinker's book *The Stuff of Thought: Languages as a Window Into Human Nature,* William Saletan (2007) summarizes one of Pinker's key points. He writes that " . . . creativity and reality-testing has taken us far beyond other animals and can take us farther. The next step is to dump our most natural and mistaken metaphor—education as a filling of empty minds—and recognize that we learn by extrapolating, testing, modifying, and recombining mental models of the world" (p. 14). In this book, we seek to create opportunities for you to experience firsthand a framework for thinking, teaching, and learning along with numerous sample-supporting strategies. Our aim is for you then to test these experiences in your own classroom, modify and extrapolate as you build, and rebuild mental models of teacher-learning practices.

Note: Why we begin with the word *evocation* will become clear as you work through the first few chapters. Once you understand how we are using evocation here, you will agree that it would be impossible for us not to use it right from the very beginning.

In this first chapter, we will share our philosophy of professional development; we hope as well to join you in a co-equal and collaborative partnership aimed at prolonging the ongoing global conversation among educators about how best to serve our children's educational needs in the 21st century. Whether you are an inservice, preservice, or other educator, we take as given your commitment to ongoing professional development as part of our shared journey toward instructional excellence. This chapter will offer a description of a professional development model and outline what will be required of you to take full advantage of the process. You will be encouraged to keep a journal of your learning experiences, as it is an extremely important part of the learning process and is one means by which you will observe the building and rebuilding of your own mental models of teaching and professional practices.

Throughout this Professional Development Sequence (PDS) you will be asked to engage in a variety of writing-for-thinking tasks. Each will be explained, and in most instances, you will write in your journal. The writings have two purposes, as does much of what you will do throughout the text. The first purpose is to engage in writing as part of a firsthand learning experience. The second is to provide a tool for stepping back to observe yourself as a learner. In doing this, try to gauge in some way how the writing tasks facilitate your own learning. Attempt to operate at both levels throughout the text, as you will be asked in the final chapter on writing whether and how your writing experiences impacted your learning.

OUTCOME EXPECTATIONS

At the end of this chapter, you should

- be aware of the underlying assumptions of the authors regarding professional development,
- understand the professional development model proposed here and what your role is in the learning process,
- have a writing journal in hand with some early entries,
- be aware of the link to critical thinking underscoring the model proposed here, and
- be engaged fully as a partner in this professional development and change process.

EVOCATION 2

Throughout the text, you will be guided to engage in specific activities. These activities are indicated by the lighthouse image in the margin. The first activity follows and asks you to first think about a topic related to thinking and learning, then asks you to share your thoughts. This pattern will be repeated throughout the text.

Let's begin by thinking about your view of the ideal classroom. It is best to do this with your eyes closed, so read on to understand the type of image you are seeking to envision, then close your eyes and bring your image to the fore. When you begin to create your image, do so in a way that enables you to create a detailed vision. Think for a moment about how your ideal classroom looks: the sunlight through the windows, the desk or table arrangement, colors, and sounds. Picture the resources available around the room. Now, imagine how you and your students interact, the kinds of interactions you have with students, and the interactions among students. Imagine how your instruction unfolds and how your students respond. There may be other elements to your vision. Think about this until you have a clear image, clear enough for you to descri be the setting along with the interactions and the teaching-learning process under way. You need take only a minute or so. Now, close your eyes and imagine until your image is clear.

RULES FOR FREEWRITING

Freewriting is a brainstorming procedure. When freewriting, begin with a fresh sheet of paper and an open mind, and follow these few basic rules.

1. Set a time limit, five or seven minutes, let's say, and write the entire time. Do not stop writing. If ideas stop flowing momentarily, doodle or write something like, "I can't think what to say right now," or "I'm stuck for now." Soon enough new ideas will come.

2. Write whatever comes to mind. Do not edit as you write. Ideas that come to mind should find their way to the paper.

3. Do not worry about spelling or punctuation. The writing must be legible, interpretable; that's all.

When your image is clear, if you are with other teachers, turn and share your vision with a partner. If you are alone, take a moment to capture your vision on paper with a quick freewrite. When you are finished, hold those images in your mind's eye, as we will return to them from time to time as you progress through this professional development journey you have joined. You may want to write your thoughts as your initial entry in your own professional development journal. We encourage keeping such a journal as it serves to chronicle changes in your thinking and your practice over time.

THE CHANGE PROCESS

Learning itself is a change process, so it is not so surprising that our profession is constantly entertaining ideas of change and growth. It is important to monitor these various changes to be certain they are in the best interest of our students. The final test of any educational change idea is always how it plays out in the classroom. How students react, their learning progress, and the satisfaction teachers have in their work and with their classroom environment are the final determinants of successful instructional change. For this PDS, we have been listening to teachers' reactions and collecting their comments for many years.

Linda, one of our colleagues, is a sixth-grade teacher. We listened to her comments during one of the monthly meetings of teachers participating in a districtwide professional development opportunity. "What most surprised me was how much my sixth graders think about things," Linda said to her fellow teachers gathered around the table in a small discussion group. "It was a total surprise so many would have strong opinions on anything, but there we were discussing topics I never dreamed we could speak about, and my kids were taking stands on issues. I am really surprised! When I left our last meeting, I took my skepticism with me, thinking there was no way my kids were going to be 'engaged' in dialogue about important topics. Now, I am here to tell my kids were great; they were thoughtful, and they notice more than we think about their world. They have great ideas. I think we just think their opinions do not matter or that they don't have any when they really do!" Matilda, sitting to her left, smiled, silently nodding her agreement.

Like so many great teachers, Linda has been teaching for years and knows her craft well, yet she eagerly volunteered to participate in the district professional development experience. Her motivation? Simply to continue to develop her teaching skills and remain informed. Linda is not about to abandon wholesale what she believes about teaching and what she knows works well and is best for her students. She is also not about to miss an opportunity to serve them better and grow professionally in the process. She always arrived at meetings full of news of the work going on in her classroom. She openly shared the good with the not so good. This day she acknowledged her discovery that sixth-grade students are critical thinkers with ideas and opinions to share. Her students, she discovered, have strong views, hold to ideas, ideals, and beliefs, and willingly offer to others. Matilda teaches second grade. Her motivation is much the same as Linda, but Matilda is quiet. To understand her, you must look for subtle signs: a head nod, a smile, a slightly furrowed brow, or raised eyebrow. When she nodded toward Linda, it was Matilda shouting that her experience with her second graders was similar.

Patrick Shannon (1989, 2007) cautioned about the "de-skilling" of teachers. His concern was that "bureaucratically" developed instructional text, such as basal readers, reduced classroom teachers' role to a mere clerical function. He noted that the political and organizational response to concerns about student performance on standardized tests resulted primarily in reductions in teacher responsibility and choice along with the imposition of routines in order to standardize instruction. By controlling input (teaching), it was thought output (student test performance) would somehow be dependable and predictable. By relying on "expert authors" to develop what amount to routinized instructional texts, outputs would include increased performance on standardized measures. This simplistic formula has yet to live up to its promise, yet in many districts, the illusion that there exists a single simple "remedy" for low student achievement drives instructional design (Darling-Hammond & Bransford, 2005). Our teacher, Linda, as you could probably predict, was not about to become a clerk. She knew, as almost all good teachers do, that student performance is primarily a function of teacher instructional practices, classroom interactions, and teacher decision making.

You are about to embark on a professional development journey. There are many approaches to teachers' continuing professional development, and each one operates from a set of assumptions, beliefs, and expectations. For many, these are implied but not made explicit. Here, we will attempt to lay some assumptions on the table so you will know and understand the basis for your experience. We will attempt to make transparent the beliefs about teaching and learning upon which this experience is constructed. We will also clarify expectations by describing the change process as it is applied here, how the PDS is delivered, and the role you will have in this professional development process.

ABOUT THIS TEXT

You have already learned that this text is written for use in several types of settings and with several audiences. The content of the text includes a discussion of an instructional change process that began in the United States and was eventually implemented successfully in over 30 countries and with well over 75,000 teachers (Meredith, 2002; Klooster, Steele, & Bloem, 2002). The instructional change model begins with a framework based on sound, well-documented instructional theories of practice (Steele, 2001). The framework acts as an umbrella under which an array of practical instructional strategies is organized. The framework guides the instructional process, leading students from a pre-awareness level through genuine and thoughtful encounters with academic content, resulting in genuine learning experiences—the kind that enable practical applications of content and thorough understandings that facilitate critical thought and the creative reordering of knowledge.

The instructional model we are encouraging cannot simply be discussed. The model advocates that learning occur at two levels simultaneously: *process* and *content*. (See Figure 1.1.) *Process* refers to the means and procedures by which information is introduced to a learner and the steps the learner takes to take ownership of content, making it personal, practical, applicable, and accessible within multiple contexts.

Figure 1.1   Learning on Two Levels

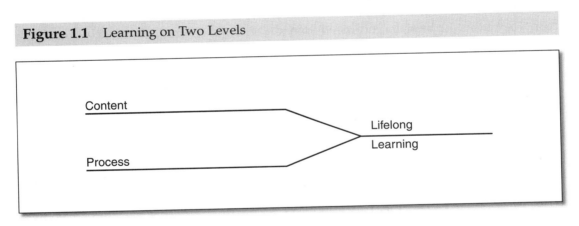

Content represents the ideas, information, and concepts, the nitty-gritty, to which learners are exposed both formally and informally. Content includes both the intended information and material developed purposively for instruction and considered to represent the intended curricular content and the content that emerges through dialogue within the learning community, what Eisner (2002) called the operational curriculum. Content also includes the prior knowledge relevant to curricular content held by learners at the outset of instruction. In this text, content and process will be presented on parallel tracks, as they are intrinsically linked. While reading the text, remain cognizant of the content and process connection and be actively experiencing both during the various model lessons. As a participant, you will be both a student of that particular content and a student of pedagogy, interested in the instructional process as it unfolds. Engaging as a learner allows you to experience and understand how your students will learn when you apply the teaching-learning approaches with them.

As suggested in this text, instructional practices will be modeled then described. This is most often accomplished in an inservice context but can be accomplished through text if we agree to be partners in this process and work together. It requires your commitment to active participation in the various guided strategies that make up the preponderance of the text. We believe strongly that learning is an active, involved, and demanding process. Yet learning is also personal, driven primarily by seeking answers to your own questions, connecting what you know to new and perhaps different or conflicting knowledge, and engaging in experiences that create a larger, richer universe of understandings and possibilities. This text will lead readers through an experiential learning sequence to both model and inform an instructional framework and companion strategies that, in aggregate, define a way of thinking about, organizing, and implementing instruction. Rather than as separate subjects, the model defines reading, writing, speaking, and listening as tools for learning across grade levels and content areas. Consequently, the model framework offered here, though literacy based, is intended for application across content areas.

As will become evident, we place high value on learning communities and believe in the power of dialogue and shared experiences as a way to facilitate discovery and long-term learning (Yangchen, 2009). We encourage critical inquiry and spirited discourse. In life, it is essential that we ask hard questions, seek solutions to our most vexing problems, and attempt to resolve our most intractable dilemmas in order to move forward to better ways of thinking and living. So too must we encourage academic communities to address their most pressing issues.

ASSUMPTIONS, VALUES, AND BELIEFS

> *Students need to tell each other and the world what they know—in order to find out what they know. Through the telling, they will learn. Through the telling, they will interpret the world as they see it to the rest of us.*
>
> —Judith Renyi

As we have suggested, this PDS experience is best described as literacy based in that it employs reading, writing, speaking, listening, and thinking as tools for learning across all content areas. There is tacit acknowledgment that the central component of learning is language based, social, and centered on the mediated construction of meaning between, say, an author (teacher) and learner. Relying on the work of Rosenblatt (1978) and many others, teachers and students will be actively engaged in the social act of creating and sustaining dynamic learning communities where responsibility for teaching and learning is shared. Often, the proclamation of a literacy-based PDS centered on reading and writing alarms content teachers, concerned they may be expected to become reading teachers. This professional development construct does *not* suggest this and encourages content teachers to remain focused on content and determine how best to apply the framework and strategies constructively and creatively to that content.

The premise here is that effective content teaching involves grounding instruction in the effective application of the framework and strategies so students gain not only specific factual information but also working knowledge of content. In other words, students will be able to reforge information into resources for problem solving, for practical or creative application, independent analysis, or opinion formation. Alfred North Whitehead (1957) wrote in *Aims of Education* something about what to avoid in higher education that now seems to apply to all of education today. He said, "So far as the mere imparting of information is concerned, no university has had any justification for existence since the popularization of printing in the fifteenth century" (p. 138–139). What he deplored, of course, was the idea that teaching or learning is somehow complete with the sharing of facts. We agree and view learning as the process whereby we develop agency, in the way Maxine Greene (1994) speaks of agency as the capacity to act with knowledge in ways that utilize knowledge to advance our own constructive purposes.

Content knowledge, then, is compressed into two symbiotic elements or attributes. The first comprises the vocabulary, concepts, and information base on which the content area is defined and constructs itself as a quasi-identifiable entity. The second element contains the language and thinking skills necessary to successfully understand, assign meaning, manipulate, judge, create, and apply. In other words, content must come to us, to borrow a word from the tech world, bundled. That is, for content to be made meaningful and lasting, it needs to be packaged and presented with a process that leads to an increased capacity for learners to connect to the knowledge encountered and make it useful as an agent for advancement. When this is not accomplished, there is overwhelming evidence that long-term learning is less likely to occur. Here we seek to provide the means for bundling content, if you will, to make the outcome of study not simply the acquisition of information but the development of informed thinkers and doers.

In the book *The Discoverers* (1983), David Boorstin wrote, "The greatest obstacle to discovering the shape of the earth, the continents, and the oceans was not ignorance but the illusion of knowledge" (p. 86). In the final analysis, our students will join a global culture. They will be confronted by new technologies, a continuing information explosion, unprecedented cross-cultural global encounters, unimagined career paths and skill expectations that will demand both a sound information base and advanced independent thinking and learning skills. Preparing young people adequately for this reality requires an educational experience rich with opportunities to reconceptualize knowledge to accommodate heretofore unforeseen demands, new discoveries.

EXPECTATIONS

We begin with the basic assumption that most teachers are engaged in teaching at a highly professional level and are typically applying instructional strategies believed to be effective methods for teaching and learning. This PDS begins with the idea that most participating teachers do not need to radically alter their teaching, nor should they consider tossing out those approaches they know to be effective. Rather, we are building on a foundation of solid instructional practice. To be sure, this PDS represents a change process. There are clear expectations that teaching practices will change. What is anticipated is that instruction will evolve as a cogent, comprehensive, and systematic activity that addresses the fundamental needs of today's learners and raises their learning horizons.

Thomas Szasz (1974) wrote, "Every act of conscious learning requires a willingness to suffer injury to one's self-esteem. That is why young children, before they are aware of their own self-importance, learn so easily" (p. 18). Change is threatening because it is fraught with personal risk and uncertainty. Yet we are asking you to take these risks. The instructional model requires students to be active, engaged, and co-responsible for their learning; so too does the PDS you have now joined. Best results demand you be fully engaged with your learning community and in the experiential components offered. Your contribution is vital to your development and to your learning community. Your thoughts, opinions, experiences are all essential content. The good news is that many colleagues have already completed this process, and they suggest the risk is minimal while the rewards are great.

THE ROLE OF CRITICAL THOUGHT

There is reason to believe one of the highest goals we have for our students is for them to develop the skills of critical thought and with them the capacity to apply their knowledge and experiences to solve the vexing problems facing humanity. And vexing problems there are. In an article in the *Chronicle of Higher Education* (June, 2009) McArthur and Sachs suggest that " . . . the world faces many . . . challenges that will require concerted and highly skilled policy efforts in coming years. Those interwoven challenges include the mitigation of climate change, the control of emerging diseases, the reduction of extreme poverty, the development of new and sustainable energy sources, and the sustainable management of water and food systems" (p. 64). If we agree that teaching students to think critically is essential, then it must be introduced into teaching practice systematically (Zelina, 1994). It cannot be assumed that students will come to thinking critically naturally. It is also not enough to simply make critical thinking a part of the content of the curriculum. We have learned that critical thinking does not occur by teaching, say, "the seven steps to critical thinking" or other prescriptions for thoughtful behavior. It comes when students are first modeled critical-thinking processes, guided to think critically themselves, and then given time to do so. Thinking is a process similar to reading, writing, speaking, and listening. It is an active, coordinated, complex procedure, involving thought about something. Critical thinking is best learned by experiencing thought as a way of approaching content—that is, as something that is part of and an expected outcome of the daily curriculum. Research concerning critical thinking and learning suggests that a model focusing on teaching isolated skills and fact learning minimizes critical thinking. One group of researchers (Brown, Palincsar, & Armbruster, 1984) argued that learning skills separate from real-world tasks and purposes may allow students to do well on an objective test but leave them unable to apply those skills in new situations. The reality of high-stakes testing and satisfying multiple stakeholders dictates that critical thinking come packaged with content mastery. What we do know is that we learn and remember better that which we think about and link to our own contextual frames. Throughout this text, thinking will be incorporated with reading, writing, speaking, and listening for learning.

OUTCOME EXPECTATIONS

General

Successful professional development sets target outcomes and goals so participants understand where they are headed and are clear when they have arrived. Setting target goals is not always as simple as it sounds. This particular PDS seeks to facilitate change by guiding readers through an orchestrated change process. However, the outcomes will vary from one reader to the next as settings and practices differ. Furthermore, in a collaborative model, dictating specific outcomes in advance removes from participants the power to set individual and group outcomes. We prefer to see the process as one of "unfolding design," a phrase coined some years ago by a colleague, Brian Shirley, responsible for professional development for schools in Augusta County, Virginia. That is, we have a set of outcome expectations but encourage readers to set personal outcome expectations and modify them as needed in response to individual professional development progress and the subsequent reality of changing goals as a result of working in learning communities.

Stop Now. In your journal take 5 to 10 minutes to think about and then write your own set of target outcomes for your work with this text. Some are listed below, but we suspect you have goals of your own that will help you measure the success of your work.

Some expectations for participants are that you will do the following:

1. Increase the capacity of students to think critically, engage in critical reflection, take responsibility for their own learning, and form independent opinions

2. Successfully apply practical methods of teaching based on philosophically consistent and theoretically sound ideas, which fully engage students in the learning process

3. Teach within a comprehensive instructional framework that guides instructional decision making and reflects the true value and purpose for lessons and context

4. Experience increasing confidence in your own teaching based on successful implementation of the framework and strategies in your own educational setting and content

5. Become master teachers, able to serve as instructional models and resource people within your own professional setting

CHAPTER REFLECTION

In this chapter, we discussed the need for continuing professional development. We also disclosed our philosophy of professional development as supportive of a practical yet theoretically sound model that thrives best within a partnership where all partners are active and fully engaged. We began by detailing some basic assumptions and beliefs that underscore the model implemented here. Those include the notion that whether you are an inservice or preservice teacher, you have a commitment to professional service. For inservice teachers, the basic assumption is that your professional practice is already highly skilled, yet you retain an appreciation for the importance of ongoing professional development. We have made a commitment to offering a pragmatic, experience-based PDS readily implementable in your classrooms with the intention of improving student learning. This chapter also offered discussion on the importance of critical thinking.

Finally, with journal in hand and your image of an ideal classroom in mind, dive in. The succeeding chapters will engage you in learning activities at both content and process levels. Be prepared to think on both levels.

JOURNAL ENTRY

At this point, you may have some questions about this chapter, your role, how the process will unfold, or something else you are wondering about. Before you turn to Chapter 2, ask yourself if you have any questions at this point, and write down any that come to mind.

2

A Framework for Teaching and Learning

Knower and known are joined, and any claim about the nature of the known reflects the nature of the knower as well.

——Parker J. Palmer

EVOCATION

Consider for a few moments that you are now about to teach a content you have never before taught. You have some time to prepare, so you know you will become knowledgeable of the content, if you are not already. With mastery of the content, you now need to decide how to teach it to your students. There are many decisions to make.

For now, though, think a bit about how you determine what to do first, second, and so on. What will you do to introduce your students to the content? How will you go about selecting particular teaching strategies? Why do you choose one over another? After you have thought about these questions, write down your thoughts, and in small groups, share what you have written. See if there is consensus as to how you all might start. If not, is there a pattern or perhaps no apparent method in the madness? Hang on to your ideas about putting a lesson together. We will now experience a content lesson together and then take it apart. You can compare your approach to this one. Be sure everyone shares his or her approach; then read on.

Developing a practical understanding of a framework for teaching and learning requires experiencing the framework within an instructional context. Chapter 2 presents the foundational framework for teaching and learning on which this professional development process is built. The framework is experienced within a guided instructional lesson. Following an introductory rationale, readers are led through using a brief content text. Taking active part in the lesson will give you the learning experience you need to understand what your students will experience when you use the framework with them. Discussion of the lesson and framework in which it is embedded leads to considerations regarding instructional implications for teaching and learning. Chapters 2 through 8 are organized in this fashion so you will first experience the framework strategies modeled and then reflect on your experience in order to analyze their pedagogical structure and the steps to implementation. You will also be asked to reflect on how you felt as a learner as you experienced the lesson.

OUTCOME EXPECTATIONS

At the conclusion of this chapter you should be able to

- understand and describe the three stages of the framework for teaching and learning;
- place various teaching strategies presented in Chapter 2 in the appropriate phases of the framework;
- prepare classroom lessons based on the framework, using present curriculum and available materials; and
- apply the framework and the various teaching strategies in your classrooms.

Drawing from many teachers' experiences with implementation, we offer one caution. When students' learning history is defined primarily by passivity and deferred responsibility, students may, when first invited to become actively involved, hesitate to do so. It is not uncommon for teachers to be confronted by silence when interactive instructional practices are first introduced. Students conditioned to a more teacher-directed instruction will not know how or whether to respond. Reactions vary: Students are sometimes cautious, sometimes distrustful, or refreshingly responsive from the start. Younger students respond more quickly than older students, as they have not spent as much time being silent and passive in school. Usually, several attempts are required before students accept that expectations for their active participation and shared responsibility are real.

RATIONALE

No one questions the importance of factual knowledge. There is a great deal people must know to successfully negotiate daily commerce. However, the idea that a specific knowledge set exists that will adequately prepare students for their future becomes less and less supportable the more rapidly societies change and information flow multiplies. Furthermore, this rapidly expanding knowledge base is increasingly available to everyone. With electronic communications extending into almost all cultures around the world, every school and home is an information center with immediate access to the global information base.

What is required of students to be successful in our changing world is the ability to sift through information and make decisions about what is and is not important. They will need to understand how information is linked and how it can be manipulated to serve multiple purposes. Their future success will be determined by their ability to place new ideas and knowledge in context, to assign relative value to new encounters, and to reject irrelevant or invalid information. Students will be challenged to make meaningful—in critical, creative, and productive ways—that part of the information universe they encounter.

To manage information well, students have to be adept at applying a set of practical thinking skills that enable them to sort information efficiently and transform it into practical behaviors. Students will develop this capacity when instruction is embedded in a framework for thinking and learning that is systematic and self-evident—systematic so students can come to understand and apply the process consistently, self-evident so students can recognize where they are in their own thinking and learning in order to monitor and manage these processes independently. When students independently apply the framework to their own thinking and learning, they are able to

- contextualize their knowledge by adding new information to what they already know,
- actively engage in new learning experiences, and
- reflect on how new learning experiences change their understandings.

The model presented is based, in part, on a model first described by Vaughn and Estes (1986) and modified and expanded by Meredith and Steele (1997). Actually, the model is quite similar to many learning cycles. In his seminal work, Herber (1970) introduced an instructional framework for content area that incorporated both the content and literacy objectives of a lesson. The phases had different titles from the one presented here but were similar in that the ultimate goal of instruction was student independence.

Science educators proposed a learning cycle early in the 1960s (Atkin & Karplus, 1962). Their three-phase model, based on the psychological theories of Piaget, was used as the basis for instructional design in Science Curriculum Improvement Student (SCIS). The 5E Instructional Model (Bybee, Powell, & Trowbridge, 2008) is based on the early learning cycle work and has five phases: engagement, exploration, explanation, elaboration, and evaluation.

Although the various cycles have different numbers of phases and different names of the phases, the rationale is basically the same. The major difference here is that the framework is presented experientially first. We present the model experientially first because we know that you will learn it better and understand it more fully if you experience it yourself. The model is both a teaching and a learning framework. We will not say more now because we want you to experience it first. In debriefing the experience, you will be asked to reflect on how you responded as a learner and what you observed pedagogically as you went through the lesson. It is presented at the outset to provide coherence for all subsequent experiences.

EXPERIENTIAL FRAMEWORK LESSON

You are about to begin the first experiential lesson. Whether you are a participant in a professional development inservice, independently created learning community, class, or are an individual reader, please follow the text instruction so your experience will be genuine and serve you well as a source for later reflection.

In a moment, you will read a short article titled "The Sea Turtle." Before reading the article we will do some thinking about sea turtles. Begin now by choosing a partner for discussion. In the next three or so minutes, first independently and then with your partner, make a list in your journal of all you *know* or *think you know* about sea turtles. It is important to write down everything that comes to mind about sea turtles. It does not matter if what is written down is accurate or not. What is important is to write down all that comes to mind, thinking about what you already know or think you know about sea turtles. Please begin making your list now, and when you and your partner have completed your independent lists, share and discuss. Look for similarities and for new ideas. When this is done, return to this text.

Now, partners, share your knowledge of sea turtles with the larger group. Have someone keep track of *all* the ideas shared on a board, overhead, poster paper, or some other medium. Any disagreements should be brought to the surface by checking from time to time whether all agree with what is being said. For example, there is often disagreement over the number of eggs sea turtles lay, what sea turtles eat, how large they grow, or how long they live. If these issues do not surface, it is fine to speculate about these questions now. It is quite good to encourage discussion, friendly disagreement, and taking stands on one side or the other. Where there are disagreements, indicate with a question mark by the item in your brainstormed list.

When the class ideas are all out, it is time to *prepare* to read the article. There are some actions you should be taking while reading. As you read, you will be making some marks in the margins of the article using the Interactive Notating System for Effective Reading and Thinking (INSERT) developed by Vaughn and Estes (1986).

INSERT

The marks should be used as follows:

"√"   Put a "√" (check) in the margin next to something you read that *confirms* what you knew or thought you knew.

"–"   Put a "–" (minus) if some information you are reading *contradicts* or is different from what you already knew or thought you knew.

"+"   Put a "+" (plus) in the margin if a piece of information you encounter *is new information* for you.

"?"   Place a "?" (question mark) in the margin if there is information that is *confusing* to you or there is something *you would like to know more* about.

As you read, you will be placing four different marks in the margin according to *your own* knowledge and understanding. You will be marking in the margins using "✓," "–," "+," and "?" as appropriate to your own knowledge base. It is not necessary to mark each line or each idea, making your mark reflective of your relation to the information in general. You may end up with three or four markings per paragraph, sometimes more or less. "The Sea Turtle" can be found in Appendix A. Now read the article, making sure to mark as you read.

Once you have read the article, pause for a moment to recall and consider what you read; then turn to your partner and discuss the article. Discuss what knowledge was confirmed for each partner and what beliefs or understandings were disconfirmed. Check with each other to determine what was new or surprising. Also determine what you have questions about. Take time to look over your lists and go back over the article to look at your marks. Your markings will serve as convenient reference points for information confirming or disconfirming your previous knowledge. Your markings will also reference new or confusing information or ideas about which you would like to learn more.

When discussion is finished, make an individual chart of the markings to categorize information similar to the example in Figure 2.1:

Figure 2.1   INSERT Chart

(✓) Confirms	(–) Contradicts	(+) Is new	(?) Question or more information
Young left to survive on own Lays eggs Returns to same beach each year	Lays 50 to 100 eggs Lays eggs several times per year	Eats plants and fish Travels great distances Sheds tears	Where do the young go? How do they find the same beach each year? Are mothers really crying to keep sand out of their eyes?

Now, as a group, discuss the article, returning to the large-group brainstorm written on the poster paper on the wall or overhead. Review agreements and discuss disagreements. Discuss whether the article resolved them or other sources are needed.

This can be an elaborate and enjoyable conversation if questions arise or disagreement persists. This entire experiential lesson should take no more than one to one and a half hours and can be shortened with practice. If questions persist, various members of the learning community can take responsibility for finding answers to bring back to the group. If fact, this is the last step in this lesson, with the exception that new information will be brought back to the group for later discussion.

EXAMINING THE FRAMEWORK

Evocation Phase

You have now experienced firsthand instructionally and in terms of strategy application a brief application of the framework. Let's examine what has occurred. To do this, first, think back to the very beginning just before reading about sea turtles. What were you asked to do? Take some time now to recall your experience. Try to list everything you recall from the lesson in the order it happened. Think what was asked of you and what you experienced as a learner. Then, share your list with your partner. Keep your list, as we will go over it together. You might want to make a T-chart with learner responses and pedagogical observations as headings for the columns.

As you remember, after introducing the topic, sea turtles, the very first thing you did was to recall everything *you knew or thought you knew* about sea turtles and you made a list. Then, you shared your list with a partner. Next, you followed a group discussion and sharing. So what was going on at this point? At this point in the lesson, it was important to bring to awareness everything you thought or understood about sea turtles without concern for whether it was right or wrong. Raising awareness of prior knowledge is a primary objective of the first phase in a three-phase framework for teaching and learning that will guide our thinking about teaching and learning for the remainder of the text. This first phase is referred to as the *Evocation (E)* phase.

During the evocation phase, students are introduced to new material or new learning experiences through questioning or through other connected themes that prompt thought about a topic or issue. In the sea turtle lesson, brainstorming was used first individually, then in pairs, and finally with the large group. With the large group, brainstorm ideas were written on a board or poster, and, as was modeled here, all ideas are accepted without concern for their veracity. Minimal direction was offered by eliciting some ideas or by exploring issues not raised otherwise but relevant to the text. In our example, we suggested considering what sea turtles eat, how many eggs they lay, and other qualities. This enables teachers to guide readers to the content of the reading. Despite these brief assists during this stage, it was important that you did your own thinking, generated your own lists of known or thought-to-be-known information. The teacher's role was mostly to listen carefully to students' ideas and guide occasionally.

Rationale for Evocation Phase

The first purpose of the evocation phase is to energize students to learn. Learning is an industrious enterprise not well supported by student passivity. Yet students often view learning as a passive endeavor. So energizing them to be active and then sustaining that energy is what will drive the learning process. Students' learning experiences often resemble a subway ride. Students hop on, let's say, the Sea Turtles line. They sit for a while before hopping off at the next station. A while may pass before the train comes by again, and they hop on for another short journey, only to exit at the next attractive station.

Early on in the sea turtle lesson, learners were *actively engaged* in recalling what they knew or thought they knew about the topic. This helped turn attention toward the topic you would soon be exploring in detail. Active engagement of this sort illuminates students' *prior knowledge* of the topic, making it available for scrutiny and for scaffolding to higher or richer understandings. Of primary importance in *E* is that through this initial activity, learners establish a momentary baseline of personal knowledge to which new knowledge can adhere. Learning is a process of connecting the new with the known. Learners build new understandings from the foundation of previous knowledge and beliefs (Roth, 1990). As Figure 2.2 illustrates, learning is essentially a process of building bridges between what we know and the new we encounter. Thus, when we prompt students to rediscover previous knowledge and beliefs, the broadest foundation can be established on which long-term understanding of new information is built. Bringing prior knowledge to light also serves to illuminate misunderstandings, confusion, and misconceptions that might otherwise go unnoticed without active examination of held knowledge and beliefs.

Figure 2.2   Building Bridges Between Known and New Knowledge

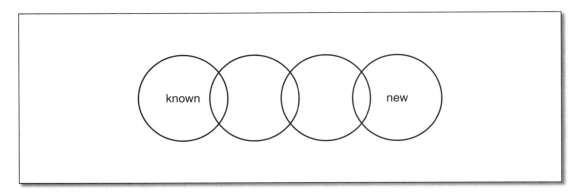

Equally useful, prior knowledge comes to us as contextualized thought in the form of schema. Schema represents our previously established constructs about our assembled thoughts or ideas (Rumelhart, 1982). Schemata, the plural of schema, are the capsules our ideas travel in, but as Marshall McLuhan (1964) might suggest, the medium here is also the message; that is to say, as prior knowledge becomes accessible, so too our schema for that knowledge is in part revealed. The importance of this is understood when we realize that learning is ultimately all about altering our schema. So enabling learners to make conscious attributions and modification to existing schema is necessary for the incorporation of new knowledge. Schema helps to connect new information to known because the context for understanding is made self-evident. Facilitating permanent changes in understandings to reflect new knowledge requires linkages between new information and existing schemata.

The next purpose of the evocation phase is to *set interest and establish purpose* for study. Interest and purpose sustain engagement. However, as with cholesterol, there are two types of purposes, one better than the other. Teacher or text driven is one sort, self-directed another. Self-directed purposes are more powerful than those imposed from external sources. Self-directed purpose is more easily sustained both in and away from school. Without sustained interest, motivation and the energy required to reconfigure schema are less likely committed to the task. In our sea turtle lesson, prior to reading the passage, it is not likely you were thinking much about the lives of sea turtles. But brainstorming a list of thoughts and ideas and creating questions to answer generated interest. Discovering alternative hypotheses, even about the lives of sea turtles, can be intriguing and spark interest when deliberated within a context of exploration and personal growth.

Evocation activities also serve another function. They are also useful to discern students' levels of understanding, the class knowledge base, and their various perspectives and opinions. Divining student variations in knowledge and understanding helps develop questions of interest and helps make instruction personal, which can be a powerful motivator for reading for understanding. In fact, Pearson and Fielding (1996) have suggested that the definition of comprehension is having your own questions answered. Knowing students' topic knowledge informs teachers as to students' readiness to engage the topic productively as well. Where there is evidence of insufficient prior knowledge, a base must be built from what students already do know.

Realization of Meaning (R)

The second phase of the three-phase framework for thinking and learning is *Realization of Meaning (R)*. It is in this phase that the learner first encounters the new—new information, new ideas, or new experiences. This encounter can involve text, as in the sea turtles example. It can also be through watching a film; listening to a presentation; conducting an experiment; participating in a field trip; engaging in debate; teaching with an interactive DVD, website, or video; involvement in a round table discussion; or any other medium where we encounter something new. Significant for instruction, this phase of learning offers teachers the least opportunities for influencing learner behavior. What happens in Realization of Meaning occurs in the mind of the learner, and what is happening in the mind of the learner is not readily transparent. It is here that learners must share responsibility for sustaining active engagement.

Rationale for Realization of Meaning Stage

Recent studies are disconcerting regarding student learning from text (NEA, 2004). Studies examining the learning outcomes of students following reading from informational text suggest that many students in the upper elementary and high school grades are not benefiting sufficiently from text. In fact, it seems often when students read scientific or other narrative materials that directly contradict or correct student factual errors and misunderstandings, they are unaffected by their reading, leaving their erroneous conception and misunderstandings intact. This rift between student "reading" and student comprehension is a major obstacle to achievement.

To understand how a reader can be so disconnected from text content while reading, recall your own reading experience. Can you recall a time when you read a page or perhaps many pages of text only to suddenly realize you have absolutely no recollection of what you just "read"? More frightening are those times, and we all have had them, when while driving, we are jolted by the realization that we have no real awareness of the last 10 miles or so. Both are examples of operating without active cognitive engagement either with text or, in the latter case, with the road. For reading, this precludes the possibility of comprehending what we are reading, not to mention the possibility of monitoring comprehension while reading. A second inhibitor of comprehension is that we all look first for that which agrees with what we already know or believe. Most people find disagreement, well, disagreeable. Too often, students approach reading and other learning experiences anticipating no real cognitive engagement or need for change. The significance for teachers of the realization of meaning phase comes first in recognizing how ineffective student encounters with any content are without students' active cognitive engagement with the content coupled with persistent comprehension monitoring and an inclination to learn.

The essential tasks of the realization of meaning phase are to sustain engagement, maintain interest and momentum created during the evocation phase, and support learners' efforts to monitor their own comprehension and change. Passive learners often ignore lapses in understanding, unaware of or indifferent to their confusions or misunderstandings. We know good learners are efficient learners, busy monitoring their own understanding as they encounter new information (Pressley, 2002). When reading, good readers reread or apply other effective strategies if comprehension wanes. Listeners, attending to a presentation, will ask questions or note confusions or misunderstandings for later clarification. Students monitoring their own comprehension actively reference new information against their established schemata, purposively connecting the new with the known.

Practicing teachers know well how often students become lost as they wade into new content. A mask is seemingly drawn down over their otherwise alert faces. We know that without activation of prior knowledge and setting purpose for learning, there is little hope the shade will lift, yet these steps alone will not sustain engagement. Many students fail to understand that they are bored by their learning experience precisely because they are disengaged. They look to outside sources for their disenfranchisement and see only that their classroom, their text, or other medium, no matter how cleverly developed, offers no cure for their detachment. The realization of meaning phase is a partnership phase intended to bridge the gulf between teacher control of the learning process and student responsibility for contributing the energy and intention needed to fully engage with content.

There are a number of teaching strategies available to assist student efforts to sustained engagement. In the sea turtles example, the reader was instructed to apply the INSERT method to sustain cognitive involvement during reading. The INSERT strategy is an excellent tool for helping readers monitor comprehension (Vaughn & Estes, 1986). Asking students to consider whether the information they are encountering is new, confirming, counter to present understanding, confusing, or intriguing as they read demands attention to content and ongoing interface of the new with the known. Some may struggle with the idea of marking a textbook. We suggest students mark lightly in pencil so marks can be easily erased and have had success with this with students as young as third grade. However, a colleague of ours, Victoria Ridgeway, uses sticky notes—a practice that can work once students have experience with and understand how to use the method. Incidentally, the number of marks students use in classrooms varies according to the age and maturity of the students. It is recommended that students in Grades 1 to 4 initially use no more than two marks. In our example, we suggested using four. It may take some practice for students to attend to four marks without distraction. What the marks represent may also vary, depending on the purpose for reading and student experience with the marking system.

What students mark, what they are looking for in text is dependent on what you decide is most important in the text. It is up to you to decide what your goals are and what you believe students should take from their reading of the text.

Too often, we take for granted that students will somehow benefit from reading no matter what. The evidence is clear that this is not the case, so we need to consider how we involve students as we engage them in planned learning experiences. Work now in small groups or pairs to discuss the realization of meaning phase of learning. Think about the importance of cognitive engagement for your own learning and the necessity of metacognitive engagement to sustain what Rosenblatt (1978) referred to as a stream of aha moments. Share your thoughts with colleagues and list some ways you already work to sustain student engagement.

Reflection (R)

The final phase in this three-phase model of teaching and learning is the *Reflection (R)*. Recall now what was done following your reading of the sea turtle article. You will recall you first completed an individual brainstorm. This was followed by a paired brainstorm and then, if in a large group, you did a group brainstorm. You then read the article employing the INSERT method. When finished reading the INSERT, markings and group brainstorm served as the basis for further discussion of the topic. Revisiting the group brainstorm, you looked for confirmation of previously held beliefs, reconciled some unresolved questions, and acknowledged inconsistencies or errors in knowledge as a group. INSERT offered an opportunity to categorize these observations at an individual learner level and generated a number of still unanswered questions for future research. In the process, you also looked for anything surprising in what you read.

Before reading on, take a minute to consider the discussion following reading the sea turtle text. What did it do for you as a reader and learner? How did the various activities impact your connection to the topic and the text? What effects were there on short- and long-term learning? What was required of you to complete the INSERT chart in terms of revisiting the text? Share your thoughts and keep them and your own experience with these strategies in mind as you explore the purposes of the reflection phase.

The reflection phase is most often omitted from the learning process, yet it is equally critical to long-term learning. During reflection, learners consolidate new learning by actively restructuring their schema to accommodate new learning. In this phase, learners truly make new knowledge their own. Learning is an act of changing, of becoming in some way different. Whether that difference is seen in terms of new understandings, a new set of behaviors, or new beliefs, learning is characterized by genuine and lasting change. This change occurs when learners restructure their schema and develop the necessary vocabulary to assure schema accessibility. So it is in the reflection phase that lasting learning is secured. In the sea turtles lesson, the reflection phase came following the reading of the article and involved all the subsequent activities related to the brainstorm, INSERT, and any further research done to answer additional questions.

Rationale for Reflection Stage

There are several essential purposes for the reflection phase. They include the following:

- Maintaining student engagement in the lesson and, in the sea turtle example, with text

- Orchestrating overt efforts to connect what is already known with new information

- Encouraging student ownership of new knowledge

- Becoming different

- Creating opportunities for multiple encounters with essential content

- Facilitating expression of new knowledge in students' own language and making new vocabulary part of expressive vocabulary

- Allowing time for students to actively process new learning so that it moves from awareness to long-term memory

The Reflection phase is best understood by understanding its intended outcomes. There are two primary outcomes. The first is change. Teaching is foremost about guiding students to become someone other than who they are. This is why teaching carries such great responsibility and why it is critical that before each lesson, we have a clear sense of why we are teaching what we teach and what change we are seeking. For all learners, lasting learning is reflected in the changes that occur in our schema as it is altered to accommodate to the new. The second primary outcome is ownership. For learning experiences to be lasting and practical, students must consciously believe the knowledge is theirs and under their control, and that they can act or build on that knowledge with confidence.

We have all experienced those times when we use our knowledge to accomplish a new task. It might be mastery of a new digital camera, learning to salsa dance, the troop movements during the battle of Gettysburg, how to cross-stitch, or crossbreeding plants in a lab. The knowledge is truly owned when learners use the requisite knowledge to make something happen.

Orchestrating the Reflection phase of the framework requires attention to students at multiple levels. As with evocation and realization of meaning, reflection requires a sustained commitment to the task. Altering schema, becoming different, is energy intensive and tiring. Successfully propelling students through the process of change relies on energized students who remain fully engaged to the end of the lesson.

We know from experience and learning research that multiple exposure to new information dramatically enhances long-term learning. Yet we also know that simply insisting students review or memorize lists will not get this done. One need only guess at the number of lists we have all learned throughout our schooling and how many we can recall today. Repeated encounters with the new are useful when they are purposeful and driven by interest.

Some students seem naturally inclined to build connections between held knowledge or understanding and new experiences that require reconfiguring those understandings. "Hey, demoting Pluto to a lesser planet makes the jingle I learned for the planets obsolete." "The melting polar cap does make me think differently about the possibility of global warming." But for many, especially those who perceive learning to be random acts of memorization, the process of building connections is not automatic and needs conscious facilitation.

When we express new learning in our own words, we lay claim to this new territory as part of our own knowledge base. Just as our use of new vocabulary makes it part of our functioning lexicon, opportunities to elaborate on our knowledge give form to new schema.

We learn to remember when new learning comes to us as a part of something larger and more conceptually clear. Knowledge of details is more likely secured if it underscores our understanding of something bigger, more categorical. Taking ownership of knowledge and moving learning experiences to long-term memory are most often the result of deliberate action. We can facilitate the process by involving learners in actions we know are necessary for long-term memory. Repeated encounters and incorporating new learning into expressive language are two early steps of long-term learning. The first serves learning by moving new from new to familiar. The second provides accompanying personal conceptual frames that enable retrieval and application. Contextualizing knowledge offers learners understanding about what sort of change is required to make knowledge permanent (Pearson & Fielding, 1996). I do not need to change my global thinking about the solar system, but my notion of what constituted a planet needs to change if I am to understand what is being said about Pluto and the larger moons of the larger planets.

Since reflection is a time of change, of reconceptualization, another goal of this phase is in generating a robust exchange of ideas between students. Exposure to multiple ways of integrating information offers exposure to creative, thoughtful constructs and solutions, which might be more practically applied or might represent intriguing ways of thinking.

THE ERR FRAMEWORK REVISITED

Teacher Experience

You have now experienced the beginnings of what we will refer to as the ERR framework. Understanding ERR is foundational for your understanding of the teaching-learning framework, for the application of strategies, and for the model of critical inquiry instruction to follow, so some considerations of its worth to instruction and the benefits to teachers and teaching from implementing ERR should be shared. Students come to class mostly occupied by their own lives outside of class. They do not walk into class hoping to examine the secret lives of sea turtles. We can all easily imagine, however, students walking into class thinking about something that just happened in the hallway between two friends and the ripple effect of that event during the lunch hour to come. Our task at this point in their lives is to persuade our 20 or 25 or 30 or more students first to refocus their attention on sea turtles or Shakespeare or the Civil War or algebra or weather systems or whatever else and to allocate enough energy to compel them through their study to an endpoint of change and growth. Not an easy task with the sheer number and power of competing distractions that fill the lives of students. The ERR framework provides a mechanism for organizing instruction and applying systematically the best strategies for teaching your particular lesson, enabling you to engage students in an effective learning sequence that is intended to energize students' involvement and solicit them as partners in their own learning experience.

Teacher time is limited. ERR offers teachers a means of organizing lessons in a timely way that provides an instructional guide through the phases of learning each student must pass through to learn permanently. Lessons often seem to emerge out of the ether or fade at the end without a sense of a real purpose or at least a beginning, middle, or end. This leaves teachers and learners wondering whether anything was accomplished. Through application of the framework, a clear beginning, middle, and end unfold, and in many instances, a clear transition to succeeding content emerges rather self-evidently. The ERR teaching-learning framework provides instructional routine, allowing management of the basics of teaching: good lesson planning, well-conceived goals and objectives, targeted standards, and support for all students to perform well on assessments by creating relevance for content through instruction linked to individual experience and learning history. It offers an instructional approach teachers are comfortable modeling because students typically respond with increased interest and energy, making instruction more enjoyable and classrooms more creative, constructive, positive communities.

As discussed earlier, there are numerous instructional frameworks for engaging students actively in their own learning (Vaughan and Estes, 1986; Vacca & Vacca, 2008). The ERR framework offers an instructional paradigm that employs reading, writing, speaking, and listening as tools for learning as described by Meredith and Steele (1996); Meredith, Steele, & Temple (1998); Steele (2001); and Meredith, Steele, & Kikusova (2001). The model integrates practical instructional methods into a framework for thinking and learning that embody the fundamental findings of literacy research about teaching and learning across grade levels and content areas.

ERR provides teachers with a context in which they do the following:	
Activate student thinking	Help students to ask their own questions
Set purposes for learning	Provide rich discussion
Motivate student learning	Stimulate change
Actively engage students in the learning process	Stimulate reflection
	Encourage self-expression
Expose learners to varied opinions	Facilitate critical thinking

These models all seek to accomplish similar instructional goals of a practice that actively and equitably evokes voice, establishes purposes for learning, shares power, and recognizes the need to allow time for taking ownership of knowledge. By facilitating the transfer of contextualized knowledge (Meredith & Steele, 1997) students can practically apply, teachers are transformed from lecturer to partner, and classrooms are neither teacher nor student centered but learning centered. In such a setting, students are expected to bring to the learning environment active minds and sufficient energy to make the personal changes required for the acquisition of lasting knowledge.

The ERR framework is a concise, transparent, yet powerful instructional model. Students moving through the framework routinely experience a definitive sequence of learning behaviors, which lead them toward successful integration of new information with previous knowledge. Student time in the classroom is limited, with the preponderance of learning ultimately taking place outside formal instruction. Through a transparent instructional model, students learn the skills and processes necessary to become effective and efficient learners throughout their lives. Because it is transparent, ERR allows students to come to understand the steps required for their own learning and what to do to transition through the learning process.

Furthermore, by using the ERR framework, teachers plan lessons based on how people learn. Hana Kostálová (2003), Director of Reading and Writing for Critical Thinking (RWCT) of the Czech Republic, describes how she sees the framework infused into lesson planning.

> The framework for teaching learning: *Evocation—Realization of Meaning— Reflection,* permeates the whole RWCT program (see http://www.rwctic.org/ for more information). It helps us to plan the lesson, and when we as teachers experience it fully, it becomes our "educational nature." We stop to think about ERR, and we plan instruction so that it respects natural processes that take place in a learner's brain. Our instruction becomes effective because it corresponds to the needs of the learners giving them enough intellectual and emotional stimuli in a way that stirs students' interest in learning. Thanks to the methods through which the individual phases are realized, students get an opportunity to practice their skills critical for their life in a democratic society, and at the same time, they learn a lot of factual information and understand their relationships. (p. 3)

CRITICAL THINKING AND THE FRAMEWORK

How is this framework for teaching and learning linked to critical thinking? Chapter 4 will examine critical thinking in greater detail. However, here it is useful to build a link between the framework and critical thought as an evocation for Chapter 4. Critical thinking requires the ability to understand and reflect at multiple levels on what one knows and thinks. To some extent, critical thinking requires a level of command over our knowledge that enables us to manipulate, defend, promote, or hypothesize. For this to happen, students must bring their knowledge and understandings to an awareness level, the central purpose of evocation. Failing to activate prior knowledge and the schemata in which it is embedded, learners end up entertaining vague, confusing, or even conflicting thoughts simultaneously. The beginning point for thought, then, is coming to know what one already knows.

Critical analysis of what we know, think, and believe requires thoughtful, often inventive deliberation over new knowledge and how applicable it is to previous understandings or about how previous understandings may be accommodated. Students are most motivated to thoughtfully deliberate when they sense they have some control over their learning. When students realize they have control over their own cognitive and metacognitive processes, they become better able to hear and understand new ideas and new ways of integrating information and concepts. They are then more able to manage new information because they have greater confidence in their ability to successfully integrate new knowledge with previous knowledge.

Confident students able to engage in metacognitive processes are typically more open to new ideas and influences that can be productively incorporated into their existing schemata. Some worry that students will too easily alter their belief system if left to their own devices. Actually, the opposite is the case. David Wong (2007) writes, "In my opinion, though, metacognitive experience is a feeling about whether something makes sense or not, rather than a feeling about what sense something could make" (p. 5). It is the metacognitive that opens our minds, makes us receptive by determining that we sense sense. It is active cognition in a reflective process that helps us determine beliefs. It is far more possible to toss away all we presently believe in if we are not cognizant of our existing beliefs, thoughts, ideas, or ideals and constructs supporting them. By becoming more cognizant of our knowledge, understandings, and beliefs, we also take more ownership of them and are less able to disregard them in the face of flimsy alternatives. Finally, critical thinkers are able to more freely combine ideas and information because they are starting from a familiar and self-evident knowledge base. By being aware of their knowledge, which starts with evocation, students are better prepared to make creative use of that base to solve problems, formulate opinions, and generate new ideas, which is the outcome we seek in reflection.

FRAMEWORK STRATEGIES ORGANIZATIONAL CHART

As a concluding activity, make a chart similar to the one below to organize the strategies encountered so far. Turn your journal lengthwise and place the phases of the framework at the top of the page and list the strategies in the appropriate phases (see Figure 2.3). You are encouraged to maintain this chart throughout your work with the text, adding new strategies to each phase as they are experienced. The initial charting is done below. As strategies are presented, it will be a useful exercise to always consider where in the framework the strategy best fits. You will see strategies that may fit in several phases. Where they fit depends on how they are applied instructionally and what goals for instruction you intend. So, for example, the strategy *Group Brainstorming* was used in our sea turtle example in the **E**vocation phase. It can be applied equally effectively in the **R**eflection phase, the determining factor being whether the intent of the strategy application is to provide a means of organizing prior knowledge or to categorize new knowledge and prior knowledge as a means of integrating the new with the known.

Figure 2.3 Framework Strategies Organizational Chart

Evocation	Realization of Meaning	Reflection
Paired reading Group brainstorming Individual brainstorming	INSERT	Individual brainstorm Group and paired discussion Group brainstorm INSERT chart

CHAPTER REFLECTION

Chapter 2 began with a discussion about how you organize content into a sequence of effective lessons. We thought about how to sequence encounters with content knowledge, what strategies to select to effectively deliver instruction, and why. This chapter then offered an experiential application of the ERR framework. Foremost, the framework serves as a conceptual umbrella under which we can assemble an instructional sequence that reflects the learning process all learners must pass through before they are able to take full ownership of new learning. As such, the ERR framework provides a flexible structure for planning and implementing instruction. At its core is a clearly articulated learning sequence, yet the strategies used may be as varied as the number of effective strategies a teacher has in her or his quiver. What the framework offers at a basic level is a way of understanding why one strategy may serve better than another at a particular point in the teaching-learning process.

There is an old, wise, and familiar saying, "The road to hell is paved with good intentions." This can easily be rephrased, "The road to instructional disaster is paved with great teaching strategies." The right strategy at the wrong time will lead to disappointing outcomes every time. As we go through the text, you will encounter increasing numbers of teaching-learning strategies. It will be important to situate these within the ERR chart so their utility as facilitators of instruction and learning will be evident.

However, before proceeding, stop to consider the implications of the framework; think how its implementation might change your own teaching. Share your thinking with a partner and speculate some about how the framework can facilitate your own lesson development. Think about what you already do or how you already conceptualize your lessons that might incorporate the framework at some level.

Then think about a content area and a one-class-length topic you already teach, and with your partner, develop a lesson plan for this content using the framework and strategies from this chapter or others with which you are already familiar. Then, share these lessons with the large group and discuss how they might or might not work.

3

Narrative Text and the Power of Questioning

Perhaps the most effective way to involve a large number of learners is through vivid, dramatic narrative.

—Howard Gardner (1999)

EVOCATION

In Chapter 2, we read from an informational text. It is important that informational text be introduced to even the youngest readers. There is evidence (Yopp & Yopp, 2000) clearly indicating that young students can manage such text and, in fact, find it motivating (Kleitzen & Dreher 2003). Sill-Briegel and Camp (2000) described a "twin text strategy," blending thematically similar narrative and nonnarrative text so students will come naturally to see the link between nonfiction and narrative text.

In Chapter 3, we will explore working with narrative text, experiencing a narrative text lesson in which the ERR framework is applied at multiple levels. This somewhat more complex framework application yields a more layered lesson, enabling students to examine text in greater detail while developing more complicated images and understanding and, consequently, a more intrinsically rewarding outcome.

As with the sea turtle lesson, as you proceed through this lesson, attend to it at two levels. One is as a student of literature, so attend carefully to the text and participate in the conversation regarding the text, building understanding as you read. The second is as a student of pedagogy. At this level pay particular attention to the teaching-learning process as it unfolds during exploration of the text and the subsequent instructional activities. Be mindful as well of the ERR framework and how it is applied. Finally, for this lesson, pay some attention as well to the way in which questions drive the lesson. Observe how they guide your thinking and the kind of thinking you are asked to engage in as you read or consider content. Attending to all these variables is a tall order, so you will be busy.

As with sea turtles, when the lesson is complete, we will take time to examine the lesson in some detail. You will be asked to think about how you responded as a learner during various points in the lesson and your view of the strategies and the lesson in general pedagogically. We will also examine the role of questioning in the lesson and its impact on learning.

OUTCOME EXPECTATIONS

At the conclusion of this chapter readers should

- be able to engage a class in guided inquiry using multiple question formats;

- understand the value of questioning students at various levels;

- understand the thought processes associated with various question levels;

- understand the relationship between questioning and critical thinking;

- understand the importance of teacher questioning for promoting critical thinking; and

- be able to present a narrative text to a class, blending the ERR framework with skilled questioning practices, stimulating various types and levels of cognitive processes necessary for students to interact with text at increasingly sophisticated levels.

TEACHER QUESTIONING

Think for a moment about the typical questions you ask your students. What prompts those particular questions? Where do they come from? That is, what makes you ask one question and not another? What are your purposes for asking questions? Think about these questions for a few minutes; then discuss with a partner or enter your thoughts in your journal.

Now, as you read this next section, see if what you thought about questioning and its sources and purposes connects with the text.

Questioning is a powerful tool for eliciting information and ideas, for setting great acts in motion. Used properly, questioning propels thinking forward, uncovers underlying beliefs, strikes at the heart of issues. Television talk show host Larry King's long and successful career is built around his capacity to use questions to drive compelling conversation and tease out new information, new revelations, or new insights. Over and over, we have examples of how a single question set an enormous chain of events in motion. During the Watergate hearings, the basic question asked over and over again was, "What did you know, and when did you know it?"

But the question that changed the nation was, "Are you aware of any recording devices recording conversations in the Oval Office?" The lives of the authors of this text were forever changed by a single question. Following the fall of the Berlin Wall, the Education Minister for the then state of Slovakia in the Czechoslovak Republic came to America to an education forum and asked, "How do you teach democracy?" This single question led these authors to implement a national school reform effort in Slovakia (see http://www.zdruzenieorava.sk/xmap/index_en) that ultimately reached over 32 nations around the world.

The kinds of questions teachers ask establish the intellectual climate of the classroom. Questions determine what is most valued; how right and wrong are defined; and who and what are, or are not, sources of information and knowledge. The types of questions asked can teach students that knowledge is not fixed and that ideas are malleable. Or questions can limit student thinking to simple recitation, constraining thought and informing students that their own thinking is superfluous. Questions that invite students to reflect, speculate, reconstruct, imagine, create, or weigh carefully elevate the level of student thought and confirm for students that their thinking is valued, that their views constitute a contribution to their learning community.

Studies of classrooms in the United States suggest that over 60% of the questions teachers ask students are literal-level or factual questions, 20% are procedural, and the remaining 20% are at a higher cognitive level (Cotton, 2003). Whether the subject matter is science or literature, the questions students confront most often require only single-word or simple-phrase responses. Questions like name a four-legged animal; what is the name of the village in a story just read; or how many, what color, how far, what date, and so on exemplify classroom questioning. With so many literal-level questions being asked, it is no surprise that students value factual information above all other forms of knowledge and attend most to this level of thinking.

However, literal-level questions require only minimal use of language, do not involve meaningful conversation, and demand only a superficial awareness of content along with words or phrases borrowed from a text. Many students develop the capacity to recall factual information without ever coming to understand the central ideas for which the factual information is provided in the first place. They are able to memorize without being meaningfully challenged or changed by their learning experience. Yet having been fed for years on a strict diet of literal-level questions, we find that altering our pattern of questioning is nearly as difficult as giving up an addiction. Despite the difficulty, it is imperative that we give up our dependency on recitation questions so our students will develop the necessary skills to think through the hard questions 21st-century life presents.

Turn to your partner or to your journal and review what you thought already about questioning and then discuss how the ideas shared here concur with, disagree with, or perhaps add to your thinking about classroom questioning purpose and practice. We will return to questioning later, following a narrative lesson, so keep your ideas about questioning in your mind as you engage in the next lesson.

MODEL ERR LESSON WITH A NARRATIVE TEXT

The following guided reading activity is intended to engage students in reading text while involving them in critical analysis of the text. The ERR framework, demonstrated here with narrative text, is the same as that presented in Chapter 2, though implemented differently using expository text. As you experience this model lesson, note the differences and similarities between it and the expository lesson.

In this lesson, you will again play two roles: first, as a student, by participating fully in the guided lesson. This way you will be prepared to reflect on it as a learner. The second role is that of a student of pedagogy. Notice how the various activities within the lesson impacts your learning so you will be able to recall these experiences during part two of the lesson. This model lesson uses the short story "The Sniper" by Liam O'Flaherty (Appendix B). (Our thanks to Beth Whetmore for developing the segmentation of the story and many of the prompt questions while she was at the University of Virginia.)

In a moment, you will begin this lesson by reading a short story. The text is divided into four segments. You will read one segment and stop to reflect on and discuss that segment before reading further. Do not read ahead in the story, as you will be reading in a particular sequence. Reading ahead will distort your learning experience.

Before you start reading, we need to say something about the author. If you are in a learning community, someone should read aloud the introductory piece about the author. If not in a learning group, read the author information and then stop. This should take only a few minutes. Then take a few minutes to speculate about how the author's life experience might inform you about his writing. After this deliberation and some brief additional instruction, you will read only as far as the indicated first stop. In this first reading, read only the first two paragraphs. Again, it is important not to read past the stopping point. Please read the introductory comments about the author now and think about how his life experience might influence his writing.

Now, as you prepare to read the short story, notice the sensory contrast between the first two sentences and the last three sentences of the first paragraph. The first paragraph seems to present a deliberate contrast. Please go ahead and read the first paragraph. If you are in a learning community, signal one another when you have finished reading.

Now that you have read these first two paragraphs, let's think about them. How did you feel after reading the first few sentences? Did you feel any sensory changes? What did you see? What did you hear? (*Translation*)

There is no correct answer, of course, so share your feelings and sentiments. In groups of responders, it is important to listen and acknowledge the credibility of all responses. So what is the contrast as you understand it? Is there something here about the natural world and the human world?

Based on your brief reading so far and your knowledge of the author, wonder for a time about what you think might be the main problem in this story. What big issue or issues might be at stake? Why do you think so? (*Interpretation*)

In a moment, read to the next stop. As you read, try to picture the scene in your mind in as much detail as possible. (*Translation*) Remember to read only to the stopping point and signal others when you are finished reading.

Now that you have read to the second stop, take a few moments to reflect on what you have read. When done, conjure up the image you have created in your mind. What do you see? (*Interpretation*) In your group, share images of the scene. Be detailed so others can see vividly the images imagined. Think now as well about the main character, the sniper. What do you think the sniper was feeling? How do you feel about the sniper? Do you like him or not like him? Was it okay to shoot the "old lady"? Why or why not? What must it have felt like to pour iodine on the wound? Oh, do you know what a parapet is? (*Memory*)

Now, before reading on, ask yourself what you now think this story must be about. What do you think will happen next? (*Analysis*) Do you think the sniper will get out alive? What makes you think so? (*Synthesis*) When you have thought and perhaps discussed your responses, think about what is to come. You may guess this story will develop a bit of a twist and then another close after the first. Look for those points in the next section of the story where you sense a twist of some kind. (*Interpretation*) Read now until the next stop. Signal colleagues when done.

Well, there is certainly a lot to consider and a lot going on for such a short story. Did you see the twist and then a bit of a twist again? Yes, what about the sniper's change of mind both times? What do you think was going through the sniper's mind? Is there something good about what is happening? What might not be so good? Why do you think so? (*Evaluation*)

Well, everything is now almost done in this story, but the author will not finish for another 200 words or so. Thinking of what has happened up to now, can you predict how the story will end? Jot down some thoughts or share how you might end this story. Why? Discuss different views and why you think as you do. Do not limit this conversation, as it can be full of fascinating insights and informative perceptions.

As you now prepare to read the last section of the article, think about what is at issue in this story. If you were the sniper, how would you feel right now? What would you do and why? (*Synthesis*) Okay, read on and signal when you are finished.

Well, it's done. Did it end as you thought it would? Share your thoughts with others or jot down your immediate reactions and read them aloud to see and hear them. This will bring more clarity and power to your own thoughts. Now, wonder if this story were to continue what would happen next. What would the sniper do? Will the sniper survive? What evidence is there in the story to support what you think? How do you feel about the sniper now?

Now, consider what you think the big issue is in this story. Is it warfare, civil war, brotherhood, or something else? What about the concept of brotherhood? Is it limited to blood brothers, or is it inclusive; can we attribute brotherhood to all humankind? Share your thinking with others and listen to what others say and think about "The Sniper."

"The Sniper" is a powerful story. O'Flaherty has managed to say a lot in a short amount of time. The story ending typically strikes readers viscerally. It is clear the author has written the story to make a point beyond the detailing of the events in the tale itself. O'Flaherty had a larger purpose. Certainly, he intended to stimulate thought about war and peace. This is one reason why we would want our students to read the story. So our work with this story is only just beginning. So now, we want to expand our thinking by contemplating how this story fits into our thinking on the broader issue of war and peace. To stimulate our thinking and to lay our ideas out where we can view them to perhaps understand more precisely their implications, we will do some writing. Read first the following two quotes. Think about them for a few seconds and then select one of the quotes to respond to.

> "The tree of liberty must be refreshed from time to time with the blood of patriots and tyrants." Thomas Jefferson

> "Suppose they gave a war and nobody came." A poster commonly displayed during the Viet Nam War.

After selecting a quote, consider how it might relate to "The Sniper" and your views on war and peace. Write for no more than eight minutes. However, for this writing, use the freewriting technique discussed in Chapter 1. Remember to follow the three basic rules of freewriting.

Begin writing now and write for eight minutes.

In your learning community, take time now to share your writing with a partner. Partners should read their writing. When reading, *do not* paraphrase but read what is written. After you have read all your writing, begin a discussion about why you believe as you do. Following this paired sharing, as a larger group, determine how many have written from each of the quotes. Listen to the writings of some volunteers willing to share. You can then begin a larger discussion of the various beliefs expressed by colleagues. Be sure to reflect on "The Sniper" and the messages you might have drawn from the text.

If you are working independently, you will find it useful to consider now the quotation you did not originally select and try to take the stance this quotation encourages. When done, examine the two positions, attempting to negotiate a point of view that accommodates the two disparate beliefs.

NARRATIVE LESSON ANALYSIS

Recall the application of the ERR framework for the sea turtle lesson. Think for a moment how the elements of the framework, as you understand that at this time, are evident in this lesson.

This lesson contains two primary elements. First is the application of the framework for learning from narrative text, and the second is the systematic use of questioning as a guide to learning by prompting thinking at various levels and from various perspectives. We begin our analysis by recalling first what happened in the lesson. Take a moment to reflect on the lesson just experienced. In your journal, make a list of the instructional steps you recall. Remember, this lesson began with a reading of introductory remarks about the author. What followed? Continue your list, and with it, we will deconstruct the lesson with an eye on how it incorporates the ERR framework. With your list at the ready, look at the lesson.

The first activity, discussing the author and his context, was done as a general evocation activity. Its purpose was to stimulate thinking about the universe of the author, the time, location, and some likely themes as possible clues to meaning. It was intended to be general, as more specifically targeted Evocation activities were to be introduced during the reading. It represents a means of approaching the story globally. We will say more about this later.

Instructionally, the next step was to ask readers as they read to look for some specific shifts in the text, some contrasting sensory images. Why these questions? These questions are intended to invite readers to begin to immerse themselves in the text, alerting them to read carefully, to be watchful of content and mindful of their capacity to connect to text at multiple levels as they build understanding. This was a prompt for the Realization of Meaning phase. It is intended to activate readers' cognitive and metacognitive processes so reading for meaning becomes a conscious, almost physical act.

Next, you read to the second stop and where you were asked to reflect on the contrast and how the reading made you feel. Stopping to deliberate meanings and implications and discuss reactions involved you in the work of the Reflection phase.

You can see, then, that the ERR entire framework was applied to the first reading segment. Activating engagement through these microapplications of ERR as exemplified here, by working through the entire framework sequence within segments of text, is a robust means of maintaining engagement with text while instigating critical analysis from the beginning. There is little justification for postponing cognitive engagement with either narrative or expository pieces, or any other lesson format for that matter. We know comprehension is a process of mediating meanings between what an author or composer may intend and what the learner ultimately constructs. The less artificially confined and more critically considered we approach text, the greater the potential for more elaborate, more eloquent constructions.

As reflections regarding the reading were concluding, you were invited to think about the big picture idea. You were asked what you think might be at issue in the story. This constitutes the Evocation for the next reading segment. After answering questions about the first reading, you were asked, again while reading, to create a detailed vision of the scene unfolding in the story. This story is particularly visually powerful, so a visual prompt is appropriate for this author. Readers cannot help generating mental images while reading if they are involved, but encouraging attention to this act brings it to a more conscious, potentially more vivid, level thereby serving to sustain reader engagement at a more thoughtful level. The image is, of course, personal, intentional, and malleable, adjusting to the story line as the reader proceeds through the text.

Immediately, questioning, at the next stop about your vision, helps to keep your vision fresh. Beginning in this way also confirms that the task assigned during Realization was serious, reinforcing expectations for engagement. Furthermore, discussing your vision requires transformation of your visual image into descriptive language and places the representations in the public domain for other students to consider and respond to. Gathering feedback offers opportunities to see if your image is a shared image or a unique representation. This comparative experience enlightens readers to the array of possible of interpretations.

Interestingly, it was during this stop that the only literal-level or memory question was asked. Do you recall what it was? It was, "Do you know what a parapet is?" Juxtaposed here in the lesson against the richness of the preceding questions, this question stands in stark contrast to the others. It is easy to see in this context how literal- or memory-level questions neither promote nor assess meaning making at a thoughtful or critical level. Understanding what a parapet is may be informative, but it is certainly not essential to understanding the story.

Next, readers were invited to engage in continued critical analysis by preparing for plot twists or a change of some kind. The intention here of course is to make uncovering the mystery an added purpose of reading. When this reading was completed, questions were asked to capture the full consequences of this section of text.

By your own list of sequenced lesson activities, you can see that the remainder of the reading portion of the lesson unfolded through a series of framework applications. The lesson then ended with a writing-for-thinking task. Presented with two quotations, you were asked to make a choice and write in response to your choice. Juxtaposing these quotations within the context of this particular story creates a fund of immediate experience with the issues raised by the quotes from a literary source. The story immediately becomes a resource supporting thinking, in this case about war, and aids in the development of opinion formation. Employing reading in service of critical thought personalizes the experience and reinforces students' understanding of the role of reading as a powerful resource for personal growth and intellectual development. The reader now makes use of the message of this short story as the author intended, that is, as stimulus for thought and a medium for posing questions for conscientious deliberation.

In a moment, we will engage in a further analysis of this lesson as there are a number of elements to this lesson that are less apparent. Before we continue, walk back through the lesson once more and recall what you did and how it affected you as a learner. Consider at each step whether the process increased your motivation to read or your engagement with the text. That is, were you more engaged in the text as you read than you otherwise might have been? Think as well about how your students will respond. Do you think they might be more involved, intrigued, engaged? Were you eager for the questions to stop so you could continue reading? When you have thought about those matters, consider how this model lesson differs from the one modeled in Chapter 2 using expository text. How are they similar? Share your thoughts with your partner or in a small group.

ERR AS A MULTITIERED MODEL

At first glance, this lesson appears rather straightforward and perhaps unremarkable. However, much is happening here, and when the various elements of the lesson become transparent, the lesson is more sophisticated than it might initially appear. It offers a multipurpose guide to content lesson development. As your own experience attests, this lesson sustains reader engagement as it guides learners through a complicated text. It enables readers to monitor their own comprehension, provides opportunity for feedback about their thinking as meaning is being constructed from the text, and builds connections to personal understandings and beliefs. These are all actions good readers perform to comprehend text.

Let's examine the details. In this lesson, the ERR framework is applied at two levels. The first is at an overarching or global level. Reading about the author and speculating on possible themes represent initial engagement in the evocation phase. Global Realization of Meaning unfolded through a guided reading framework. Finally, Global Reflection occurred during the final writing and discussion activities. This global framework application walked us through the various learning phases and would by itself serve us well. However, careful reading of complex text offers readers a more richly textured understanding and enables students to consider the central issues and themes, the big ideas of a curriculum, so it is important to commit the time needed to a more complex instructional process. In our example, we examine the text in greater detail by applying the ERR framework to text segments. Consider the flow of the lesson. The text was divided into four segments. Each segment contained, in some fashion, a whole idea or story element, with stops situated at a poignant point or when there was some element of suspense. Within these segments, questioning guided the reader through the ERR process so readers engaged in evocation activities by speculating on what was to come by making predictions. Then readers explored the text, looking for particular themes, visions, answers to questions, challenges, or points of interest. This was followed by reflections on the implications of that segment for character, story and/or broader themes, and always involved revisiting the initial Evocation and the Realization of Meaning reading goal.

Applying the framework in an increasingly complicated manner is possible because the framework is nonlinear. Most content and certainly human thought are decidedly nonlinear, so instruction is most effective if it too is structured to accommodate to this nonlinear reality. In the sea turtle example, we applied the framework globally. That lesson followed a course represented by something like Figure 3.1.

Figure 3.1

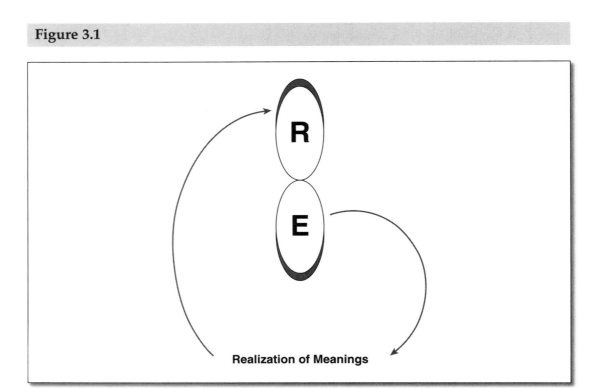

Realization of Meanings

The sea turtle lesson concluded with learner recognition of both new knowledge and the difference between what learners understood after learning relative to their prior knowledge. In ongoing learning environments, say, a biology class, the study of sea turtles may be part of a larger lesson on reptiles or ocean life or endangered species, or the effects of the recent oil-well blowout on the ecology of the Gulf of Mexico. The arrow leading away from the initial ERR cycle leads to the next concept or topic.

Let's imagine the study of sea turtles was part of a lesson on ocean life with the next unit of study examining ocean currents and how they support ocean life. The sea turtle study then serves as an evocation activity for the larger study of ocean life (see Figure 3.2).

The ERR framework represented in Figure 3.1 becomes part of a larger representation of a more complicated instructional process in which the sea turtle is embedded but with the same basic elements. "The Sniper" lesson application of the framework represents another variation and can be visualized differently. Using the framework as guide to a series of text encounters, the framework application in "The Sniper" lesson is represented by Figure 3.3.

In this latter configuration, Realization of Meaning becomes a series of whole framework applications because we want the benefit of all the various learning phases throughout the text. This enables us to continuously evoke ideas and

Figure 3.2

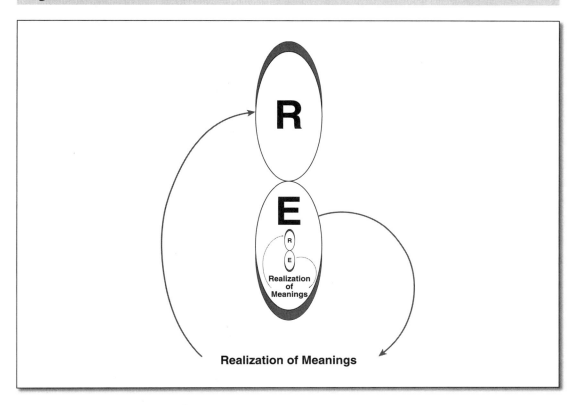

Realization of Meanings

Figure 3.3

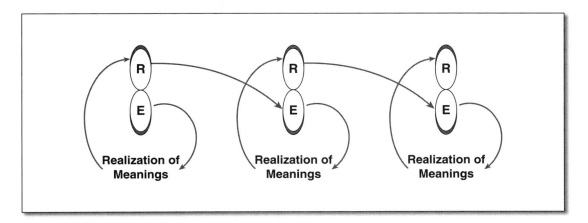

understandings to maintain text-reader connections. The text is certainly compelling but also dense with implication. It is important that readers monitor comprehension, but we can enhance this by focusing attention on the various themes as they emerge. We facilitate deeper understanding by targeting our gaze at elements of particular interest as complex understandings evolve. With complicated text, it is helpful to know what you know, think, and understand as you travel from start to finish. Hikers, meandering along a challenging mountain trail, must, from time to time, stop to catch their breath. So too, readers, engaged with difficult text, must stop for a comprehension breather, reviewing where they have been and pondering the trail ahead. With some chance for renewal, they are better prepared to set out again for the summit. The periodic reflections and evocations of "The Sniper" lesson serve this purpose. They also serve as opportunities to orient learners' attention toward the concepts and issues that drive the lesson in the first place. There must be a learning purpose for everything in the curriculum. This process makes this transparent while retaining teacher and learner focus.

"The Sniper" model also reveals how integrated continuous application of ERR can be. As you think about how you will implement the framework, it will become increasingly apparent that the model provides a mechanism for facilitating fluid transitions from idea to idea and from one topic to another when sequenced carefully. The model demonstrates how evocations and reflections are blended so that reflections, resulting from one content, concept, theme, or experience, become evocations for another. Figure 3.4 offers a model for thinking through a coherent sequence of learning experiences that will move students through a purpose-driven course, while offering individual learning experiences that are in themselves coherent. The model allows instruction to explore tangents—immediate interests or passions—and detours yet maintains focus on the intent of, let's say, the course and the desired outcomes of instruction. More important, this model offers a vision of how to engage students in what Dewey (1987) would describe as a complete learning experience that embodies both the rational and the emotional or aesthetic. Wong (2007), referencing the work of Dewey and Rosenblatt, speaks of motivation as "that which animates the learner" (p. 8). Citing Dewey, Wong described learning as the relationship between elements of active learner control and receptiveness to environmental input, or "doing and undergoing." Wong wrote,

> . . . motivated learning involves both the rational and the nonrational elements, and learner control and its opposite, there is also something distinctive about the relationship between these elements. Dewey (1987) describes the relationship this way. "Moreover, at each stage, there is anticipation of what is to come. This anticipation is the connection link between the next doing and its outcome for sense [meaning]. What is done [action] and what is undergone [reception] are thus reciprocally, cumulatively, and continuously instrumental to each other" (L. W. 10.56). In other words, deep engagement is more than doing and undergoing, or acting on the world and the world acting on us. Deep engagement also requires a contingent, coherent, and evolving relationship between these elements. In each interaction, there is movement and direction toward some kind of culmination. And although the culmination is by definition at the conclusion of an event, its presence is felt throughout. According to Jackson (1998), "This consummation, moreover, does not wait in consciousness for the whole undertaking to be finished. It is anticipated throughout and is recurrently savored with special intensity. We anticipate the possibility of what might be—new perception of the world or a new way of being in the world—and are energized to move forward." Anticipation is embodied in readers who cannot put a book down and must keep turning pages to learn whether an imagined possibility becomes a sensible actuality. Anticipation is the tension in the dramatic line that connects the "what if" to "what is." The excitement of sensing and

opening to a possible world and the irresistible urge to move into the world best describes the motivation of a student who suddenly sits bolt upright in class and exclaims, "I have an idea! What if . . . ?" (pp. 8–9)

Take a moment now to think about your own curriculum. Identify a reading task and think through how the ERR sniper model from Figure 3.3 might be applied to the passage. Or consider Figure 3.2. Think how you might construct a lesson sequence across some related themes that would resemble the lesson sequence exemplified by Figure 3.4.

Figure 3.4

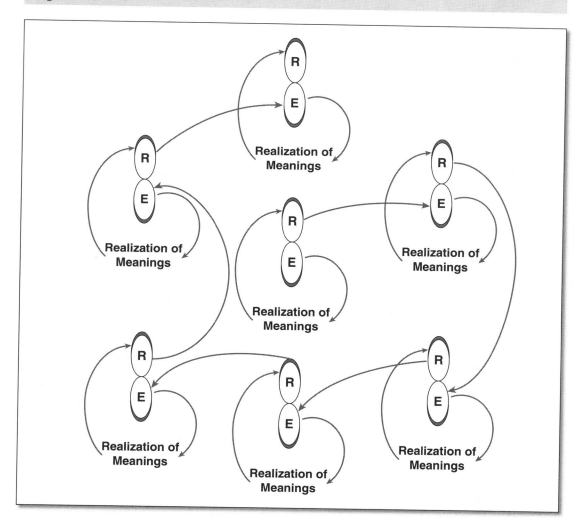

QUESTIONING

Recall now your thoughts about questioning from earlier in this chapter. Remember your thoughts about your own questioning history and how critically questioning is linked to learning. Have your early thoughts out for reflection as you read the next few pages. You will want to return to them at the end of this reading. ERR served as instructional subtext for "The Sniper" lesson. Questioning served us differently. Like wind powering a schooner on the sea, questioning propels readers through a learning experience. Compelling questions motivate learners to think, stimulate curiosity, sometimes anger, or perplex, or trigger imagination. Yet with so much potential, classroom questioning is often conducted haphazardly, with little or no thought given to what kinds of questions to ask, when to ask them, or why. The example lesson in this chapter was driven by questions. The composition of those questions and their timing were not accidental. Rather, they were calculated to accomplish the following:

- Link reader experience to text
- Provide catalysts for ongoing comprehension of text
- Sustain motivation to understand
- Engage readers in multiple levels of cognition dependent on various types of thought processes

You will see that understanding the power and purpose of questioning provides yet another layer of sophistication to the lesson and, when implemented with care and purpose, provides teachers with a powerful instructional tool.

Adapting Bloom's Taxonomy of Questions

The questions posed in this narrative example are derived from Sanders's (1969) revision of Bloom's taxonomy of questioning. You probably noticed while reading the text that many questions were followed by a term in parentheses. They represent the various types of questions Bloom and Sanders describe from the cognitive domain. The taxonomy also represents only one way of organizing questions. There are many other conceptualizations of question types. All are intended to guide learners through a variety of thought processes, preventing instruction from narrowing to a single or limited range of approaches to inquiry. Bloom's and Sanders's taxonomy suggests that guiding inquiry requires students to interpret information, synthesize ideas, analyze information, reconstruct or translate images, and evaluate and then apply their understandings and constructs to text or other instructional media as it evolves. For Bloom and Sanders, these various types of questions form a hierarchy, with memory or literal-level questions representing the lowest form of questioning and, consequently, a minimal type of thinking. Evaluation or judgment questions, in their view, invoke the highest level of thinking (see Figure 3.5).

Bloom (1956) addressed three domains: cognitive, affective, and psychomotor. Much has been written about these domains, and there continues to be considerable attention paid to Bloom's work. The following websites offer a review of some recent discussion as well as applications of Bloom's taxonomy.

While there is certainly minimal thought associated with memory questions and much more sophisticated thought is required for evaluative questions, we believe it more beneficial instructionally to think in less hierarchical terms. As we have suggested, well-considered questioning leads to different ways of thinking, prods differing thought processes, resulting in more enriched learning experiences. So it may be more productive to view questioning as a circle of options (see Figure

Figure 3.5

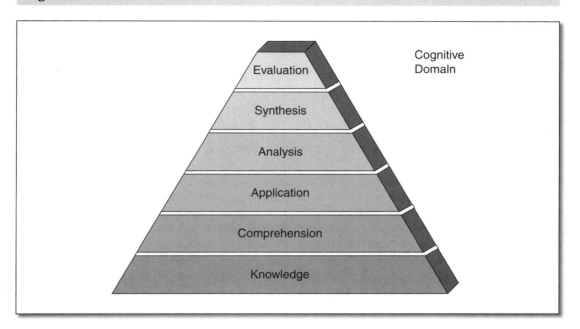

Explanation of Bloom's Taxonomy:

http://www.eoun.unic.ca/learning/exams/blooms-taxonomy.html

http://krummefamily.org/guides/bloom.html

http://www.odu.edu/educ/roverbau/Bloom/blooms_taxonomy.htm

Excellent site for visualizing a reworking of Bloom's categories:

http://projects.coe.uga.edu/epltt/index.php?title=Bloom%27s_Taxonomy

A chapter on Bloom's Taxonomy:

http://eduscapes.com/tap/topic69.htm

Critical and creative thinking and Bloom's Taxonomy:

http://edtech.clas.pdx.edu/presentations/frr99/blooms.htm

A table of verbs associated with Bloom's Taxonomy:

http://www.gdoe.net/ci/CurriculumGuides/K-12%20Math%20Curriculum%20Guide%
5CSection%20IV%20-%20Appendix%5C2%20Bloom%27s%20Taxonomy
%5Cbloom%27s%20taxonomy.pdf

3.6) to draw from, understanding that each question type represents a unique angle of vision that provides access to different realities, which in turn may contribute to more elegant, more richly textured understandings. One legitimate goal of instruction is to engage students in all manner of thought as they deal with content. When questioning and thinking remain primarily at a literal or memory level, students' knowledge represents only data storage, demonstrating no real evidence of understanding. Perhaps the best way to determine what questions to ask is to start with the big idea for the lesson and ask, "How can I lead my students to consider this big idea, and how do I want them to think about or approach the idea(s)? "What do I want them to do with the idea?" Or we find it helps focus questions on the big ideas by asking, "What do I want my students to know and be able to do in 10 to 15 years as a result of this lesson?"

Figure 3.6

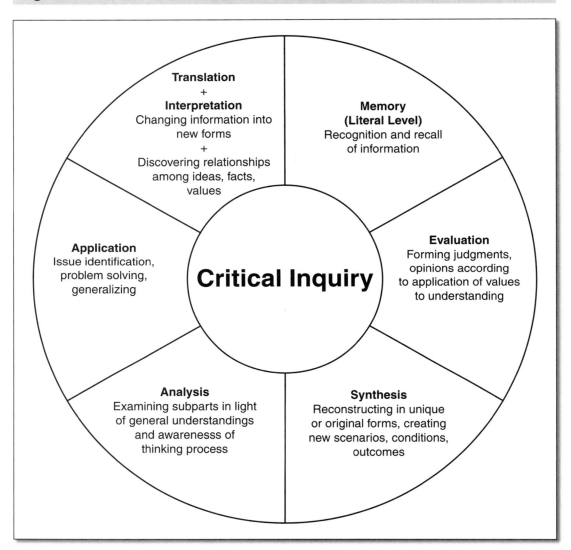

Multiprocess Questioning

Since various types of questions engage thinkers differently, understanding the thought processes underlying question types enables better decision making about what questions to ask when making questioning a more powerful tool for guided inquiry. Following are brief descriptions of the various question types included in

Bloom's and Sanders's taxonomies and question prompts to stimulate the desired thinking.

Literal level questions—for example, "What is a parapet?"—seek factual information. They typically require simply rote recall. Respondents need only short-term, fragmented knowledge to successfully respond. Answers to literal-level questions are typically found in the text or presentation and require students merely to recite what has already been stated. Define, describe, duplicate, label, list, match, memorize, outline, quote, recall, repeat, recognize, reproduce.

Translation questions require reformulation of information. They ask students to picture in their minds a situation, scene, or event and describe what they see. Translation questions encourage students to restructure or transform information into different images. Students responding to translation questions imagine the sights, sounds, smells, or other sensations conjured up. "The long June twilight faded into night. Dublin lay enveloped in darkness, but the dim light of the moon that shone through fleecy clouds, casting a pale light as approaching dawn over the street and the dark waters of the Liffey. Around the beleaguered Four Courts the heavy guns roared" (from "The Sniper" by Liam O'Flaherty). Students translating text have to create their own sensory experience and then use their expressive language to describe their vision to others. It is an active, creative process of engagement. Picture, re-create, script, illustrate, imagine, invent, charge, draw, act out.

Interpretation questions seek to discover connections between ideas, facts, definitions, and values. Students must think about how ideas or concepts go together meaningfully, building various contexts into which ideas can fit. Interpretation questions ask students, "Why do you think the main character waited until her father came home?" or "What was the reason that catastrophe struck when it did?" This kind of questioning stimulates speculative thinking. Sanders (1969) considers interpretation questions to be core questions for higher-level thinking, and many (Vaughn & Estes, 1986) have suggested comprehension is interpretation. Why, how so, explain, defend, estimate, extend, predict, summarize.

Application questions offer students the opportunity to solve problems or further investigate problems of logic or reason encountered during reading or learning experiences. For example, "How does what we know so far help us understand why the decisions being made make sense?" Apply, change, choose, construct, demonstrate, dramatize, employ, interpret, operate, schedule, produce, show how, solve, use.

Analysis questions ask whether events are adequately explained or if information or circumstances might explain outcomes more reasonably. Might there be a better explanation for what is happening? For example, a reader might question a character's motives or an experimenter's research plan, or question the reasonableness of a historian's conclusions. Analyze, appraise, compare, contrast, criticize, diagram, differentiate, deduce, discriminate, distinguish, examine logical consequences, outcomes, question, test what follows.

Responding to *Synthesis* questions involves creative problem solving using original thinking. While application questions ask students to solve problems based on available information, synthesis questions allow students the opportunity to bring the full range of their knowledge and experiences to a problem to solve it creatively. Synthesis questions ask students to create alternative scenarios. For example, "Given the evidence we have so far, what is another way this crime might have been committed?" or "What might the victims have overlooked in their immediate environment if they were looking at their resources creatively that could have saved their lives as the *Titanic* was sinking?" Combine, compile, devise, design, generate, induct, reorder, reorganize, reexamine what's missing.

Evaluation questions ask students to make judgments about good and bad or right and wrong according to standards the student defines. Evaluation questions may seek judgments about the behavior of a character in a story, determining whether a character acted rightly or wrongly in a situation or if a character acted fairly or unfairly. Such questions necessitate thorough understanding of content encountered along with its integration into a personal belief system from which judgments can be made. Evaluation questions ask students to judge the quality of information they have learned or, in some cases judge their own behaviors in light of new information, like, "Why don't I brush my teeth every night before bed after what I just learned about tooth decay?" This level of integrated comprehension makes the learning process personal and enables learners to readily take ownership of cognitively agreeable new ideas and concepts. Appraise, assess, argue, criticize, critique, defend, formulate opinion, judge, justify, support, value, evaluate.

Returning for a moment to "The Sniper" lesson, recall that from time to time, some parenthetical terms were present following a number of questions. You probably noticed that those labels reflect the various question types found in Bloom's taxonomy. Tracking the questions through "The Sniper," you will observe that there was no obvious order to the questioning. In other words, there was no attempt to follow some specific sequence, say, from lower to higher level. Two ideas drove the questioning process here. First, the belief that text content will, to some degree, define the question sequence. A second guiding idea involved simply acknowledging the importance of including multiple forms of questions so students engage in various ways of thinking about the content.

As questioning expands beyond basic memory or literal-level questioning, students begin to respond to instruction with meaningful thoughts and ideas, integrating their own expressive vocabulary and learning histories with the language and vocabulary of the specific content area. The dialogue that develops out of such questioning exposes students to a broad range of perspectives and differing expressions, expanding their conceptual knowledge along with their capacity to articulate new and perhaps creative ideas.

Some suggest that complex thought is developmental and that young students should not be expected to engage in synthesis or evaluation or even interpretation activities. This is not the case. These questions do not simply represent a developmental sequence. Certainly, the sophistication of children's responses reflects developmental characteristics. However, even kindergarten children eagerly respond to synthesis, evaluation, or interpretation of questions. Young people continually engage in synthesizing ideas, making judgments within their social, physical, intellectual, and emotional environments, actively applying newfound knowledge to understanding and negotiating these landscapes. It is what children are in the business of doing until we tell them to stop. Again, Kathleen Cotton (2003) in her meta-analysis of cognitive questioning research offers a more sophisticated view of the developmental nature of questioning. It seems lower-level cognitive questions can benefit primary-level students, provided the questions are at a level that enables most students to respond correctly to most (70%) questions. But there is no support for exclusivity of lower-level questions for this age group. For older students, increasing higher-level questioning beyond 20% substantially enhances learning and achievement.

Return to your own thoughts and experiences with questioning. See if you can detect a pattern in your own questioning approach. Do you tend to concentrate in one or two areas? If so, think about why this is so and how you might broaden your questioning processes. Share with your partners.

Discussion as a Learning Tool

Several teaching principles are important to note in the process of understanding the sample lesson. First, one of the primary types of thinking being encouraged in the example is prediction. Throughout "The Sniper," you were asked to consider what you thought would happen next. The phenomenon of prediction is a powerful factor, affecting comprehension and critical thinking. Prediction increases interest and obliges learners to examine what is already known and not known, raising existing knowledge above the horizon, making it serviceable knowledge as opposed to merely accumulated knowledge. Prediction establishes learners' purposes for reading and is a primary mechanism for promoting comprehension. Prediction poses a singularly purposeful question, "Will my prediction come to pass?" The act of seeking confirmation of our own thinking, having one's own questions answered is, according to some researchers, the very definition of comprehension (Steele & Steele, 1991). Thus, prediction, hypothesizing, can serve as a central contributor to increasing comprehension. It is important to note, however, that it does not matter if predictions are correct. It only matters that one makes predictions, thereby beginning the process of searching for answers.

The second principle for directing learning experiences toward expanded levels of thinking is that there must be a coherent plan to guide student thinking. It is important, especially when teachers are just beginning, to develop an action plan for working through a text or learning experience that compels students to engage in various thought processes. However, any plan should be used only as a guide, as teaching is also reactive, so student responses should also guide classroom discussion. When we read a story with students, we follow a basic plan but let students' ideas lead discussions to points of interest for them.

Teacher as Commentator

One additional important point about questioning has to do with teacher behavior and how it influences student thinking. Since teachers initiate the questioning process, students tend to respond directly to the teacher. Students look toward their teacher, paying less attention to classmates. If genuine classroom dialogue is to occur, this interaction pattern has to change. Teachers engage in several behaviors that support classroom behaviors that limit dialogue. The first and most important problematic teacher behavior is that of classroom commentator. When students speak, teachers typically believe *they* must respond. What emerges is a predictable conversation pattern. First, the teacher speaks, then student A, then the teacher, then student B, teacher, student C, teacher, and so it goes. What this amounts to is a series of one-on-one conversations between the teacher and a student. As long as teachers engage in this response pattern, students will not speak to one another. Students will continue the one-on-one conversation. What is more effective is for teachers to moderate and guide discussion among their students. So student A speaks, then student

B, then C, with teacher interdiction to redirect when necessary, provide corrections where appropriate, prod further exploration, challenge students to think more deeply, or simply act as one party to the discourse rather than as a conversational clearinghouse.

The second teacher behavior that sustains teacher-centered interaction patterns is the instant evaluator. We have all been there. It happens when a student speaks and we immediately pass judgment with such phrases as "Yes! That's right." or "No, someone else?" or "Excellent!" The latter of course crushing any further commentary, as who is going to follow up with a different thought when the previous utterance received the ultimate reply? This scenario is an easy trap when we are asking students to guess what is in the teacher's head, when we are asking for the one right answer. More facilitative comments include "Who else has something to share?" or "What do others think about this?" or "Do we all agree with this?" or "Is there something we are missing? Let's think this through some more and see if there might be another way to look at the situation." The goal is to remove the overriding evaluative context to free students to express their ideas.

Stopping Points

Important to "The Sniper" narrative text approach is determining how and where to segment a text. While stops should occur naturally, it takes practice to identify appropriate points. It is not as easy as it looks, and care should be given to selecting stopping points that allow students to reflect on the text and make predictions. Text segments should have a self-contained quality yet precipitate forward motion. That is, if at all possible, the end of one segment should in some way foreshadow what is to come. This of course facilitates prediction. The best examples of this come from television series where the segmentation of the story is intended to sustain interest sufficiently to secure viewer loyalty through the abundance of advertisements, from week to week and even season to season. For those old enough to remember the television show *Dallas,* "Who shot J. R.?" is perhaps the most dramatic example.

Wait Time

An important issue to consider when engaged in student questioning is the issue of "wait time." Wait time refers to the time teachers wait after asking a question before they intercede by asking another question, moving on to another student, or answering the question themselves. Research on this topic suggests there is a direct relationship between the amount of time teachers wait after asking a question and the level of students' thinking (Steele & Meredith, 1991). Teachers usually wait on average less than one second. But when teachers increase wait time to three seconds, levels of thinking and student response rates increase significantly (Dillon, 1983; Gambrell, 1980). It is only common sense that when thought-provoking questions are asked, students need time to think.

Finally, when teachers engage in multiprocess questioning, it is important to encourage all students to participate. To accomplish this, teachers must call on the less outgoing students by name and sometimes overlook the students who believe they must answer every question. Many students do not respond freely to classroom questioning because, as we have mentioned, it is typically evaluative rather than stimulus for discourse. As teachers move away from evaluative questioning and toward questioning for critical thinking and learning, students more freely engage in open discussion. As students become accustomed to true discussion questions where ideas are valued, they are eager to express their thoughts.

Deciding What to Ask

It takes time and practice to divide text successfully and ask the kinds of questions that guide students through text. The multilevel questions presented here are intended to model possible types of questions and to underscore the type of thinking they elicit. When teachers prepare their own questions, it is not essential to use every question type for each lesson. We tend to approach questioning with a few basic ideas in mind. First, rather than attempting to create a series of questions that include all types, it is much better, as we have suggested, to let the natural flow of the content and the compelling purposes for examining the content in the first place determine the most appropriate questions. The second comes from the first and involves determining the purpose for investigating the particular content. This is truly the hardest part. Questions should emanate from the purposes we set for students, so careful thought must be given to "why." Why read O'Flaherty? Certainly, it is an example of great literature, but what makes it great? The powers of language, the skill of the writer to say so much so quickly are important considerations. More important perhaps is how O'Flaherty inspires readers to think and what he inspires readers to think about. O'Flaherty was not writing a historical piece to capture a moment in the Irish civil war. He was using this tragedy to confront readers with some realities of war, perhaps a caution when war is being considered a possible solution to a problem.

Before moving on, it is important to begin classroom implementation to see for yourself how what you have learned can work for you. Begin with a genuine text you are using in class or will use in class. By yourself or in small groups, segment the text and develop questions appropriate to these materials using the guide below. Ideally, your small group should be composed primarily of colleagues at the same instructional level or content area. Take time to examine the text and then plan a lesson, as the first implementation is always the most difficult.

Once reading material is selected, ask the following questions:

- Why do I want my students to read this material?
- What, if any, big issues or questions are posed by the text?
- What do I hope my students will understand when they are finished studying the text?
- What do I want my students to do when they have finished reading the text?
- What experiences do I want my students to have and share as they read?
- How will I determine students' academic success with this text?
- Where will my instruction take me from here, and how can I link to what is to follow?

Answering these questions will guide many of the questions asked during the reading of the text. As your small groups begin working, keep the following in mind:

1. There are no right or wrong dividing points.

2. Nothing is fixed after dividing the text. If it becomes obvious with use that other places would work better, then re-divide the text.

3. No questions are right or wrong.

4. Recall the question types presented and remember the importance of asking a variety of types.

5. Let the framework guide the process so students will be continuously engaged in evoking, anticipating, understanding, constructing meaning, and reflecting.

6. Do not subdivide the text into too many parts. It is important to maintain the flow of the text.

When done, if there are other groups working together, share the basics of your work, what text you are using, why you subdivided as you did (what guided your decision for this particular text), and what questions you will ask to guide reading. Also, speak to how you will follow this lesson. That is, what will you do to expand the impact of the reading beyond the text itself? Finally, go back and check to see that your lesson incorporates a global ERR framework application as modeled with "The Sniper."

REFLECTION

Chapter 3 covers a lot of instructional ground. Beginning with some initial thoughts on questioning and common practice, the chapter leads through a narrative text ERR application that is much more complex than was the case for the sea turtle experience. Questioning is then re-examined in light of "The Sniper" lesson. When seen through the lens of a real narrative lesson, the critical pedagogical role of questioning emerges. From our point of view, questioning is central to instruction at two levels. One level is core to any lesson. At this level, we must ask ourselves what the fundamental questions we are seeking to answer are with this particular lesson. "What are our purposes?" At another level, we are using questions to guide learners toward our overarching goals while encouraging student questions that might, just as well, head the lesson in unanticipated directions.

We then took some time to consider the pedagogical and cognitive significance of question types. Using Bloom's taxonomy as our departure point, we examined what various questions bring to the discussion, how they inspire particular kinds of thinking and facilitate broader understandings.

These two complex strands of narrative ERR and questioning were integrated within the context of a genuine instructional experience. It is useful, though, to take some time to consider them separately with respect to their instructional implications. Take time now to review and reflect on the various ERR models presented. See if the instructional implications, indeed curricular implications, for the various ERR representations are clear. Share in small groups your conclusions about these ERR applications and what they mean for lesson planning for daily lessons, for thematic lesson planning, and even for a term or for the academic year. It will be good to take some notes from this conversation in your journal, as the discussion is likely to touch on some intriguing ways to organize lessons and instructional sequences. Also, we will revisit this thinking near the end of the text, so a record of your thoughts at this point will be helpful.

Advancing Critical Thought

It is through listening that you will be able to cultivate wisdom and be able to remove ignorance. . . .

—His Holiness the Dalai Lama

OUTCOME EXPECTATIONS

At the conclusion of this chapter you will

- be able to implement an "Enhanced Lecture" strategy and understand the essential elements of the strategy, including how the ERR framework generates the strategy application;
- be able to use and teach others how to effectively employ the cluster notes strategy;
- understand some critical issues related to critical thinking and some steps for incorporating critical thinking into everyday classroom instruction;
- relate critical thinking to rigor and relevance rubrics;
- be able to implement the "10-Minute Essay" strategy in the reflection phase of instruction; and
- understand how critical thinking can be enhanced or inhibited through teacher behavior, classroom environment, and student psychology.

EVOCATION

Much has been said about the importance of critical thinking. Almost everyone writing about education today speaks to the essential need for students to develop critical thinking skills. But what is meant by critical thinking, and why might it be so essential? Here, we will spend some time examining critical thinking. In so doing, we will also model several instructional strategies in a manner similar to our work with the sniper and our sea turtle friends. This discussion of critical thinking will be presented within an ERR framework application as a coherent lesson. As we have done previously, here, you will be asked to fully engage in the lesson to experience the framework delivered using a different combination of strategies and with new content. Also, take care to observe your own learning experiences as the lesson progresses so you can reflect on its relative worth for teaching and learning.

Before we begin our more detailed examination of critical thinking, it is important that we share, in brief, our ideas with respect to pedagogy. We see critical thinking as a process. Thinking is a process similar to reading, writing, speaking, and listening. It is an active, coordinated, complex process that involves thinking about something genuine. It is not something that can be taught out of context. Critical thinking is not best learned when it is separated from the general context of the school curriculum or daily life. Thinking critically in school is best learned by experiencing this type of thought as a way of approaching content, as something which is part of and an expected outcome of the daily curriculum. Research concerning critical thinking and learning suggests that a model focusing on teaching isolated skills and fact learning minimizes critical thinking. For example, Palinscar and Brown (1984) argued that learning skills separate from real world tasks and purposes may allow students to do well on an objective test but leave them unable to apply those skills in new situations.

We have spoken of the utility of the ERR framework across various instruction mediums. Whether instruction employs text, lecture, video, a field trip, or laboratory work, ERR offers a framework for the teaching-learning process. Here, we are limited to text. However, for the next model lesson, it will be useful to imagine the presentation delivered as an "enhanced lecture." This form of lecture is explained more fully in the box.

The critical thinking presentation will be accompanied by some PowerPoint slides to give you a sense of the flow of the presentation. Let's begin our exploration of critical thinking.

Think for a moment about a time when you where trying to solve a particularly difficult problem or situation. There are no limits here. The problem might be social or academic. It could be related to organizing something for your children or your class. It might be a problem with friends or relatives or children, anything really. First, recall the problem and then try to think through what you thought about and what you did to solve the problem. Maybe you did not solve it. Think about what steps you took or processes you went through to try to solve it. When done, take four or five minutes to share the details of this experience with a partner or small group. Then, with a partner or a small group, list the different approaches taken to reach a solution. Keep the list, as it will be useful later to compare this list with the list of steps or processes others suggest constitute evidence of critical thought.

Now, one more evocation activity. With a partner or a small group, talk for a few minutes about "critical thinking." Your conversation can be general, thinking about what is meant by the phrase. Eventually, come around to a discussion of why critical thinking might be a worthy goal of schooling. In other words, speak to why all the fuss about critical thinking. Remember your conversation as the presentation to follow begins.

In addition to remembering your discussions, prepare to take notes during the "lecture." Not unusual of course, but here you will take "cluster notes." This note-taking strategy mirrors the clustering strategy presented in Chapter 5. However, this cluster is constructed as the lecture unfolds.

How to Take Cluster Notes

Borrowing the same concept and processes as brainstorming, begin by drawing a circle in the center of the upper half of a piece of note paper. In the circle, write the title or topic of the lecture, in this case, "critical thinking." As the lecture proceeds, draw lines connecting the central topic to subsequent themes. Remaining true to the clustering strategy, you will be able to write only single words or brief phrases—only enough to remind you of the idea. Your cluster can be as full and complex as the presentation and your organization of the information suggest. Figure 4.1 below provides basic rules. Chapter 5 details clustering and presents an example.

As you cluster (this takes practice), you will have questions. Be sure to add question marks as these questions arise so you can ask them later. In fact, the lecture will pause after about 10 minutes to allow time for you to fully articulate your questions and to share with your partners what you are taking from the presentation.

Now, remembering to take cluster notes, let's continue with our lesson on critical thinking.

Enhanced Lecture

Lecturing has been shown to be a rather ineffective instructional approach. Yet it is the most frequently used instructional approach to teaching in schools. One primary shortcoming is that students are usually passive recipients of information. Another is that the human capacity to listen and concentrate with real benefit is limited. Ten minutes is a good guide. Here, we will examine a means of enhancing a lecture by addressing these two obstacles to learning from lecture. There are times when a lecture can be useful. They include the following:

- When you want to provide students an introduction or an overview of a topic they are about to investigate actively
- When there is no easily readable written material available on the topic and direct inquiry is not feasible
- When you want to elaborate on a point that students have just encountered in an inquiry lesson
- When students' prior knowledge of a topic is not yet sufficient to read a text on the topic

Figure 4.1 Rules for Cluster Notes

1. As concepts emerge in the presentation, use "key words" to capture them.

2. Build as many connections as needed.

3. Avoid long phrases.

4. Do not let process interfere with attention to content. Links can be retrofitted if they are unclear at the time.

5. Using multiple pages is fine.

6. Be sure to mark questions or uncertainties as they emerge.

REALIZATION OF MEANING

Critical Thinking "Lecture"

To discuss critical thinking, it is useful to understand what it is. It is also useful to know going in just why thinking critically might matter. So we will begin first by discussing a possible outcome of critical thought, with an eye to identifying potential benefits as a way to drive our inquiry.

One outcome of critical thought proposed here is innovation. What is proposed is that critical thought creates a pathway from a collection of individual or group understandings and insights through a creative process to a unique, innovative conceptualization. With this view, various pieces of content knowledge are ordered, like beads on a necklace, in some creative composition, which results in a unique pattern or design, resulting in a pattern effect that, taken as a whole, represents a new direction or new conceptualization of some kind.

In this way, critical thinking is linked to innovation via a creative process. What about innovation? Is it a worthy goal? Some suggest that innovation is central to survival, perhaps our most essential tool for survival. The capacity to innovate enables us to respond to unforeseen challenges that may even threaten our existence. Thomas Friedman (2005) in his book *The World Is Flat* suggested that innovation would be the key to economic survival. Whoever develops key innovations will determine which economies flourish and which do not.

How we arrive at innovations remains open to question, but it seems, for the most part, it comes at the intersection of mostly conscious critical thought. There is some indication that innovation arises rather spontaneously and with only limited conscious control. However, there has always been control over input and how inputs, that is, information and experience, are processed and stored for recall, manipulation, and use.

So what does critical thinking seem to involve? Many suggest it involves some or all of the following:

- Understanding or developing logical connections between data points, ideas, or constructs
- Identifying, constructing, and/or evaluating rationales
- Detecting inconsistencies and common mistakes in reasoning
- Developing and applying systematic problem-solving strategies
- Culling problems or component elements to identify and sequester essential elements
- Suspending, at least momentarily, any unnecessary self-induced limitations or constraints to thinking to the extent one is aware

Critical thought then seems to be coupled with a creative process that simultaneously seems to engage thinkers in the process of the following:

- Envisioning familiar things in new ways
- Seeking in the familiar previously undetected patterns
- Connecting previously unconnected phenomenon
- Sequencing multiple forms of thought such as the following:
  - Synthetic–divergent thinking, making connections
  - Analytic—convergent thinking—evaluative

○ Transformative—reconfiguring, imagining across mediums
○ Practical—from abstraction to application

There are some wonderfully illustrative examples of critical and creative thinking processes coming together for innovation. For example, Alexander Fleming's discovery of penicillin, Archimedes' discovery of displacement, or Röntgen's discovery of radiation. Each discovery involved observing everyday events and asking, "What is really happening? What alternative idea(s) explain what is witnessed?"

We will review Alexander Fleming's discovery process below. In the next day or so (*Reflection*), do some research to learn how Archimedes and Röntgen made their discoveries.

Alexander Fleming discovered what is regarded as the most efficacious, life-saving drug ever developed. He discovered penicillin, which transformed the world of medicine and incubated the now enormous pharmaceutical industry. Within a few decades, previously fatal diseases such as gangrene and tuberculosis were conquered. Like many discoveries, this one was partly luck and partly a good dose of critical thought. Fleming left a culture dish with *Staphylococcus* bacteria on a bench in his lab and left for a two-week vacation. Fortunately, a *Penicillium* mold found its way to the desk as well and began to grow in the dish. The *Staphylococcus* bacteria grew as well, and when Fleming returned, he noticed the mold growth and where there was mold, there was no bacterial growth. He could have tossed the dish aside, but he did not. Instead, he asked if there wasn't some underlying reason why bacterial growth was inhibited near the mold. He correctly deduced that the mold released some sort of substance that retarded bacterial growth. Finding that substance, the active ingredient, turned out to be the most effective antibacterial agent known. Interestingly, he was not the first scientist to notice the same event surrounding the presence of mold. What was special about Fleming was that he saw this familiar event and acted on his observation in ways no one else had done previously. Equally intriguing, because Fleming lacked a background in chemistry, he was not able to take his discovery further. Not until more than 10 years later did others move Fleming's discovery forward with the kind of breakthrough experimentation that would prove the curative powers of penicillin.

Stop now and look at your cluster notes. Add anything you think needs adding that you recall from the presentation so far. Check to see if any connections need to be made between ideas you might have missed originally. Look to see what questions you have. When done, turn to your partner and share your notes, discuss the connections you made and why. Ask any questions that have arisen and see if the two of you can answer them. If not, write them down for later discussion with the large group. Remember as well your earlier thinking on this topic. Discuss with your partner, exploring whether innovation as an outcome makes sense and how it connects in any way to your original thinking.

Before proceeding (*Evocation*) imagine someone engaged in critical thought. What is that person doing exactly? How is his or her mind operating? In what cognitive activities is he or she engaged? Keep this image as we move forward (*Realization of Meaning*) and be sure to take cluster notes.

Let's continue now by looking at some examples that require problem solvers to alter perceptions or think more expansively. These examples

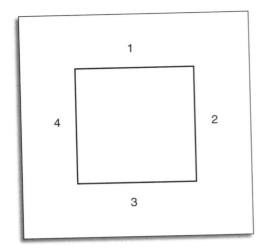

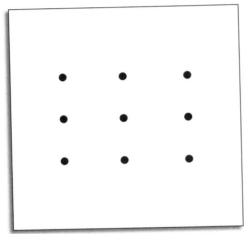

may be familiar. If so, recall your approach to problem solving the first time you encountered these problems.

Example 1: These four lines below form a figure with four 90 degree angles. Arrange these four lines, without bending or altering them, to create a figure with sixteen 90 degree angles.

Take some time to try to resolve this challenge. Try to remember as well your thinking as you tried to solve this puzzle. If you do not solve the problem, look in Appendix E. Monitor your thoughts when you first see the solution. This may reveal some reasons why you did not solve the puzzle. Often, the reason is rooted in self-imposed limitations.

Let's try another one.

Using only four, straight lines and connecting them end to end, arrange the lines so they pass through all the dots but each dot only once.

Take a few minutes to solve this puzzle. If you solved correctly, try to remember how your thinking progressed. If a solution escapes you for the moment, and this is so for many people, note your reaction when you first see the solution and speculate on what prevented you from reaching this solution independently. (The solution is found in Appendix F.)

It is not unusual for our own thought processes to interfere with our ability to think critically and innovate. Recent brain research offers one reason that this is so. Evidence suggests that what we often assume to be our own unbiased "objective" observation and recording of an event, a stimulus of some kind, is anything but. Examining brain activity levels when a stimulus of some sort is presented, we have learned that before information reaches our higher-level interpretive centers in our brains, our brains have already sent information from the interpretive center to the site of initial sensory reception in the brain to provide a preliminary interpretation of the raw data. In so doing, our brains are already "shaping" the information to fit preconceived notions or expectations before we engage in the kinds of cognitive work we do to make use of the sensory experience. In fact, we commit 10 times more brain activity to preconceiving the information than we commit to sending the information to our higher-order interpretive centers. In other words, we see or hear what we want to see and hear, making us potentially our own, in many cases, greatest inhibitor of critical thoughts. (Remember to keep cluster notes.)

So how do we teach to critical thought and innovation? Some simple steps include the following:

1. Teach beyond simple awareness to deep understanding. Knowledge is power for creative thought and innovation, though full mastery of information is not a prerequisite for innovation.

2. Demystify knowledge. All knowledge is transient, representing what is known at a given point in time. No knowledge is sacred, so nothing is off-limits for reconsideration.

3. Minimize rote recitation and recognize it as the lowest level of thought and of limited utility.

4. Integrate ideas across boundaries and borders. Demonstrate how ideas are linked across areas of study and fields of thought, and engage learners in active applications.

5. Help students understand that information is categorical. More complex language captures more sophisticated concepts. Teach to development of an active categorical vocabulary.

6. Demonstrate to students that knowledge is both content and a medium for understanding. That is, information can be concrete, but it can also serve as a means to understanding other concepts and content. As such, information is not static but represents a language of learning that is intellectual currency students use to invest in the construction of ensuing realities.

In classrooms it is possible to create psychological conditions that favor innovation. These involve the following:

- Encouraging students to see themselves as responsible initiators of ideas and actions
- Creating in students the sense that they are able to exercise considerable influence over their own learning and thinking processes
- Ensuring a psychologically secure and relatively risk-free learning environment
- Assigning projects that are challenging yet sufficiently contained for teams to work on effectively and see through to completion
- Providing structured opportunities for innovators to also share insights and knowledge with others in an atmosphere of respectful engagement

Finally, the cognitive psychologist Csikszentmihalyi (1975, 1997) speaks of the primary dynamic for innovation. He writes, "Understanding that innovating at the highest level requires personal reformation. That is, we must come to understand that who we are and how we think about and understand our world, even how we come to know, must be reorganized into something that has not yet been before" (p. 157).

Let's stop here for a moment to reflect. Look over your cluster notes. Make any additions; draw any links you think appropriate. Review the prompts to see if they trigger any recollections of ideas or terms you want to include in your notes. Once you have made any changes or additions, turn to your partner and share your notes. Where necessary, be sure to explain and/or elaborate on your various notations.

As evocation for the next part of the "lecture," begin a conversation within a small group about the implications of the critical-thinking presentation for your own teaching and for your students. What practical steps come to mind that you can take to increase student engagement in critical thought and innovation?

CREATING AN ENVIRONMENT FOR CRITICAL THOUGHT

Continuing our lecture, on the PowerPoint, you will see a list with some additional ideas for stimulating critical thought. Though there are no credible lists of steps leading to critical thought, there exists a set of classroom, teacher, and student activities and conditions that may promote the development of critical thinkers. As you hear them (*Realization of Meaning*), consider whether you think the list is exhaustive or you can add to the list.

Teachers Must Do the Following:	*Students Must Do the Following:*
• Provide both predictable and spontaneous time and opportunity for critical-thinking experiences • Give permission for students to speculate • Accept various ideas and opinions as plausible • Promote students' active engagements in shared deliberation and contemplation • Assure students a risk-free environment, including a ridicule-free environment • Express belief in students' capacity to make critical judgments • Overtly value critical thought and its occasionally "messy" outcomes	• Develop self-confidence • Appreciate the worth of their own opinions and ideas • Actively participate in the hard work of thinking • Be prepared to either formulate or suspend judgments • Take responsibility for their own intellectual engagement as well as their own response to the learning environment and the learning of classmates

Teacher and Student Responsibilities

What comes next is a brief elaboration on the activities and/or conditions that may make critical thinking a reality in the classroom. Take a moment to consider the brief list of teacher and student activities and conditions just presented, as many will now be elaborated. The discussion again speaks to teacher and student roles and responsibilities. With what you have encountered and discussed already, read through the following suggestions for fostering critical thought. See if they are consistent with you own beliefs about what is needed to successfully encourage critical thought. As these ideas are shared, consider as well obstacles to implementation.

ESSENTIAL CLASSROOM ELEMENTS OF CRITICAL THINKING

Time

Critical thinking takes time. Before thinking through something new, we must first take time to discover what we already think and believe about a topic. Discovering our own thoughts involves some exploration of previous ideas, beliefs, encounters, and experiences (Pearson, Hansen, & Gordon, 1979). Time too is needed to express thoughts in our own words to hear how they sound. Without time to think and share, there is no opportunity for hearing how well our ideas hold together. This also enables us to examine our biases and prepare us for processing new information.

Permission, Respect, and Responsibility

Students do not always speculate freely. More often, they wait for their teacher to give out the one "true" answer. Critical thinking is speculative, involving the development of tentative hypotheses, uniquely stringing together ideas and concepts. Some of these combinations will be more productive than others; some may seem reasonable at first but, upon reflection, become less so. Still other conceptualizations may appear foolish at first, only to become more valuable with refinement or changes in perspective. For this kind of thinking to occur, students need permission to speculate, create, state the obvious or the sublime. When students understand that this is acceptable, even encouraged, they will begin to engage in speculative thought.

We all learn from experience, and when teachers grant students permission to become critical thinkers, they must do so advisedly. That is, they must draw distinction between granting permission and being permissive. Granting permission to speculate does not grant students license to be frivolous or inconsequential thinkers. Not all contemplation is worthy contemplation; students deserve to be held accountable for the genuineness of their thought and the purposefulness of their contributions. This is done by providing honest feedback. Permission to think critically implies granting permission within the context of both a supportive and productive environment where there is genuine purpose for speculating and genuine student intent to learn and grow.

Certainly, there are occasions when there is one right answer, and we must be honest with our students. In these cases, what may differ is the means or processes by which individuals arrive at the answer. In most cases, process is as important as the answer itself. What is important to consider is that if most class time is spent looking for the one right answer, then thinking is not likely occurring at a meaningful level, and the outcomes of instruction will reflect these limitations. Limiting expressions of opinion, of course, limits student thinking. This does not suggest all ideas are acceptable, all views tolerated. Class is socially embedded, and conventions are an essential part of the prevailing social context. They too are to be respected, though conversations at the boundaries of convention often generate the most energy, bring the greatest clarity, or broaden those boundaries so that they are inclusive of community members.

The responsibility for engaging in critical thinking and learning ultimately rests with students. The classroom environment may enable students to engage in critical thought, but students themselves must act. We know when our students are engaging in critical thought as there are attributes and behaviors critically engaged students exhibit. Some behaviors we see include being more focused and, consequently, less distracted. Students ask questions and seek alternative resources, and they engage in topic-related conversation. The attributions to self-critically engaged students often make include identifying themselves as self-motivated, self-confident, and believing in self-control, and the capacity to manage their immediate environment.

Communicating to students that the outcomes of their own critical analysis are of value is essential to supporting critical thought. Schools, by the nature of the demands they place on students in terms of student performance feedback, communicate a great deal about what is most valued. When students are asked most often to simply retell what they have been told, either through classroom dialogues or testing, they quickly understand that basic recall of someone else's ideas is most highly valued. If recall is not the only educational outcome we value, then, we must demonstrate what it is we do value by interacting differently with students, setting different expectations, and asking them for different kinds of feedback. The true measure of what we value is the amount of time we commit. The more time committed to thinking and sharing, the more evident it is that these are valued.

Confidence

Interest, investigation, beliefs, and opinions are what guide a thoughtful life, underscoring our everyday decisions and actions. It is through our beliefs, understandings, and opinions that we project ourselves into the world of others. They also provide the footings upon which individuals stand as they are buffeted by the overwhelming flood tide of information, ideas, and opinions young people confront today. When we are uncertain about the worth of our own thoughts and beliefs, when our footings are poorly constructed, we are unduly susceptible to the persuasive arguments of others. We hide our own ideas from view and can lose touch with them altogether. Confidence in our ideas and beliefs coupled with confidence in our capacity to weigh new ideas carefully and mediate our belief system in self-sustaining ways frees us to share with others and opens our mind to alternative views, without concern that they represent potential threats. Self-confidence enables learners to participate fully in discourse and experience the personal development derived from encounters with knowledge from a position of personal strength.

Active Participation

Mihaly Csikszentmihalyi (1975) demonstrated that when learners are actively engaged in the learning process at an appropriately challenging level, they express great pleasure in their engagement and experience an increased capacity for understanding and mastery. Students who experience complete absorption in a task, what Csikszentmihalyi describes as "flow experience," come to understand that when they commit sufficient energy and effort to sufficiently challenging tasks, they will derive not merely a sense of pleasure but a powerful sense of personal fulfillment. Teachers are responsible for presenting students with challenges at an appropriate level. That is, challenges students are able to meet successfully when they commit themselves fully to a task. Students, however, must be responsible for supplying the energy and all of the skills at their disposal to accomplish that task.

Sharing

Sharing is a disciplined behavior. It requires the sharer to give up something for the sake of others. Parents teach sharing to young children as an important social and survival skill. Children come to accept the idea of sharing, however, not simply because parents expect it, but because they eventually experience the intrinsic rewards of sharing. That is, they understand that in giving up something, there are certain benefits to be gained. When learners commit to sharing, they are making a commitment to the learning community, to their class, to their school. Sharing beliefs, ideas, and opinions is risky, requiring learners to show themselves to others as thinkers and believers, capable of great thought and humbling mistakes. Yet, when sharing their thoughts responsibly, they learn more about what they are thinking and the impact of their thoughts on others and their world.

Listening

Sometimes the best kind of sharing is sharing our attention by attending to the thoughts of others. Wise sayings abound with the same basic theme, for example, "When I am speaking, I am not learning," or "I do my most active learning when I am a most active listener," or "The wise man listens loudly and speaks softly." All this wisdom simply suggests that learning and listening are companions. The kind of listening we speak of is active listening—the kind of listening where judgments are momentarily suspended as is the impulse to impose order on what is being said, and where we actively, if only temporarily, accommodate our thinking to the message being communicated so that we can interact with it constructively.

Now that the presentation is finished, take 10 minutes to write your reactions to the critical-thinking presentation. You can use your cluster notes to support your writing. Use them to summarize your thoughts and then include some thoughts on what you will do to improve the classroom environment to support students' critical thinking and what can be done to overcome obstacles.

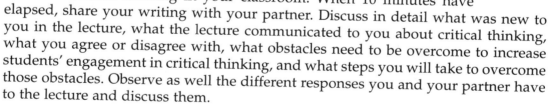

Now take 10 minutes to write your "10-Minute Essay" on critical thinking. You will share this with your partner when finished. Remember to include thoughts on how you will work to increase students' critical thinking in your classroom. When 10 minutes have elapsed, share your writing with your partner. Discuss in detail what was new to you in the lecture, what the lecture communicated to you about critical thinking, what you agree or disagree with, what obstacles need to be overcome to increase students' engagement in critical thinking, and what steps you will take to overcome those obstacles. Observe as well the different responses you and your partner have to the lecture and discuss them.

LESSON ANALYSIS

As is always the case, two lessons are occurring here simultaneously. One is about critical thinking, and the other is about teaching, using an enhanced lecture format. First, we will look at the critical-thinking lesson.

Evocation

This lesson began by asking the "listener" to examine his or her own problem-solving history. You were asked to consider how you approach challenging situations. To capture these thoughts, you were then asked to list and discuss with your partner the approaches and/or steps to problem solving each of you employs. As part of a Realization of Meaning phase, you were then asked to hold onto this list for comparison purposes when listening to the details of the lecture to come. A second evocation task was then assigned. You were directed to discuss quite directly your thoughts on the specific topic of critical thinking. You were also encouraged to remember this conversation, as it directly relates to the content of the lecture.

Realization of Meaning

This phase of the framework was orchestrated in several ways. First, as mentioned above, listeners were encouraged to recall the content of thought and discussion about problem solving and critical thought and use it as a base understanding against which lecture content was to be held in relief, a conceptual backdrop, if you will. To this, a realization of meaning strategy was added in the form of cluster notes. This strategy is intended to enable listeners to remain engaged in the lecture while avoiding the distraction of lengthy narrative note taking. It also offers listeners opportunity to link information in a nonlinear format more conducive to how we speak, more reflective of how our minds work, and more flexible in more accurately depicting the complexity of the topic.

Reflection

The first reflection came at the midpoint of the lecture. Responding to the reality of listeners' capacity to attend, the enhanced lecture strategy includes opportunities to engage in shorter, more deliberate ERR applications that help listeners process the information they are hearing by engaging them more actively in the learning experience.

At the first stop in the lecture, listeners were asked to review their cluster notes and share them with a partner. Listeners were also encouraged to recall their own thinking about critical thinking. This was done to link existing perceptions and beliefs with incoming information. A story was also offered as part of the reflection processes so listeners could be witness to a rather famous example of critical thought leading to innovation. This brought together the basic tenets of the presentation in a memorable and readily accessible form. A follow-up assignment was also given to extend student involvement.

Evocation

The lecture continued with an invitation for participants to imagine someone engaged in critical thought.

Realization of Meaning

Students were then exposed to two problems requiring application of critical thought in order to engage in the process themselves. They were encouraged to be observers of their own problem-solving approach in order to be informed thinkers but also to discuss with others and compare approaches. Participants were able to experience firsthand how we sometimes limit our thinking unwittingly. Cluster note taking was also encouraged.

Reflection

Participants in this lesson were again asked to stop and review their notes and discuss what they mean, ask any questions, and build appropriate links.

Evocation

Listeners were then encouraged to consider implications for implementation of critical thinking strategies in their own classrooms. This was in anticipation of the discussion to come on implementation strategies.

Realization of Meaning

Beyond continuing to take notes, participants were asked to attend to a listing and determine whether it was complete in their view or if they might add to the list.

Reflection

A 10-Minute Essay was then assigned with specific expectations set for what the essay should include. Discussion ensued with partners to go over in detail each partner's written response. In this manner, the ERR framework was employed to guide learners through a complex lecture, all the while intending to keep learners engaged yet recognizing the limits of the human capacity to attend.

The second piece to this lesson is the process lesson. Here *evocation* for the lesson appears in various guises. It was included, in part, in the introductory paragraphs and the expected outcomes. Here, it was made clear where the lesson was going and provided insight into what should be taken from it. There were also links built to previous applications of the ERR framework.

Realization of Meaning was manifest in the lecture itself, the application of cluster notes and the embedded discussions, while *reflection* was evident in the lesson analysis and discussion of future implementation of the strategies. Along the way, three strategies were presented. The more comprehensive strategy is the enhanced lecture strategy. This can be added to your chart as a Realization of Meaning strategy. Cluster notes, a strategy embedded here within the enhanced lecture, is also a Realization of Meaning strategy. The 10-Minute Essay is the third strategy and in this instance was employed as a Reflection strategy.

CHAPTER SUMMARY

Chapter 4 offers an approach to a frequently employed, and therefore important, instructional approach, lecturing. This approach enables application of the ERR framework, mechanisms for full student engagement, and mechanisms for monitoring student engagement. This chapter offers examples of how to implement three new strategies. They include the umbrella strategy known as Enhanced Lecture. The other two strategies implemented here to facilitate the enhanced lecture are Cluster Notes and the 10-Minute Essay. The enhanced lecture strategy is similar to the ERR for Narrative Text strategy applied earlier in the sniper lesson. Both strategies are implemented within the Realization of Meaning phase. Enhanced lecture is, of course, applied during the body of the lecture presentation and involves cycling through the ERR framework. As with the sniper lesson, this approach provides repeated ERR cycles for multiple benefits. Those benefits include the following:

- Enabling the content to be segmented so learners can engage with manageable amounts of information
- Respecting the reality of limitations to the human capacity to attend and concentrate
- Providing opportunities to sustain engagement or re-engage learners as needed
- Maintaining the instructor's role in guiding learners' attention to essential content elements and primary purposes for learning
- Leading learners toward practical learning outcomes that sustain the relevance of the lecture content for learners

This chapter offers an overview of critical thinking and its link to innovation. Information was presented regarding the nature of critical thought, why it might be important to consider, and how critical thinking can be more effectively encouraged in classrooms. Ways by which thinkers themselves inhibit their own thought processes were described, and some practical solutions delineated. Student and teacher roles related to setting value, providing time, taking responsibility, and eliminating risk were discussed as essential elements in the construction of a classroom conducive to engendering critical thinking and innovation. In the end, it is clear that incubating critical thinking requires teamwork, trust, practice, and the understanding that knowledge is not stagnant and thinking is not painful. Rather, knowledge is effervescent and thinking a genuine and lifelong source for personal fulfillment.

5

Framework Strategies

Today, the Knowledge Society and the Knowledge Economy place cognitive resources at the center of human activity and social dynamics.

—Mary Louise Kearney

OUTCOMES OF USING THE ERR FRAMEWORK

Evocation

As we have already discussed, the ERR Framework is an excellent tool for guiding students at all grade levels through learning experiences. We have shown how thoughtful questioning practices guide student learning, lending an overarching sense of direction and pointing toward specific learning goals, when offered within the framework. Providing such structure does not inhibit student inquiry, as carefully considered, well-targeted questions more often invite thoughtful speculation and reflection. The ERR framework, as we have seen, accomplishes several other important instructional tasks, including the following:

- Allowing students to clearly set purposes
- Maintaining students' active cognitive and metacognitive engagement
- Provoking rich discourse
- Encouraging students to create avenues of inquiry
- Facilitating students' expression of opinions
- Maintaining students' interest and motivation to learn
- Creating a setting for reflection on what to value
- Serving as stimulus for change
- Setting expectations for students' critical engagement
- Facilitating critical thought at increasingly sophisticated levels

Once you automate the process of thinking through the lens of the framework, an array of teaching strategies can be implemented at the various phases, allowing instruction to be altered to meet specific demands of the content or to satisfy student needs or specific instructional purposes. This chapter offers a set of strategies you can implement immediately within the ERR framework with almost any content. They include writing-for-thinking strategies that too are placed within the framework's specific phases, facilitating their immediate implementation.

The following section includes a discussion of what is meant by writing for thinking followed by a discussion of three writing-for-thinking or more traditionally, writing-to-learn strategies: clustering, cinquains, and cubing. The section concludes with some general writing-to-learn strategies that can be used in content classrooms.

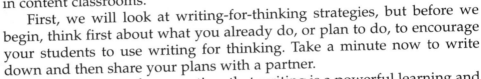

First, we will look at writing-for-thinking strategies, but before we begin, think first about what you already do, or plan to do, to encourage your students to use writing for thinking. Take a minute now to write down and then share your plans with a partner.

We have known for some time that writing is a powerful learning and communication tool (Langer & Applebee, 2007). We also recognize the numerous ways we can use writing in the classroom and in the learning process. Yet students do not come to these forms of writing naturally. They must be shown how writing contributes to their learning and how they can use writing at various stages in understanding and learning in order to move to more complex learning. Gunning (2007) wrote,

> In writing, students don't make progress until they are challenged to compose more complex forms and are given instruction in how to do so. Students need careful guidance, direct instruction, and experience writing in a variety of modes. (p. 160)

Here, we will discuss writing-for-thinking strategies as one form of writing that facilitates readiness for study as well as advancing comprehension and the contextualization and communication of knowledge.

Clustering

Many may already be familiar with clustering (Rico, 2000). If you're not familiar with clustering, then perhaps you are familiar with webbing or concept mapping or the many online web applications such as www.graphic.org/concept.html and http://classes.aces.uiuc.edu/aces100/mind/c-mz.html. Clustering is different from these but within the same family. (For a delightful description of an application of clustering to a civics lesson, read *The Thinking-Writing Connection: Using Clustering to Help Students Write Persuasively* by Steele and Steele, 1991.) Clustering is a teaching strategy that encourages students to think freely and openly about a topic. It entails only enough structure to stimulate thinking about an idea and the connections between subsets of related ideas. It offers a nonlinear organizational strategy more closely aligned with how our minds actively work rather than linear strategies for thinking.

Clustering has several uses. It can be used to stimulate thinking about a topic or used to summarize what has just been studied. It can be used as a way to build new associations and as a way of graphically representing connections between ideas or themes. It is, as well, a prewriting activity that serves as a powerful tool for initial engagement with the writing process, especially for reluctant writers. (We will discuss this role more thoroughly later.) Clustering is also a powerful study tool, especially in preparation for testing. Mostly, however, clustering is a strategy for gaining access to prior knowledge, understandings, and beliefs.

As is our usual practice, we will first set the rules for the strategy; then you will experience clustering firsthand before we discuss the strategy further.

To begin, the steps for clustering are few and easy to remember:

1. Write a nucleus word or phrase in the center of a piece of paper, overhead transparency, chalkboard, or other writing surface (depending on whether you are doing an individual or group cluster).

2. Begin by writing down, in linked associations, words or phrases that come to mind about a target topic or the growing array of associated subtopics or attributes that emerge.

3. As ideas come to mind, write them in proximity to related ideas, draw a circle around each word or phrase, and draw connecting lines that link related ideas.

4. Write as many ideas as come to mind. Keep writing until either time is up or all thoughts are exhausted.

Every cluster is different, but the example here is representative.

There are just a few basic rules to follow when using clustering:

1. Write everything that comes to mind. Make no judgments about the thoughts; just put them down.

2. Do not be concerned about spelling or other writing constraints.

3. Do not stop until enough time has elapsed and all ideas are out. If ideas stop flowing for a time, doodle on the paper until new ideas come.

4. Let as many connections build as possible. Do not restrict the number of ideas, the flow, or connections.

Experiencing Clustering

Clustering can be performed individually or with a group. Now, select a topic that you or the group has interest in and some knowledge about. For demonstration purposes, it can be a topic such as your country, state, or a topic of study from your teaching. The sample in Figure 5.1 is a cluster done by a group of Slovak teachers on Slovakia. To begin, select your topic and place the starter term in the middle as instructed above. In your group, select your prompt now and begin

generating responses. Encourage random comments from all until the ideas ebb. Be sure to link responses to prompts or associated ideas.

Figure 5.1

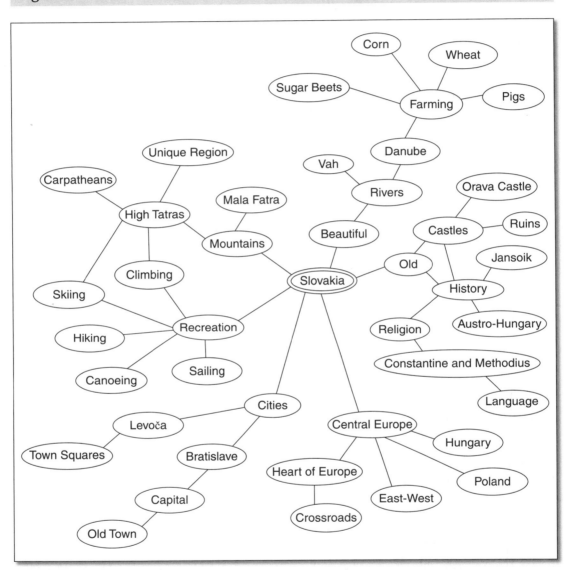

After the initial group cluster, it is useful to do an individual cluster on a separate topic. This is an important next step, as it is through this that you can see the power and value of the process. The topic is important here, as it will need to be something familiar so you will have enough information for a full cluster.

For this experience, think of a loved one. You might consider a spouse, a significant other, a parent, sibling, friend, pet, car, or other object of affection. Recall the steps and rules again. Look at the example (Figure 5.1) and take five to seven minutes to develop your own cluster. When you are finished, share with your partner. Then, discuss your experience with both the individual and group clusters. How they are similar and different. Speak as well about how this strategy might relate to writing for thinking and your own ideas about this you considered earlier. Consider too how this strategy might serve the beginning writing process. Then, discuss how you might use this in your teaching in the near future.

Debriefing Clustering

Steele and Steele (1991) described clustering as a flexible writing-for-thinking strategy. As a group activity, it can effectively capture a group's ideas, providing students with exposure to the associations and relationships other students draw from a particular prompt. Clustering complements group brainstorming tasks since it is quick and permits all students, not just those who always put their hands up first, to actively engage in thinking. Experience has taught us, however, that when clustering individually, the topic should be one students know a fair amount about since they will not have the shared experience of the group to draw from. The benefit then for learners comes from bringing their own knowledge and schema to an awareness level to prepare them for further learning experiences.

Now, develop plans for using clustering in your own class. If possible, speak with a partner about the uses for clustering and discuss how you can implement the strategy in your class tomorrow. Consider the content of your next lesson. Imagine how students can be drawn into the subject matter by first accessing their own knowledge for consideration and seeing how their existing knowledge is organized.

When completing individual clusters in class, we suggest you cluster as well. Doing so shows you take the process seriously, and it prevents students from interrupting to ask questions, disrupting the thinking of others.

Finally, before moving on to the next strategy, think now about where in the ERR framework clustering should be placed. Take out your ERR chart and place clustering in the proper location. If you assigned clustering to either the evocation or reflection phases or both, you would be correct as clustering works well in both phases of the learning process. As mentioned, it works well in evocation as a strategy of activation and engagement with prior knowledge. In reflection, it serves as an organizing and restatement tool.

Cinquains

The capacity to summarize information, to capture complex thoughts, feelings, and beliefs in a few words can be terribly useful. It requires rich understanding and the ability to engage in thoughtful reflection about a particular strand of content and/or experiences. Constructing a poem requires a writer to express in the most parsimonious terms the outcome of reflections on complex matter. A cinquain is a poem that requires synthesizing information and experiences into concise expressions reflecting understanding. The cinquain poem was invented by Adelaide Crapsey (1876–1914). The cinquain used here is a modified version referred to as a modern or didactic cinquain.

The guidelines for writing cinquains are as follows:

1. The first line is a one-word description of the topic (usually a noun).

2. The second line is a two-word description of the topic (two adjectives).

3. Line three is three words expressing action of the topic (usually three *ing* words).

4. The fourth line is a four-word phrase showing feeling for the topic.

5. The last line is a one-word synonym that restates the essence of the topic.

Cinquain Format

Title (usually a noun)   _____

Describe (usually adjectives)   _____ _____

Action (usually *ing* words)   _____ _____ _____

Feeling (phrase)   _____ _____ _____ _____

Restatement of essence   _____

Experiencing Cinquains

Cinquain comes from the French word for five and is a five-line poem. To understand the thought process involved in writing cinquains, it is necessary to write some to experience the process firsthand. Examples are always helpful, so here are two examples to give a flavor of how cinquains look and sound.

Sample Cinquains

Mexico

Hot, tropical

Mining, fishing, drilling

Cultures, languages, history, together

Spicy

Baseball

Pastime, rivalries

Pitching, hitting, fielding

Greatest game of summer

Home run

Take out a piece of notebook paper, or in your learning journal, find a clean sheet of paper. For your first cinquain, think of some event in which you have recently participated. Any event will serve here. It could be a show of some kind such as a play or musical event, a sporting event, or perhaps a party or other social event. A walk in the park or swim in a lake could serve as well. Think about the event: your reactions, feelings, sensations, and perspectives. Now, take a few minutes and, following the guidelines listed above, create one or two cinquains. When those are complete, share with a partner and discuss how you decided what to write.

During your sharing, be specific and detailed. Explain why you selected the words that appear in your poem. Recall as well some words of phrases that came to mind that you did not select. In this discussion, you will begin to see the language involved in this strategy and what learners do to create their poems. Now select a topic in your content area. A seventh-grade class we worked with completed their study of Mexico by writing individual cinquains on the topic "Mexico," another on volcanoes. Your topic can be as general as Mexico or more specific, but be sure it is content based.

Debriefing Cinquains

When introducing cinquains to your students, first present the guidelines for writing the poem. Then offer some samples (as provided above in this section). Then have your students write cinquains on a single topic. Cinquains can be difficult for some in their first attempts, so an effective means of introducing them is to have the group divided into pairs. Provide a topic with which students are familiar. Allow five to seven minutes to complete the task individually. Next, ask partners to share and then assign them the task of creating a single cinquain by either taking from each cinquain terms or lines they both like or writing a totally new cinquain. This prompts conversation about why they wrote what they did, enabling further reflection and critical review of the topic. It also requires listening to others and pulling from the work of others' ideas both partners can relate to and agree with. These paired cinquains can then be shared with the whole group. It is often useful to have the paired cinquain written on the overhead and presented by the pair to the group. This can engender further discussion.

At this point, for our purposes, it is important to take a moment to think how you will use this strategy in your classrooms. Cinquains serve well as a tool for synthesizing complex information, a means of evaluating student understanding, and a means for creative expression. A cinquain is a quick yet powerful tool for reflecting on and summarizing concepts and information. As you might conclude, cinquains are most often used in the reflection phase of ERR. However, they are sometimes used during evocation but only on a topic students already know quite a bit about. Take a few moments now to think how you will use this strategy in a content lesson. Share your ideas with a partner. Remember to add cinquains to your ERR chart.

Cubing

Cubing (Cowan & Cowan, 1980) is a teaching strategy, like cinquains, that requires examining a topic from varying perspectives and encourages student thinking about a topic by using a variety of question types. It is called cubing because the mechanism for prompting student response is a six-sided cube students can either hand around, toss softly from one to another, or simply be rotated from side to side by the teacher or another student, exposing the various prompts written on the six sides. The cube is made by covering a small box, preferably four to six inches on a side, with paper. The standard cube has one of the following six prompts on each side:

Describe It. Think about the topic and describe it as you envision it. Perhaps your vision is similar to others; perhaps it is unique. Let's see.

Compare It. Write about what it resembles and what is does not resemble. This could refer to its shape or function of operation or implication.

Associate It. What is the first thing that comes to your mind when you hear the word or topic? Does it prompt some connection to something else familiar or perhaps strangely linked in your history? It can be events, inanimate objects, places, or people. Think freely, and see what comes up.

Analyze It. Describe what it is composed of, what happens in its inner workings, what its source of power or purpose is, how it came to be.

Apply It. State its use. You might state its intended use or some other purposes it might serve other than what it was originally designed to do. For example, a coffee can can be used to bail water out of a canoe.

Argue for or Against It. Judge whether you believe it is useful, thoughtful, appropriate, helpful, well constructed, well considered, harmful, clever, efficient, or whatever you might decide about the topic and state your belief.

There are a few ways to use the cube. Here are two.

One. With a cube you can draw students into a circle and toss the cube gently around. The rule for this is that a student who catches the cube looks to see what prompt is facing up (or is under her or his left thumb or some other designation) and then hands the cube to the student to the left or right for his or her response.

Two. Teachers lead students through the process of cubing by having students freewrite for a brief period (2–4 minutes) from a given perspective on a topic. First, a topic is selected, then, students are directed to the first prompt, *describe it*, that is, look at the subject closely and describe the vision, including colors, shapes, or signs. With these directions in mind, students freewrite for the specified period of time. The process continues as above through all six sides of the cube.

Experiencing Cubing

It is your turn to try this strategy. The first application should be using timed freewriting, let's say three minutes for each prompt. The first topic should be interesting and familiar and should be something useful as a model to get the idea across, as you will see how cubing can be applied to almost any topic. So have a blank sheet of paper ready and be prepared to cube on the topic: *Teaching*. Move through the various prompts, responding to each with your focus on teaching. So you will *describe it*, compare, associate, and respond to the other three prompts in turn as you consider teaching and what teaching means to you.

Following writing, share your responses to each side of the cube with your group. Have each person read her response to the first prompt. Discuss briefly and then move to the next. Discuss what is similar, different, surprising. In class, you would have your students share in this manner as well. It is likely time would not allow all to share each side, but a good sampling of responses for each side would be informative. Often, sharing is done first with a partner. Each person selects three sides of the cube to share and reads his writing to his partner.

Next, get in a circle if you are in a group. Here, you will use a cube (so someone will have to make one). With the various sides labeled with the prompts, gently toss the cube across the circle to differing respondents. As each prompt comes up, speak to how it relates to the topic: *escalator*. A strange topic, but you will see clearly how cubing can work for just about any topic. After each side of the cube has been responded to two times, stop and discuss what you noticed about the strategy from a pedagogical perspective.

Debriefing Cubing

There are usually a few questions at this point. Do you have to go through all six sides with small children? No, often three sides are enough with small children, but it depends upon the topic and the group.

Do you have to do the sides of the cube in a particular order, or can you just roll the cube? You probably noticed the prompts in the cubing modeled above closely follow Bloom's taxonomy presented earlier. There may be some rationale for following the order, as it would lead learners from less through to more complex thought processes. However, it is not essential to order responses. Sometimes, you may use different prompts altogether. For example, we have used cubing after reading a play. In this instance, the sides of the cube represented characters from the play. In one example, the play students read was about a teenager who became pregnant. Sides of the cube were the young girl, the boy, the mother, the friend, the father, and the teacher. Students were presented with a thoughtful question from Bloom's taxonomy that was applied to each character. Alternatively, one character could be selected with a set of six questions identified for that character. The question, in this case, could also reflect Bloom's taxonomy of questioning. The sides of the cube can change depending upon the perspectives you wish to have your students consider and the purposes of your lesson.

To which phase(s) of the framework does cubing apply? After much discussion with many teachers who have implemented cubing in their instruction, we have agreed that is can be used well during the evocation or reflection phase. We discussed the importance of cubing on something about which students are knowledgeable, so topics should be selected carefully. One example topic we have used in science is connected with the study of photosynthesis. We observed a science teacher use cubing to introduce this topic. The teacher asked each student to bring a leaf to school. They cubed on their leaf in the evocation stage using the prompts as we did in the example above. Then, after studying photosynthesis, the students cubed on photosynthesis in the reflection phase. The teacher began with cubing on a leaf because students would not already know much about photosynthesis, but they would have lots of observations of leaves. By looking at leaves in detail, students were preparing for a closer analysis of what is happening in leaves and their life cycle. Cubing is effective when the topic is something about which one knows a lot. Yet the strategy can be used in the evocation stage when we want students to begin understanding what they know about something quite familiar that is intimately connected to where their studies will take them next. Cubing in this way affords the opportunity for students to experience how their existing knowledge is a valuable resource they can rely on for future learning.

Take time to consider how you will implement this strategy in your content lesson. Consider what questions you will ask. You will see that if you think about the important underlying purposes for your lesson, the questions you want to ask will come readily. Be sure to vary your question types so students engage in multiple ways of thinking. Share your example with your partner.

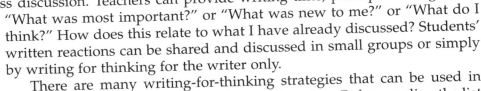

OTHER WRITING-FOR-THINKING STRATEGIES

Often, writing for thinking occurs in content classrooms where students wrestle with ideas, working hard to understand and learn. Writing for thinking is used to facilitate evaluating and reacting to instruction following a presentation, a film, or a reading or class discussion. Teachers can provide writing time, perhaps writing about

"What was most important?" or "What was new to me?" or "What do I think?" How does this relate to what I have already discussed? Students' written reactions can be shared and discussed in small groups or simply by writing for thinking for the writer only.

There are many writing-for-thinking strategies that can be used in content classes. The following list is not exhaustive. Before reading the list that follows, have a piece of paper handy, and as you read, think about the strategy and consider which strategy might work best for you. At the end of the list, write down that strategy and briefly state why you think it might work for you.

- Informing students at the beginning of class that at the end of class they will each write a paragraph describing what they believe to be the most interesting or important idea presented. Always inform students at the beginning of the class that they will have this assignment at the end of the class.
- Have students listen to a paragraph or meaningful fragment of text and write what it means to them in their own words. If students experience difficulty with the activity, have them tell another student before they write. Getting better at this will show up in improved note taking—a benefit students will see and appreciate in their own work.
- Before digging into a specific content lesson, show students a content-related picture and ask them to write an idea suggested by the picture. Or show an aerial picture of, say, a glacial river following a discussion of the forces of glacial movement in an earth sciences class and ask students to write about how they see using what they just learned to guide their thinking.
- Limit students to communicating with each other using only a question-answer format. Have each student formulate written questions derived from content material being learned. Collect papers, redistribute them randomly, and have each student answer in writing the question received.
- Have students write questions they would like the teacher to answer at a future time, stating why a question or set of questions intrigues them. When responding, give a statement recapturing the background the student brought to the question. For example, after studying about sharks, a student might write a question asking the teacher if sharks eat people. The background might be that the child had an uncle who went scuba diving and told her that

he saw a shark, but it just swam by him, so now the student wonders, "Do sharks eat people?"

Teachers in all content areas can improve students' subject learning and give them practice in the basic cognitive operations of summarizing, clarifying ideas, examining relationships, seeing errors, and remembering through writing. In addition, basic thinking processes that call on more than one operation, including inferencing, interpreting, thinking like experts, making multiple comparisons, and forming new concepts, are enhanced through the use of specific writing techniques such as those discussed above.

For the Evocation Phase

There are numerous writing-for-thinking strategies. Following is a brief presentation of a few. They are presented according to the framework. Be sure to add those you find useful to your framework chart.

Scrambled Sequences

This strategy can be used with young writers, but with complex text, the strategy can be used with older students to facilitate and/or assess understanding. With this strategy, the teacher may write five or six individual events from a sequence of events or from a cause-and-effect chain, on separate pieces of paper, which are scrambled. In larger groups or among small groups at tables, students work to assemble the pieces into the order they think best. Another way to implement is to ask students to come forward one at a time and place one item in what they think is its proper place. When that's completed, students are asked to scrutinize the text source to determine whether the students' order approximates the text.

Semantic Feature Analysis

DIET	Meat	Grains	Seafood	Vegetables	Insects
Raptors	+	−	+	−	+
Fish	+	−	+	+	+
Rabbits	−	+	−	+	−
Snakes	+	−	−	−	+
People	+	+	+	+	+

Another strategy for activating and developing background knowledge is semantic feature analysis (Anders & Bos, 1986). This strategy is useful when students are studying a topic about which they have little background knowledge. The essence of the strategy is to compare the features of the new and lesser known item or topic with those of two more familiar items or topics.

A chart to guide this activity is prepared in advance by the teacher and presented on a transparency or a large piece of paper. The names of the three to five items are listed in a column down the left side of the chart, and a series of features on which the items will be compared are listed in a row across the top of the chart (see previous chart).

As a preliminary activity (*evocation phase*), the students discuss the two familiar items and suggest the appropriate markings ("+" for "yes" and "−" for "no") for each item under each semantic feature. Then, before reading, hearing a lecture, or otherwise studying the new topic, the students also suggest marks for that topic's semantic features ("+" for "yes," "−" for "no," and "?" to indicate that they are unsure of a feature). At this time, the teacher presses students to make predictions about the topic, even when they are unsure. Students now read or explore the new topic (*realization of meaning*). Following the exploration, they discuss what they learned. As a follow-up activity (*considered part of the reflection phase*), students return to the chart and confirm or suggest corrections for the markings they made during the preliminary activity.

The semantic feature analysis works nicely with lessons that are not text based. The strategy has many applications in the sciences and in math.

For the Realization of Meaning Phase

ReQuest Procedure

When students need support reading text for information, one way to provide that support is to use the ReQuest procedure (Manzo, 1969). With this procedure, two students read through a text, stop after each paragraph, and take turns asking each other questions about it. It helps a great deal if their teacher serves as a partner when the technique is first introduced. The first time the strategy is implemented, teachers should model the procedure for the entire class. After the first paragraph of a reading is completed, the teacher can model asking questions that probe for understanding or build connections to other ideas or character or events, identifying what is most important. The questions can model skills good readers use to understand text. These skills include developing coherent representations of text, deciding on relative importance, and building connections. After answering the teacher's questions, both teacher and students read the next paragraph. Now, it is the students' turn to ask the teacher questions about the reading. This cycle is then repeated. After this introduction of the strategy, the teacher sets up pairs of students to ask questions of each other.

ReQuest may be used with a whole class. One way is for the class to read one or two paragraphs from the text, as in the example above. Students then pause and close their books, and students take turns asking the teacher all the questions they can think of. Following that, they read a new paragraph and the roles are reversed. After several such exchanges, the teacher may shift the activity to ask students to predict what the rest of the assignment will be about and to state why they think so (Vacca & Vacca, 2008).

Reciprocal Teaching

It is well known that the act of teaching is the best way to learn. Reciprocal teaching, like the ReQuest procedure, was developed to enable all students to experience the role of teacher in leading others through a text. The procedure is especially well suited to informational text.

Reciprocal teaching (Palincsar & Brown, 1984) is done in groups of four to seven students. The students all have copies of the same text and take turns being the teacher, a role that requires them to perform five tasks. After the students have read a paragraph (usually silently), the person acting as teacher

1. summarizes what has just been read,

2. thinks up two or three questions about the passage and elicits the students' answers to it,

3. clarifies issues the other students are unclear about,

4. predicts what the text will say in the next passage, and

5. assigns the next passage for everyone to read.

As an example, assume that a teacher and five students are reading text.

First, the teacher serves as discussion leader for the initial paragraph. Students are encouraged to attend to the reading and participate in subsequent discussion. They should also observe carefully how the teacher conducts the lesson. So each student will be able to play the role of discussion leader when subsequent paragraphs are read. It is useful to have a chart listing the five teacher tasks, so students can refer to it as they lead the discussion.

The text used must be read in units of paragraphs that facilitate five- to six-minute discussions. When they are finished, the teacher might give a verbal summary of the paragraph and ask if students would summarize the passage the same way. Alternately, the teacher can ask for a volunteer to provide a summary statement and then see if this is how others might summarize.

Next, the teacher formulates a question, taking care to elicit ideas that demonstrate the art of questioning. Questions might address a complicated idea explicitly stated in the text, probe an unspoken implication, or ask students to compare an assertion made by the text with their own commonsense ideas.

Next—although this often happens simultaneously with the preceding step—the teacher attempts to clarify to students any parts of the passage that are unclear, pointing out disagreements.

Now, the teacher makes a prediction as to what comes next in the text. If time allows, others may make for their predictions as well. Then, the next section of text is assigned.

If this is the first time this activity has been used with a participating group of students, the teacher may take another turn conducting the discussion. The extra turn is to make sure students fully understand how to enact the teacher role when it is their turn.

Reflection

Save the Last Word for Me

Save the Last Word for Me (Short, Harste, & Burke, 1996) is an activity that facilitates postreading reflection. It provides a framework for class discussion of either narrative or expository text. This strategy is particularly helpful in getting the quieter and more reluctant students to participate in class discussions.

The steps of Save the Last Word for Me should be explained as follows:

1. While reading a piece of text, students are asked to find one or more quotations that they consider particularly interesting or worthy of comment.

2. The student writes the quotation on an index card or small piece of paper, being sure to include the page number citation.

3. On the reverse side of the card, the student writes a comment about the quotation. The student may choose to disagree with the quotation, elaborate on it, or whatever he or she chooses.

4. The teacher calls on someone to read her or his chosen quotation aloud. (It helps if the student tells everyone what page in the text the quotation came from, so that everyone may follow along.)

5. After the quotation has been read, the teacher calls for comments and reactions from other class members. Be sure to keep the discussion on target and limit comments if they are caustic or petty.

6. To conclude the discussion of the quotation, the teacher has the student who chose it read his or her comments aloud. Here's the catch: There can be no further discussion. The student who chose it gets to have the last word. (Teachers, you will find it very difficult at times to keep from interjecting some final comment, but no fair! That's against the rules.) We have seen the discussion of controversial issues spill into the hallways and continue into the lunchroom.

7. The teacher now can call on another student to share his or her quotation and begin the process anew. It is unlikely that the teacher will want to call on every class member to present a quotation in the same class period but will select a few students each time.

T-Chart

The *T-chart* is a versatile graphic organizer for recording binary (yes or no, pro or con) or comparison and contrast or beneficial or harmful effects responses to a discussion. After reading an editorial on the benefits and detriments of television viewing, for example, pairs of students construct a T-chart, like the one shown in Figure 5.2, and in five minutes, list on the left-hand side of the chart as many benefits as they can think of for watching television. Then, for five minutes, they should list as many detriments as they can think of. Then for another five minutes, students can compare their T-charts with those of another pair. Later, the teacher can lead the whole class in developing a class T-chart.

Venn Diagram

A *Venn diagram* is derived from mathematics and composed of two or more large, partially overlapping circles. It can be used to compare and contrast ideas to show commonalities between ideas, events, and concepts. Suppose, for example, that

Figure 5.2 T-Chart

Benefits	Harmful effects
Educational	Passive, lazy
Entertaining	Poor language model
Culturally important	Violence
Local and world news	Silly stories
	Time wasting

students are comparing characteristics of sea creatures and land animals. A Venn diagram with two overlapping circles would enable the class to compare and contrast behaviors, habitat, diet, and reproduction and see the outcome on a visual representation.

The teacher might ask pairs of students to construct Venn diagrams by filling in only the two parts of the circle devoted exclusively to land and sea creatures, respectively. Then, pairs could join other pairs, and the foursomes could compare their diagrams and then list in the middle section common features (see the example in Figure 5.3).

Figure 5.3

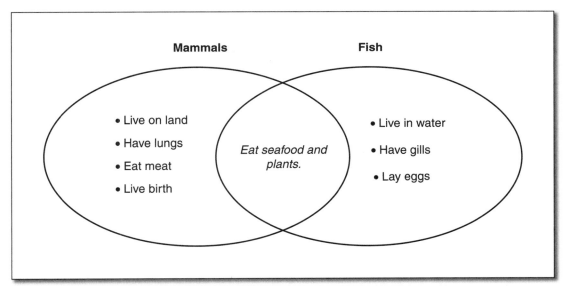

Now, select one strategy you think you would implement most successfully in your classroom. Describe the strategy; state how you would use it and why you think it to be particularly effective. Share with a partner.

CHAPTER REFLECTION

Many new strategies have been presented in Chapters 4 and 5. It is important to include them in your ERR chart. Go back through the chapters and identify the various strategies presented. Make a list in your journal and, if possible, compare it with a partner to be sure you have them all. Once listed, go through them and decide where on the ERR chart they best fit. Come to consensus with your partner before placing it on the chart. One bit of advice. You will notice that sometimes it might seem a strategy, or part of a strategy, might fit in all three phases of the ERR framework. Think about where in the learning sequence you would first introduce the strategy. Also, some strategies may be applied in the evocation or reflection stage equally well. However, their application to either phase is in response to differing outcome expectations for learners. Be sure to think these differing outcomes through and note them in your journal.

6

Cooperative
Learning

*Reading is not only a cognitive and affective activity but also an intersubjective,
social process, not only a personal act, but also a communal event.*

—Mingshui Cai

EVOCATION

In previous chapters, numerous strategies were modeled along with the detailed
ERR lessons. We also spoke of the need to be aware of our own process of constructing reality.

With these strategies and ideas in mind, first think, then take five minutes for a freewrite on how you think student thinking and learning can
be served by having students work in cooperative groups. You may also
think of some limitations to cooperative work. Be sure to note these as
well. When you are finished, share your response with your colleagues in
small groups. Keep track of similar observations, both pro and con.

This chapter outlines instructional methods that promote cooperative
learning among students. As in the previous chapters, the presentation will
follow a similar pattern. A discussion will be offered about establishing a
classroom environment that promotes critical thinking and encourages cooperative
learning among students. Your earlier thoughts on this latter issue will serve as a starting point for examining the utility of cooperative learning and ways to successfully
facilitate cooperative-learning experiences. Our discussion is followed by sample
lessons that support cooperative leaning. The sample lessons involve practical class-
room-ready strategies that can be applied directly in classrooms or that my serve as
guides for developing other strategies. As usual, the lessons are presented as they
would be experienced by students and then are followed by a detailed discussion.

What is important to attend to while working through this chapter is the kind
of classroom environment teachers create when employing cooperative-learning

83

approaches as well as the kinds of outcomes teachers seek for their students through cooperative-learning applications.

The underlying assumptions of this chapter are that classrooms should be

- intellectually stimulating centers for thinking for students and teachers;
- purposeful places where students engage in meaningful, perhaps inspirational learning experiences;
- places where expectations for student development are clearly defined and openly shared with students; and
- safe settings for innovative thought and multiple voices.

The philosophy underpinning this chapter embodies what Arthur L. Costa (1992) suggested about thinking and content. The process of thinking must also become the content of instruction. Student decision making, opinion formation, problem solving, working collaboratively, learning to learn from many sources, and creatively integrating ideas and information must always be considered part of the content of curriculum and never separated from the content. Students learn how to learn by using thinking and learning processes in the study of specific curriculum content and use the content as fuel for thinking.

The teaching strategies presented here are consistent with the authors' philosophy presented previously. They are placed within the frame of critical thinking presented. Strategies presented fit into one or more phases of the ERR framework.

OUTCOME EXPECTATIONS

At the conclusion of this chapter participants will

- understand what is meant by an environment for thinking and how cooperative-learning strategies contribute to such an environment,

- be able to plan and implement a number of cooperative-learning strategies in class, and

- be able to identify in what stage or stages of the framework various cooperative-learning strategies apply.

OVERVIEW

Presentation of cooperative learning begins with a brief rationale before moving to actual strategies. Though this section too is interactive, it requires some direct presentation. Keeping your professional response journal available and making dual entry diary notations during this discussion of rationale is recommended. Following this will be a presentation of cooperative-learning strategies, which will be experiential. This is followed by review and discussion, examining the various elements of the strategies. As is our custom, first, we determine how the strategies were implemented—what the actual process was. Next, we consider how students might respond to them, analyzing your own experience as a way of understanding what your students will experience. Finally, we will review the strategies with respect to fit within the ERR framework for thinking and learning.

As always, planning for implementation is an essential step in the learning process. The end of the chapter encourages development of actual lesson plans using your own curricular content and incorporating the cooperative-learning strategies presented here. These plans should then be shared in small groups or with the larger learning community.

To begin our examination of cooperative learning, think to yourself privately, and write a few notes about the following question: What are the two or three most important skills we can teach our students to prepare them for their future? Remember your earlier freewrite and pull from that thinking if your responses are related or relevant to this question.

Allow a few minutes for thought and then share your thoughts with a partner. In your groups, share your thoughts briefly, keeping track of them on chart paper so all can see the ideas. As a group, consider connections among the various responses.

After sharing and discussing a number of ideas about what students should gain from their schooling, there may be general but not total agreement. Total agreement would be surprising since this question has been one of the greatest sources of controversy in education since the beginning of schooling.

As you read the following text, look to see if what is presented is similar to your own beliefs with respect to the most important outcomes of schooling related to student development, student learning.

CLASSROOMS AS ENVIRONMENTS FOR THINKING

A past president of the International Reading Association, Donna Ogle (1992), stated, "One of the goals of our educational system is to develop citizens who can contribute intelligently to the resolution of issues confronting our society, citizens who can think critically and help to solve problems in local communities as well as in the national and international arena" (p. 25). We hold that one set of outcomes of schooling ought to be maximizing the intellectual growth of students and their capacity to solve problems, advance understandings, become innovative, make decisions, and communicate effectively. To accomplish these outcomes, schools and classrooms must promote active students thinking and support thoughtful discussion and the sharing of ideas, beliefs, and philosophies. In other words, schools must be intellectually stimulating centers for thinking and learning where information (content) becomes the catalyst for further thought rather than the end point of learning.

One means of creating thinking environments is to introduce cooperative-learning methods into classrooms' instructional practices. Vygotsky (1962) made it clear that intellectual growth is the product of both internal processes and external or social processes. He suggested that higher-level thinking emerged from relationships, that is to say, the dialogue between people. Costa (1992) stated, "Together, individuals generate and discuss ideas, eliciting thinking that surpasses individual effort. Together and privately, they express different perspectives, agree and disagree, point out and resolve discrepancies, and weigh alternatives" (p.177).

In schools, there is often tension between conceptual learning on the one hand and an emphasis on subject content on the other. We know that the greater the knowledge base, the more sophisticated concept development can become and the better able learners are to integrate knowledge across content areas. We also know that the more broadly and well developed our context is for information, the more information we are able to retain and use effectively. There is a reciprocal relation between content knowledge and process. In reality, it is not possible to separate content from process and maximize learning. Knowledge without the capacity for practical application is like a computer without application software. It has potential to hold a great deal of information but is without practical utility. When process and content are considered of equal importance, students understand that knowledge constructively applied gives knowledge its value, its purpose, its utility. Knowledge, then, represents a kind of stored energy source available for solving problems rather than simply artifacts of one's educational experience to be recalled and recited at indeterminate intervals.

WHAT IS COOPERATIVE LEARNING?

Cooperative learning occurs when students work together, in pairs or small groups, to address a common problem, explore a common topic, or build on mutual understandings to create new ideas, new combinations of ideas, or unique innovations.

Before we offer one view of a cooperative-learning classroom, turn to a partner and do some paired brainstorming as to what a cooperative-learning classroom might look and feel like and what teachers' and students' roles must be in such a class. Take a few minutes for discussion.

THE COOPERATIVE-LEARNING CLASSROOM

There is evidence that learning outcomes are enhanced in cooperative-learning classrooms. Johnson and Johnson (1989) suggested cooperative-learning environments are responsible for the following:

- Higher achievement and increased retention

- More on-task and less disruptive behavior

- Greater ability to view situations from others' perspectives

- Greater social support

- More positive self-esteem based on basic self-acceptance

- More positive attitudes toward subject areas, learning, and school

- More frequent higher-level reasoning, deeper understanding, and critical thinking

- Greater achievement motivation and intrinsic motivation to learn

- More positive, accepting, and supportive relationships with peers regardless of ethnicity, sex, ability, social class, or special needs

- Greater psychological health, adjustment, and well-being

- Greater social competencies

- More positive attitudes toward teachers, principals, and other school personnel

How, then, does a classroom look and function to accomplish these outcomes? Richardson (1996/1997) suggested that effective cooperative classrooms have certain general characteristics that include

- positive interdependence,
- individual accountability,
- heterogeneous membership and grouping,
- shared leadership,
- direct social-skills teaching,
- teacher observation and intervention, and
- effective group work.

Positive Interdependence

Positive interdependence is achieved when students perceive that they need each other in order to complete a group task. Teachers may structure positive interdependence by establishing mutual goals (learn and make sure all group members learn), joint rewards (bonus points for group achievement), shared resources (one paper for each group or for part of the required information each member receives), assigned roles (summarizer, encourager of participants, elaborator), and peer evaluation processes to ensure full engagement by all group members.

Shared Leadership

Students promote each other's learning by helping, sharing, and encouraging efforts to learn. Shared leadership implies that students explain, discuss, and teach what they know to classmates for greater group development.

Individual Accountability

To ensure that each group member contributes to group tasks, teachers certainly need to assess both individual and group performance. This can be accomplished in many ways. One way is to be sure each student's performance is assessed frequently relative to his or her group work, with results given to the group and the individual. Teachers may structure individual accountability by giving individual tests to students or randomly selecting one group member to provide responses to an assessment item. This must be done with care and in a positive context—focusing on demonstrating progress, not catching someone contributing less than his or her share. To substantiate the value of individual and group contribution to the intellectual climate of the classroom, procedures should be in place that allow students to actively participate in the assessment process. Group members ought to evaluate one another along a clear set of criteria. The criteria should define behaviors that facilitate group progress and are readily observable. Individual students likewise benefit from reflection on their own learning and their contribution to their group. Self-assessment is an important part of a comprehensive assessment process.

Interpersonal and Small-Group Skills

Groups cannot function effectively if students do not have and use the necessary social skills for collaborative work. Teachers need to teach these skills as purposefully as they teach academic skills. Collaborative skills include shared leadership, decision making, trust building, patience, respect, responsibility (individual and collective), communication, and conflict management.

Effective Group Work and Group Processing

Groups need specific time to discuss how well they are achieving their goals and maintaining effective working relationships among members. Teachers structure group processing by assigning tasks such as (a) list at least three member actions that helped the group be successful, and (b) list one action that could be added to make the group more successful. Teachers also monitor the groups and give feedback to them and the whole class on how well the groups are working.

> Children will only become better thinkers if they have numerous opportunities to practice the approaches to thinking to which they are introduced. We should focus on a few thinking strategies that are most useful and transferable from one area to another so that students will be likely to use the skills and strategies regularly. (Ogle, 1992, p. 26)

Like every other skill we develop, the skill of thinking critically improves with practice. Allotting time to this task is the only way it will grow so that students will engage in it in more deliberate and complex ways.

SAMPLE COOPERATIVE-LEARNING LESSONS

Jigsaw

The first cooperative-learning method we will experience is the Jigsaw method (Slavin, 1986). It is a large-group activity, so the best way to experience this is with a learning community of 20 or more people. This is because the larger group will be subdivided into smaller groups.

Procedure: First, divide the large group into groups of four. The initial grouping is called the home group. Once the home groups are formed, have members count off to four so each member is assigned a number one through four.

Once each member of the home group has a number, inform all that they will be reading an article. Direct their attention to the article titled "Halloween Thoughts: Bats Are Beautiful and Do Good Deeds" by Ken Wells (Appendix C). Explain to the group that the expectation is that everyone will understand the entire article. However, it will be taught by classmates in sections. Each person will read only his or her particular assigned part of the article, but ultimately, the article will be fully understood by everyone.

The article is divided into four parts, and each numbered group (to form momentarily) will be responsible for one part. Now have all the ones gather together; all the twos, all the threes, and fours gather in groups according to their number. These groups are referred to as expert groups. Subgroups should have no more than four individuals. If there are, subdivide the groups again to form two or more sets of each expert group. (In large classes, it may be useful to divide the class in half first, having one half work on a Jigsaw article and the other half work on another topic or article.)

These groups of ones, twos, threes, and fours are referred to as *expert groups,* and it is their task to learn thoroughly the material presented in their section of the article so they can teach others. Next, members of each expert group are to read their section of the article and discuss it to be sure they fully understand their section. The group then must decide how best to teach the material to others. It is important that each member of the expert group understand that he or she is responsible for teaching that portion of the text to the original home group. It is up to each expert group, as a whole, to determine the teaching strategies and materials that will be used for their teaching. Be sure it is also understood that several participants from each expert group will be asked to teach their section to the whole group for demonstration purposes. Ask participants to form their expert groups and begin working. This process takes time as students work through their article section, discuss the content, and develop teaching strategies.

When the expert groups have completed their work, they may return to their home groups to teach the others their specific content. Each member of the home group is now an expert in a different section of the article. It is important that individuals within each home group master the content of all sections of the article. Home group members should note any questions they may have about the material in any sections of the article. These questions should then be directed to the expert in their home group who is responsible for that section of the text. If they are still uncertain or confused, they should ask the particular expert group for that section to clarify. If uncertainty persists, their question should become stimulus for further research. The teacher's role is to monitor the expert's teaching to be sure information is being transferred accurately and serve as a resource for questions that arise.

Before you begin Jigsaw, start thinking about bats. Ask the group to discuss how they feel about bats, if they have had any encounters with bats, and if bats frighten them. As students read, ask them to record INSERT style new, surprising, confirming, or confusing information.

Now, in your group, turn to the bats article found in Appendix C. It is already subdivided for use with the Jigsaw strategy. Following the steps outlined previously, work in your home and expert groups to become masters of the bats article. When the experts have completed their teaching, ask if anyone has formed a different opinion about bats, and ask all to look over their modified INSERT chart.

Analysis of Jigsaw Lesson

After you have experienced Jigsaw, first think about then share the following:

- How the process worked for you in general
- How you felt as an expert and a teacher
- How you felt in the home group learning from your peers

Think as well about the responsibility of carrying the information back to the home learning group from the expert group and how this influenced your approach to the task as a learner.

Ask yourself the following:

- What was your reaction in the cooperative group when you were being taught by your group colleague?
- How does this strategy change the role of the classroom teacher?

Now, take some time to share these reflections. With your reactions fresh in your mind, consider how Jigsaw and its various elements fit into the ERR framework. In general, Jigsaw is a realization of meaning phase activity. When the groups begin to monitor their own learning, ask questions, and check their own understandings, they are engaging in reflection-phase activities. However, the teaching strategies the experts develop should contain elements of all three stages of the framework.

The Jigsaw method precipitates student involvement across all three phases of the framework. Its applications reflect the cyclical, "mini-framework" model experienced during "The Sniper" lesson.

Paired Reading and Paired Summaries Demonstration Lesson

Paired reading is a wonderful strategy. We have been in countless classrooms where young third and fourth graders are huddled together in pairs throughout the classroom working together diligently to understand what they are reading. Older students "sit" together in various configurations debating their understandings in order to arrive at some consensus. Here, this paired reading process is coupled with a paired summary process.

This strategy was developed by Don Dansereau (1994) and his colleagues at Texas Christian University. It is a cooperative reading strategy particularly useful when text is dense and is a helpful strategy in content courses where reading material might be complicated or laden with facts.

The steps are outlined below. This strategy is actually more complicated to explain than to do. So follow closely but engage in the strategy so you will see how much more evident are the steps when applying the strategy.

To begin, the article "The Heart Beat" by Robert I. Macey (Appendix D) will be used to demonstrate this strategy. This is a whole-class activity; before turning to the article, ask people to join in pairs. Your partner at the beginning will be your partner for this entire process. In a moment, you are going to read the article in a particular way, as with Jigsaw. You will be responsible for knowing what is in the entire article, but for now you will be focusing on just one section. Once in pairs, each pair counts off by fours. Each pair is then assigned a one, two, three, or four since the article is divided into sections one through four. Each pair will now be responsible for the section of the article corresponding to its number.

This next piece to this strategy is most important. Each member of the pair is going to play two distinct roles. Each will take one or the other of the two roles, then switch roles as they read.

1. The first role is that of reporter. The reporter's job is to read the section carefully and summarize the content. After reading the section, the reporter will tell, without looking back at the section, his partner in his own words what the reading was about.

2. The second role is the responder, which is equally important. The responder *also reads* the section and then listens carefully to the reporter. When the reporter has finished reporting, the responder asks the reporter any questions that might clarify the reading or reveal more information. The responder might ask, "What about . . . ?" or "Do you recall . . . ?" or "Was there something about . . . ?"

Each person in the pairing will play both roles, so each article section is again divided into two segments. Recall the first division is into the four sections corresponding to the numbering of the pairs, and each section is assigned to a pair according to their number. Now, within each of the numbered sections, reading is divided approximately in half.

After the pairs are assigned their section and have decided which role they will play first, they are ready to read. Each pair will be responsible for reporting back to the whole group, so they should thoroughly understand their section. The pairs should find a comfortable spot in the room to work (at desks, tables, on the floor away from others, or in corner of the classroom). Conversations must be at moderate volume, or the room will become too noisy. The process will take some time until students become comfortable with the roles. Enough time must be allowed for all pairs to complete the task.

The final step involves pair presentations to the whole group. The whole class should be made aware of this final step from the beginning so they will read with this task in mind. Reporting to the whole group can take many forms. One method that works particularly well with paired reading and paired summaries is post-graphic organizers. Graphic organizers offer an excellent way for students to summarize their understandings from the text. In the "Heart" article, a post-graphic organizer is particularly suited to the content. (See Figure 6.1.) To complete this part of this strategy, each pair, using colored markers and a blank

Figure 6.1   Post-Graphic Organizer

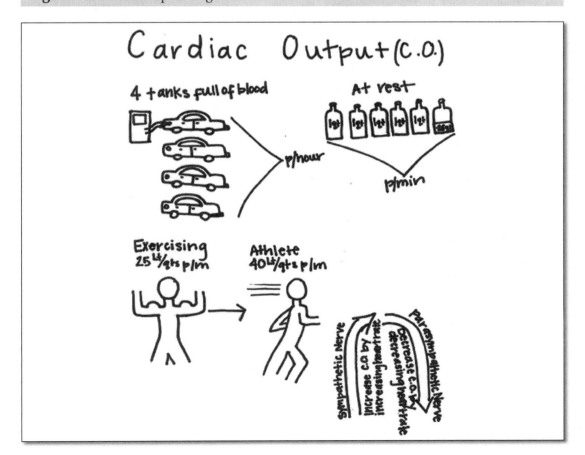

transparency sheet or laptop and graphics programs if available and the users are skilled, summarizes, using creative visuals, their understandings of their numbered section of text. After each pair has created a summary and graphic organizer, each pair should present its summary and graphic organizer to the class, beginning with the first section of the article and proceeding in sequence. Both members of the pair need to come forward, even if only one speaks.

Working with difficult text, it is possible for students to get confused or for different pairs assigned the same sections to have different understandings. The teacher's role is to monitor the work in progress by moving from pair to pair during development of the summaries to learn if there is confusion and to guide students to clearer understandings. It is useful in some instances, however, to let various understandings surface where discussion can be encouraged to determine how best to consider the information.

With these directions in mind, you can proceed to reading the "Heart" article accordingly. Before you begin reading, an evocation is required. For this reading, we often put a small dot on the board at the front of the classroom. It is so small it can hardly be seen or for some is not visible at all. We point out that this dot is there and that we are going to read about how a dot much smaller than this one can kill. At the end of the lesson, everyone should know why that is so and so much more.

Analysis of Paired Reading and Paired Summaries

To begin our analysis, in your pairs, start by describing how the process worked for you. There are many parts to this strategy, so be sure the discussion hits most of the components. Consider how you felt and behaved in the role of (1) the reporter and (2) responder. These are quite different roles, and your reactions are likely to be quite different for each. Did you feel any added responsibility knowing you would eventually teach others? Do you believe this feeling of responsibility intensified your attention to content? Do you think it will do the same for your students?

This strategy offers several instructional advantages. The first advantage is the notion that two heads are better than one when students are confronted by difficult text. Pairing students enables them to put their minds together to decipher difficult text, resolve confusions, and apply two sets of vocabulary to the task.

The second advantage is that when readers engage in the two roles, they accomplish two things. First, it sharpens readers' focus on the content and serves to maintain student engagement while reading difficult text. Second, it allows immediate opportunity for review and reflection, while giving students opportunity to put their understandings in their own words. Third, by creating joint summaries, pairs must engage in dialogue about content as they develop a concise language to convey what their section is about. Fourth, this strategy demands that students listen carefully to each other and share responsibility for teaching and learning. And fifth, having several pairs assigned to each section, the whole-group sharing presents the content in different ways, offering a variety of opportunities for understanding as well as opportunities for repeated exposure to the content. Furthermore, through whole-group sharing, the teacher can monitor understandings and correct misunderstandings.

Paired reading is a complicated strategy to describe and somewhat complicated to implement the first time. However, it becomes rather natural after several implementations, as students grow accustomed to their roles and the general procedures. At this time, take a few moments to consider where this strategy fits in the ERR framework. This may be complicated because parts of the strategy fit into different stages of the framework. The paired reading and paired summaries strategy fits into the Realization of Meaning phase, though it engages students in a considerable amount of reflection. It is primarily intended to facilitate the construction of meaning during an encounter with text. Post-graphic organizers are clearly reflection phase activities. After the presentations are complete, it is helpful to have a conversation with the whole group to check for thorough understanding. We often also view a web-based video that further summarizes the article content. One such website is http://www.youtube.com/watch?v=fLonh7ZesKs.

Corners

Corners is a cooperative-learning activity that is intended to generate debate and use group processes to stimulate constructive arguments. In fact, it is a great strategy for generating thoughtful, even impassioned debate. Every four years, we hear much about the presidential campaign and the first-in-the-nation Iowa caucuses. At its heart, this now legendary political tradition in the heartland of America is a modified Corners procedure. Caucuses come alive as supporters of the various candidates gather together and develop arguments intended to either persuade fellow caucus goers to come to their side or dissuade them from selecting other candidates. From the ensuing discourse, opinions are formed, cast adrift, and formed anew before the final tally is taken. Corners can be just as much fun, as it is used in classrooms as an active and enjoyable means of managing debates on controversial issues where two or more positions might be represented. It can be used following a class reading of a text, following a lecture or film presentation, or simply following a topic prompt for students to consider.

The directions for Corners are fairly straightforward and are intended to get students to take a stand on an issue and defend it. The strategy also encourages listening carefully to others and emphasizes the option to change opinions if the thoughts of others are sufficiently persuasive. In fact, this particular activity encourages students to change their minds as they listen to the thoughts and arguments of others.

Corners Demonstration

For our purposes here, this lesson will be on a topic offered by a prompt that follows.

In the state of Maine, there remain many unsettled lakes. For years, paper companies owned, for logging purposes, the land around these lakes. This deterred development. Now, paper companies are selling the land in large parcels of 1,000 acres or more, sometimes 30,000 to 40,000 acres at a time. These size lots are expensive, so only developers are able to afford them. Concern is now being expressed that these pristine wilderness lakes will become overdeveloped, destroying water quality, fish populations, bird-nesting areas, and other wildlife habitat. To combat this, potential ecological consequence rules are being put in place requiring developers to set aside approximately 50% of any development land and 50% of any developable shoreline, and permit lot sizes sufficient only to keep building back from the shore and out of view from the lake.

While protecting the environment, these rules drive the cost of lots up so high that only the wealthy can afford lakeside property. Now that the land is finally available, most Maine residents cannot afford to buy and are losing access to lakeshore as the land is bought by wealthy, out-of-state, absentee landowners.

The question for discussion is, "Should the rules remain in effect to protect the environment, or should they be dropped?" Environmental studies have shown that these rules represent a minimum requirement for protecting water, habitat, and land, so compromising these rules is the same as dismissing them in terms of intent. Yet keeping the rules means only the wealthy few enjoy the pristine wilderness.

After presenting the issue or topic, proceed as follows:

1. Begin thinking independently about the issue until you come to some tentative conclusion about where you stand.

2. In our example, you can be in favor of the regulations, opposed, or undecided. It is important to give students two or more options to consider. The teacher may determine the various positions students can take on an issue in advance, or students may brainstorm various stances. If "undecided" is a category, encourage students to take this position only as a last resort. Explain that they can take a stand tentatively and change their mind later. If undecided is an allowable category, at the beginning of discussion, students should be advised that by the end of discussion they will have to take a stand.

3. Next write for three minutes in support of your position, generating your own argument. Be as compelling and persuasive as possible.

4. When writing is finished, find out who supports regulation and assign them one corner of the room. Those who oppose go to another corner of the room. Those undecided could move to another corner. If there are other predetermined opinion groups (as may be the case for other discussion topics), they should have their own place to go in the room as well.

5. For 5 to 10 minutes or so, each group member should share her writing within her group and review the reasons for her positions. Arguments should be developed defending the group position and/or debunking anticipated arguments from the other group. The group selects one or two spokespersons to initially represent the group in the debate that will follow. Once debate begins, all group members should participate in the ensuing discussion.

6. Call for the debate by inviting each group to state succinctly its position and the major reasons for supporting its view.

7. Once the formal debate has been presented by the group spokespersons, other group members should now be encouraged to participate in the conversation. If the groups need encouragement, ask some probing questions:

   - Why should those of you in Group A not accept the opinion of Group B?
   - Where do you disagree with what Group B has to say?
   - What about the undecided group? What prevents you from taking a stand?

- What have you heard that moves you toward a clearer opinion?
- Why are those of you in Group B unconvinced by what Group A has said?

8. Some students may change their minds as a result of the discussion. They should feel free to change groups at any time. They simply have to walk from the group they are in to the group with whom they now agree. In fact, encourage students to move as their opinion shifts. Also, encourage members in the groups to try to persuade others not to leave their group. This puts the burden on the members within each group to be persuasive in order to keep group members as they try to draw more adherents. Students can take notes on their thinking as they listen and discuss, which will help later when they have to write about their position on the issue and defend it.

9. Once the discussion has ended and everyone has moved to his or her final group, ask each group to summarize its position and the reasons that support it. Then, ask all students to write a position paper, setting out their individual positions and the reasons behind them. (A more elaborate paper will take opposing arguments into account but defend the chosen position in the face of them.)

Analysis of Corners

Begin analysis by reflecting on the process. There are several steps to this strategy; some require individual work while some entail group work. First, consider your impressions as a learner working through the various steps along the way. Go through them one at a time with ERR as your guide.

Step 1 presented the topic and some background information for consideration. This provided a brief evocation. For this strategy to be successful, students will have to know something about a topic or issue so they can develop an informed opinion from the beginning. However, even when moving to *Step 2*, it is not necessary to be an expert on the issue. It is rare that we become experts on issues before we formulate an opinion. In reality, our opinions are often based on factors not directly related to an issue, and we discover those factors only when we are asked to defend our opinions.

Step 3 asked you to work individually to formulate your own thoughts. This requires taking a stand before hearing from others. While it may be difficult for some to do this, it is an important part of the process. We know that learners are more likely to become engaged in the learning process and learn best when they have a stake in what is being discussed. By taking a position from the beginning, students are staking their claim in the conversation. This step involves two stages of the framework, depending on whether you are looking at the strategy globally or at this particular step in the process. From a global perspective, the Corners strategy is either a Realization of Meaning or a Reflection activity or both. Everyone is already informed, though briefly in our example on the topic. They have activated awareness of previous knowledge and beliefs. Group deliberations and the discussion and/or debate that ensues constitute a genuine encounter with new information, consistent with the Realization of Meaning phase. Only here, the content is the thoughts, arguments, and viewpoints of other students, and the information source is the collective wisdom of the class. Because of the importance of valuing students' knowledge and the considerable contribution students can make to the knowledge base of their peers, we consider Corners a Realization of Meaning phase activity.

Step 4 is a powerful component of this strategy because it requires participants to commit actively to a position. A public statement of one's thinking commits an individual more definitively to a viewpoint while emphasizing the point that everyone has opinions and that those opinions count.

Steps 5, 6, and 7, as mentioned, are all considered to be a Realization of Meaning activity as students listen to the voices of their peers and consider the meanings being constructed about the issue. During these steps, it is important to monitor the conversation to be sure that many voices in the classroom are heard.

Step 8 is central to the strategy and provides participants with permission and opportunity to change their minds publicly. Understanding critical thought means understanding that thinking is a continuous process that can lead to different conclusions. Changing opinions is one legitimate outcome of thought. Changing one's opinion is a natural and predictable consequence of careful thought. This step also requires students to articulate their thoughts in ways that communicate them clearly to others. It is important to have opinions, but their value is enhanced when shared with others.

Summarizing the group's position and rationale and then writing individual position papers, as suggested in *Step 9,* are Reflection Stage activities. Asking for both group and individual activity reinforces the notion that students are ultimately responsible for their opinions and beliefs, and they must offer their own justification for their views. Certainly, their views will have, as their source, the thoughts and wisdom of others, but in the end, they must be able to express their views in their own words.

BRIEF COOPERATIVE STRATEGIES

There are many strategies that promote cooperative learning yet take little time to implement. These simple strategies offer excellent means of introducing students to working in pairs or small groups. This section will describe a number of such strategies. You are encouraged to experience them as presented and then review them in pairs in your larger group and discuss them in terms of your own experience. Be sure to discuss where and how they fit into the framework and how to modify them to fit your content area.

Paired Predictions

The first of these is called Paired Predictions, which can be used in many content areas. The following example is used in children's literature classes, where students will read a children's novel titled *Tonight by Sea* by Francis Temple. Ask if anyone has read the story previously. If yes, tell them to listen again, now. Ask students to group in pairs with paper and pencil. Explain that they should listen carefully as you read the following list of words, which refer to the characters, the setting, and some to the story itself.

| Paulie | freedom | bravery | home | Haiti | Macoutes |
| Karyl | terror | sea | life | | |

Have students form pairs and discuss with their partner a mutual idea of what this story might be about, making some prediction about the story. Allow five or six minutes for discussion for them to write their predictions so they can refer to later as they read the story. Of course, in our example, they will not be reading the story as the story is being read to them. This prediction activity can be done only at the beginning of the story. Then, as the story unfolds, the pairs come together at various points throughout the story to modify their predictions. It is likely quite clear by now that this is an excellent Evocation activity to implement before reading a text or chapter and continues to serve as evocation for subsequent readings.

Think, Pair, Share

Kagan (1992) described this strategy. It begins with the teacher telling the group they are now going to be assigned a topic for their individual consideration. The topic or issue should be something interesting and related to course content. Perhaps, for your purposes here, topics like teachers' salaries, the value of space exploration in a time of economic difficulty, or global warming might be relevant. Think individually about a topic for a few minutes; then pair with a partner and share your thinking. This should take only a few minutes. Think, Pair, Share is a quick, simple, cooperative-learning technique that can be incorporated into most content areas, typically as an Evocation activity. It works well with large groups and is excellent to use prior to a talk. Of course, this strategy has been employed frequently in this text and so is familiar already.

Summarize, Pair, Share

Recall the "Heart" article we read earlier. Just take a few minutes and write a summary of the article in two or three sentences. When finished, turn to your partner and share your summary statements. Discuss any similarities or differences to see if you can come up with a mutually agreeable summary. Allow only three minutes for each part of this activity. This simple paired activity is an extension of Think, Pair, Share typically used following a presentation, reading, or discussion of a topic as a Reflection phase activity.

Formulate, Share, Listen, Create

Johnson, Johnson, and Bartlett (1990) offered this strategy. It is a similar activity in which teammates first privately formulate responses, then share and listen in turn, and together create a new answer or perspective through discussion and elaboration. This activity has widespread application and encourages students to stretch their thinking.

We spoke earlier about the benefits of cooperative learning. There are some added benefits to using these brief strategies. By promoting focused, short-term, purposeful talk among students, informal cooperative-learning techniques such as Think, Pair, Share can ease students into cooperative peer relationships. As students learn to work cooperatively on more complex team tasks, these informal structures can be used to facilitate group interaction.

These short cooperative-learning techniques and strategies can be incorporated into instruction easily and quickly, applied to all content areas, and offer students an opportunity to work cooperatively during all stages of the framework.

COOPERATIVE MATH ACTIVITIES

Making the Target Number

Mathematicians Glenn Nelson and Earl Ockenga (1997) have developed a number of cooperative activities for use in mathematics instruction, including "Making the Target Number." This is one of our favorite math activities, and you are encouraged to follow the instructions and work through this strategy. It can be done alone but is more fun in groups.

1. Divide the large group into groups of four or five and give each group a set of digit or number cards, one through six, and a set of target cards (10, 20, 30, 40, 50, 60). Alternatively, one set of number cards and a single target card may be drawn for the entire group to work on. This is best when demonstrating the strategy to a class.

2. Place the number cards in a hat or a small container and ask a member in each small group to select (without looking) five number cards and one target card. It is important when drawing the number cards to return the selected number card to the hat after it has been drawn and recorded. It should be mixed in with the other number cards to possibly be drawn again. It is fine to draw the same number more than once.

   Example:

   Number cards   Target Card

   3 – 5 – 5 – 6 – 4   50

3. The task now is to use each drawn number indicated on the selected number cards only once (but each drawn number *must be* used) in any combination of mathematical operations to reach the target number. Once the number cards are drawn along with the target card, students can begin to find solution formulas.

   For example, looking at the cards selected from above—3, 5, 5, 6, 4—some solutions include the following:

   $$\{(3 \times 5 \times 4) / 6\} \times 5 = 50 \ \text{ or } \ \{(5 \times 5) \times 4 / (6 / 3) = 50$$

   Some students will catch on more quickly than others or find solutions to particular sets of numbers more quickly. Once they have discovered one solution, they should look for additional solutions. Most, though not all, number combinations have multiple solutions. One additional rule to help: It is fine to use exponents, but each exponent must be from a number card and counts as a number used from the five available numbers.

What's the Number?

This is a math detective task that can be performed in pairs or small groups. It also can be modified to apply to other content areas such as geography: "Where am I?" or history: "Who am I?"

First, look at the "What's the Number?" number chart and the example clues below. Form pairs and ask one member for each pair to pick a target number silently. Then he or she should lead the partner through a series of clues until the partner chooses the correct number. Try the following example:

I am thinking of a number.

1st clue: It is an even number.

2nd clue: It is divisible by eight.

3rd clue: It is between 20 and 40.

4th clue (if necessary): The sum of the digits is six.

5th clue (if necessary): The tens digit is half the ones digit.

6th clue (if necessary): The number is divisible by six and three.

The example target number is 24.

1	2	3	4	5	6	7	8	9	10
11	12	13	14	15	16	17	18	19	20
21	22	23	24	25	26	27	28	29	30
31	32	33	34	35	36	37	38	39	40

Both math examples seek to engage students in math activities that require applying knowledge to finding solutions without resorting to rote tasks that deaden math experiences. In the first instance, students must muster all their knowledge of math operations and apply them creatively to find solutions. The first strategy also demonstrates that even in math, there is more than one right answer. The second strategy asks students to recall their knowledge of the various ways numbers are grouped and described. It requires students to consider the quality of numbers, their identities if you will. Both strategies are considered Reflection phase activities.

Roundtable-Round Robin

Roundtable (Kagan, 1992) is a strategy in which one paper and pencil are passed around a group. To reach a solution to a word problem, one partner writes an idea in a single sentence or two and passes the paper and pencil to the partner on the left. That partner adds to the idea presented and passes the paper to the next. A variation of the procedure is to have each partner use a different colored writing tool when the paper is passed. This visually encourages all partners to contribute equally and allows the teacher to document individual contributions. *Round Robin* (Kagan, 1992) is the oral form of Roundtable. Each teammate verbally contributes an idea to the group in a systematic, around-the-group fashion. Both variations on this strategy are typical Reflection stage activities, but if students have enough prior knowledge, they can be used as Evocation phase activities as well.

BRIEF EXERCISES FOR PROBLEM SOLVING AND DISCUSSION

This section presents additional cooperative-learning strategies, which are described in greater detail in Baloche (1998), Kagan (1992), and Johnson, Johnson, and Holubec (1993).

Kagan (1992) called his suggestions for teaching *cooperative-learning structures.* Unlike the Jigsaw presented earlier in this chapter, cooperative-learning structures can be used without extensive prior preparation on the part of the teacher. And while some of these cooperative structures may not teach quite so thoroughly as the alternatives, they are easier to use, and thus, perhaps more likely to be used. Our advice? Don't scrimp on strategies such as Jigsaw because they are effective. Take time to prepare them, save them for reuse in future years, and share them with other teachers. But take advantage of cooperative-learning structures as well. They are lively and enjoyable, and they help students learn to think.

Stationary Group Activities

Numbered Heads Together

1. Students form small groups of three or four.

2. Students count off within their small groups from one to three or one to four.

3. The teacher poses a question or problem.

4. The students consider the problem alone.

5. The students then discuss the problem as a group.

6. The teacher calls a number, and each student with that number reports to the whole class on the group's discussion.

Pens in the Middle

This is a quick strategy for promoting small-group conversation involving all students. As students begin to share ideas in the typical cooperative-learning group (3 to 7 members), each student marks his or her contribution by placing a pen or pencil on the table in the middle of the group. That individual may not contribute again until all pens are in the middle.

With this simple approach, all members are equal in their ability to contribute, and no one may dominate or remain silent. Once under way, students often continue to comment without placing their pens in the middle. This is an ideal outcome. However, if the conversation veers from mutual levels of contribution to some dominating speakers, the teacher can remind students to use their pens.

Trade a Problem

1. The teacher gives a lecture or assigns a reading. (Appropriate evocation activities should be used.)

2. Students are assigned to random pairs.

3. The pairs identify four or five main points in the lecture or reading.

4. These pairs join other pairs to form foursomes and discuss the main points and clarify uncertainties.

5. Each pair now writes a set of questions to answer or problems to solve for the other pair.

6. The pairs link up again and quiz each other.

7. The four students reflect on what they have learned from the exercise.

Exercises That Require Movement Around the Class

Stirring Up the Class

1. Students count off within their home groups of three or four.

2. The teacher poses a question or problem.

3. The students consider the problem in their home groups.

4. All the students with the number *one* then rotate to the adjacent group and share the results of their home group's deliberations.

5. Students return to their home groups.

6. The teacher asks another question or poses another problem.

7. The students discuss their ideas within their groups.

8. All the students with the number *two* rotate two groups away and share the results of their home group's deliberations.

9. This idea continues with numbers three and four doing likewise. Number fours should not move over four groups because that will bring them back to their home group.

Mix, Freeze, Pair

1. The students stand and move freely around the classroom.

2. The teacher says, "Freeze," and the students stop.

3. The teacher says, "Pair," and each student pairs up with the nearest person, taking whatever seats are available.

4. The teacher asks a question, and the students discuss it.

5. The process is repeated several times.

6. A variation is to have students form an inner and outer circle with an equal number of students. The circles then rotate in opposite directions until someone says, "Freeze." The persons opposite each other at that point become partners.

Rotating Review

1. A number of questions (6 to 8) are written on numbered sheets of newsprint and posted around the room.

2. Groups of three or four students are assigned a question. They move to the sheet with the question on it, discuss the question for four to five minutes, and write their answers on the sheet.

3. At a signal from the teacher, the groups move to a new sheet, read the question and the answer that have been written, and add their comments on that sheet.

4. The teacher calls for the groups to move on—repeating the process, if possible, until the groups return to their original sheets.

Gallery Tour

1. In groups of three or four, students first work through a problem, preferably with varied possible approaches, and produce a demonstrable product such as a diagram on chart paper.

2. The products are taped to the walls around the room.

3. At the teacher's signal, the groups rotate around the room to examine and discuss each product. They take notes on their observations and may leave written comments on the display.

4. After the gallery tour, the groups reexamine their products in comparison to the others and review the comments left on their own work by others.

One Stay, Three Stray

1. The students first work through a problem with varied possible approaches and produce a demonstrable product such as a diagram on chart paper.

2. The students within groups count off (1 to 3).

3. Each group is numbered, as well.

4. At the teacher's signal, students rotate: Student 1 rotates one group, Student 2 rotates two groups, Student 3 rotates three groups—but one student does not move. Note: It is best to do rotations one step at a time.

5. The student who stays in the home group explains the group's work to the rotating students.

6. The rotating students ask questions and take notes in preparation for reporting back to their home groups. Each visitor makes one specific comment on the work he or she has been shown and thanks the home-group student for the presentation.

7. Students all move back to their home groups.
   a. The home-group student who did not rotate reports to the other students on the rotating students' comments on the work.

b. Students 1, 2, and 3 now report on what they observed in the other groups, noting similarities and differences with their own work.
c. The students discuss their own work further.

At this point, it might be good to stop and form groups to discuss the strategies just covered. Groups should check for understanding and ask questions if anything is unclear.

CHAPTER REFLECTION

Classrooms where cooperative-learning strategies take place are often full of the sounds of student voices. They may even look somewhat chaotic, though they are not. Implementing cooperative-learning strategies does require setting some ground rules to guide students' engagement. Some suggestions have been offered for how to manage cooperative classrooms, but each setting is different. Consider for a few minutes the rules you might set for student involvement in cooperative-learning activities. Think also how the rules you suggest might advance or inhibit cooperative-learning. After you have your list, share in a small-group setting. Discuss why you think the various rules might be necessary and their potential impact on individual students and the group as a whole.

When finished discussing cooperative-learning rules, organize in small groups according to content area if possible and have a content text available. Now, with a genuine content text in hand, plan how you would implement several of the strategies from this chapter using the selected content. Plan a lesson according to the ERR framework using cooperative-learning strategies. When finished, share your plans with the small groups where possible.

Finally, take out your ERR framework chart and add the strategies from this chapter to the chart. Be sure to talk through where each strategy falls in the teaching and learning framework.

7

Creating Thoughtful Readers

Because reading is "thinking cued by text," readers create meaning by interacting mentally with the words on the page.

—Rachel Billmeyer

EVOCATION

Have you ever stopped to consider the sheer volume of reading material available to American readers? The numbers are staggering. According to Morrow (2008), in 2002, the total number of periodical titles published in America exceeded 60,000. Barr and Harbison (2009) reported the total number of nonperiodical materials such as books, manuals, and new editions reached 185,969. Then, there are e-mail and instant messaging and text messaging and Twitter, and blogging, and on it goes. In 2008, it is estimated, publishers' net shipments to dealers was a total 3,106,000,000, and by 2011, projections are for that total to rise to 3,132,000,000 with estimated domestic consumer spending on these publications of $63,525,000,000. How do we sort it all out? How do we decide what to read, what's important, what information is dependable?

Brainstorm for three to four minutes on your own reading experiences, and jot down your ideas. Think of the number of different sources of written material you encounter in a month. Then, think of all this reading you do and how you process what you read. Does it vary with the type of text, purpose of text? How so? What, if anything, do you do cognitively to prepare for reading? Does your preparation vary according to text type or reading purpose? Share your thinking in small groups, and note similarities and differences in approaches to these varied reading tasks. Keep these ideas in mind as you work through this chapter.

This chapter has several purposes. The first is to introduce a way of conceptualizing literacy in general and reading in particular that allows us to think of literacy and reading as tools for critical thought rather than simply subjects to be studied. The second purpose is to present readers' workshop and other approaches to reading that fully engage readers in the reading process. Readers' workshop is primarily a method of approaching reading that involves extended silent reading as well as sharing and responding in a systematic and well-orchestrated way. Readers' workshop will be presented here as both a format for understanding a critical reading process and an instructional model. A third purpose is to describe and model how a critical reading process can be applied to content-area instruction to enhance student engagement and subsequent reading comprehension.

First, a brief discussion is offered clarifying the role of reading as a tool for thinking and learning. Following this discussion, readers' workshop is modeled and discussed. Then, example applications of the readers' workshop model to content-area studies are presented. It is important to understand that the instructional model, readers' workshop, is designed primarily for reading and literature teachers. However, understanding the reading processes underlying readers' workshop contributes to the effective application of the reading process to content-area studies. We believe it is useful for all teachers to experience readers' workshop, as the subsequent conversation describes how reading can become an effective tool for content learning.

Readers' workshop is a comprehensive approach to reading instruction implemented in classrooms independent of the ERR framework. However, it readily fits within the three-phase framework, and learning is enhanced when application of the reading process to content areas is considered within the various phases of the framework. Here, our discussion places applications of the reading process within the framework and includes some underlying assumptions. These include the following:

- Reading is a primary medium through which people are exposed to new information throughout their lives.
- Developing fluency is a necessary but not a sufficient skill for thoughtful consideration of text. Thoughtful, critical readers develop out of an instructional model that guides learners beyond fluency and through diverse genres of text.
- Reading is a tool for thinking and learning and not simply a subject of study.
- Reading and responding to reading are avenues for critical analysis.
- Content-area study typically requires considerable independent reading; therefore, understanding the reading process can enhance comprehension and subsequent reflection in content-area study.
- There is a powerful link between reading and writing. Both are essential tools for learning and thinking. Understanding the reading-writing connection enhances learning, enables teachers and students to more effectively utilize these tools, and increases content learning.

OUTCOME EXPECTATIONS

At the conclusion of this chapter readers will

- understand the role of reading as a tool for thinking and learning;
- be able to implement readers' workshop in a classroom;

- apply the reading process to content area studies;
- understand the role of reading, the role of engagement in the reading process, and the difference between reading comprehension and reading for thinking; and
- be able to apply both the ERR framework and readers' workshop simultaneously.

DISCUSSION OF A THOUGHTFUL READING PROCESS

Begin by forming pairs to consider the following statement and set of questions.

It has been suggested that learning is about thinking and doing, that is, about thoughtfully and actively creating new meanings, new realities. If this is true, then classrooms must be thoughtful, active, yet reflective places. What must teachers understand and do to make classrooms thoughtful, active, and reflective places while students are engaged in the reading of text? These questions deserve our attention. With your partner, brainstorm responses to these questions. Take about seven minutes to reflect on the questions and enter them in your journal. After seven minutes or so of paired discussion, share your responses, listing them on chart paper. Then in large groups, review and discuss the various points to ensure clarity of the ideas presented.

You are now about to read a brief presentation about reading thoughtfully. You will actually engage in two learning strategies simultaneously. The first will be assigned below and is a paired reading and paired summaries strategy. The second is described within the presentation. Continue to work in pairs using the paired reading and paired summaries strategy presented in Chapter 6. You will see that the following presentation has been divided into two sections (A & B). With your partner, decide who the reporter and the responder will be for each section. With this decision, read the presentation with the understanding that there will be whole-group sharing of what the presentation means and how it relates to earlier thinking about thoughtful classrooms. When reading is complete, take a few moments to write down some impressions from the reading, drawing connections to earlier paired and large-group discussions about thoughtful classrooms. Alternatively, take a few moments to write your reactions to the reading, being mindful of your earlier thoughts.

Part A

Reading Thoughtfully—A Brief Presentation

Now, before we begin, take a moment to think about your own reading history. Think back to your earliest school memories and even earlier. Try to recall your earliest encounters with print. Try to think of your literacy experiences in and out of school. What influenced you to develop as a reader? You may want to write out a few notes or just bring these memories to an awareness level for now. Later, there will be time to share your early literacy history with others.

Before we begin examining approaches to improving reading comprehension, we want to build the case for why it is essential that we take this task seriously. We also wish to share some preliminary thoughts about what we consider some requisite elements of reading instruction essential for improving reading comprehension.

Before reading, however, create a Dual Entry Diary in your professional development journal. On a blank page, draw a vertical line down the middle of the page. As you read, enter in the left column ideas that strike you as important or otherwise noteworthy. On the right, jot a few notes reflecting your thinking. When finished reading each section, first have the reader summarize the section. Next, the respondent should react to the reader's summary. Following this step, each should turn to her or his Dual Entry Diary and discuss her or his entries.

As we consider how we become thoughtful readers, it might be useful to get a context for reading in terms of the volume of reading we do and its value. We already saw earlier in this chapter the overall volume of reading in terms of publications and their commercial value, but what of individuals? Contrary to some opinions about the impact of television and other technology on learning, the medium we most depend on for sharing information and through which we learn is reading. Whether reading from textbooks, journals, manuals, web-based sources, or other written text, people wishing to be better informed, better skilled, or simply more aware of issues that effect their lives must read. Yet for some students, reading does not always provide access to new knowledge, new understandings, or new ways of doing something. In fact, Beck and Dole (1992) reported on a number of studies that demonstrated that even for good students, reading new information in science and social studies texts did not result in altered misconceptions, misunderstandings, or erroneous beliefs. This distressing failure to comprehend occurred despite direct presentation of information in the text that conflicted with students' previously held notions and beliefs. In other words, readers' schema for content is often undisturbed by their reading despite glaring contradictions.

One reason a student may not derive much from informational text may be explained by the research of Nell Duke (2003). Duke reported beginning readers spent almost no time (3.6 minutes per day) with informational text, while most reading time was occupied by reading narrative text. Students experience little preparation for responding to the type of academic text they will encounter throughout their schooling and their adult lives.

Furthermore, we may be encouraging students to stay disconnected from the reading process by focusing on low-level "comprehension" of written materials. Again, Beck and Dole (1992) suggested that "reading comprehension" is often considered in a classroom context to be simply a matter of understanding the details of what an author has written. Consequently, if students are able to recite what the author has said, they are applauded for understanding the text, when in fact, this may not be true at all. If by understanding we mean students have incorporated some form of negotiated meaning from text into their own knowledge base (schema), and dealt with any contradictions, and are able to apply these new understandings at critical points in their own lives when necessary or when so inspired, then mere recall cannot be considered understanding. If all we ask of students is to recall and recite, then we will not know if any higher-level comprehension has occurred, and we will not know if students truly understand text.

James Voss (1992), describing the Beck and Dole work in regard to the distinction between reading for low-level comprehension versus reading for thinking, wrote the following:

> The importance of this orientation distinction should not be underestimated. Literacy is a function of the person and the context. A political scientist reading an editorial, typically, will evaluate the article's contents virtually as the reading takes place. A novice will focus on what the writer is saying. Because there has been so much preoccupation in teaching with the idea of comprehending what is written, we have neglected the study of how what is written can be interpreted by different individuals. What is written . . . is . . . an opportunity for a person to provide an interpretation of meaning to what is read. (p. 1)

For reading to be useful beyond the next No Child Left Behind assessment and to become an integrated interpretive process requires actively engaged readers connecting what they are reading to what they already know. Good readers are thinking about the author's message in personal terms, filtering text through the prism of their own experiences. Our primary task is to help readers develop the capacity to become and remain engaged, thoughtful, and reflective readers, connected to and responding to text by moving beyond naive recall to complex consideration of content.

As a mechanism for conveying a global understanding of how students become thoughtful readers, we will briefly experience readers' workshop. Readers' workshop, elaborated eloquently by Nancy Atwell (1998) in her book *In the Middle*, is a method, a grand strategy if you will, by which readers develop the skills necessary for interacting continuously and meaningfully with text. It sets in motion an instructional sequence, grounded in best-practice research about reading and thinking, which moves students beyond low-level reading skills to a point where reading becomes a sophisticated tool that incubates complex thought. Readers' workshop, as described here, is implemented fully in reading class, literature class, and in more advanced language classes. However, critical elements of readers' workshop can and should be applied to all content areas and courses where reading from text is a central means of conveying content.

Regardless of setting, whether literature or science class, the reading process requires three basic elements: time, ownership, and response. We will examine each of these elements in brief to see how they contribute to reading comprehension.

Part B

Time

Reading time, the most precious commodity for improving reading, is too often the rarest of resources. Given the preponderance of evidence extolling the virtue of time spent reading, acknowledging it is the single best way for readers to become better readers, adopting instructional approaches that increase time spent reading should certainly increase student's ability to benefit from reading instruction. However, for reading time to be time well spent, some specific goals for reading need to be clearly stated.

The most critical literacy goal is creating lifelong readers. All indicators suggest we are not meeting this goal for large numbers of students. In 2004 the National Endowment for the Arts (NEA) published "Reading at Risk." This survey of 17,135 people concluded that traditional reading in America is in sharp decline. As evidence, only 56.9% of survey respondents read a book of any sort during the previous 12 months, and only 46.7% of adults reported reading literature for pleasure. More alarming, the biggest decline in reading occurred among 18-to-24-year-olds. This is the age group most recently out of school, and for black adolescent males, the picture is even more disconcerting—large segments of this population tend to disregard reading altogether (Tatum, 2005). Once out of school, people make their own choices about what is entertaining, how to gather information, what intellectually stimulating activities to pursue, and whether or not to be curious. Away from school for reading to be a viable option, it has to have a well-storied past. Prospective readers will choose to read if they know by going to that well, a thirst will be quenched. This is more likely to happen if reading experiences have been joyful, enriching, social, self-rewarding, absorbing, successful, and/or stimulating. So our goals beyond spending time reading ought to include creating reading experiences that are personally enriching, certainly social, potentially self-rewarding, absorbing, joyful, and always successful. Increasing reading time is a necessary but not sufficient condition for the creation of lifelong readers. Certainly, time devoted to readers' workshop should be sufficiently frequent, consistent, and dependable for students to anticipate and plan purposively for reading. What matters as well, though, is providing reading experiences that develop intrinsically motivated readers, students who come to think of themselves as readers.

Ownership

So often, students are handed textbooks and told what to read, how many pages to read, and by when. Seldom do students have real choice over what they read and for what purposes. When students read only the selections of others and for external purposes, they are less likely to read with engagement. This leads us to conclude that, left to their own devices, students will avoid reading and certainly will eschew good literature. Yet when offered good literature with passion and an understanding of interest, students do choose good literature, and they will choose to investigate topics in science, history, and math. This should not be surprising. As Steven Stahl (1999) wrote, "Most instructors agree that learners place more belief in knowledge they have discovered on their own than in knowledge presented by others, yet all too often, these same instructors fail to trust students to learn anything not explicitly stated by the instructor" (p. 1). When given some choice and voice over what students are reading, they are willing to explore a variety of genres voluntarily. Taking ownership is the first crucial step readers take to becoming invested, inquisitive readers.

Response

We have come to consensus that reading is a social act and not an individual process of learning skills followed by engaging in the isolated chore of reading. Fluency, we now understand, is simply the capacity to apply a skill sequence with minimal errors. Now, we believe that reading is better understood as applying complex skills that enable a conversation between an author and a reader where the construction of meaning is the outcome of the conversation. For meaning making to be contextualized and placed in long-term memory, it is critical to provide opportunity for genuine response. Responding to text within a social context energizes readers to modify, evaluate, and then locate their understandings in a viable, memorable, and accessible form. Response comes when readers tell others about what they have read and what it means to them. As adults, we delight in telling friends about the good books, interesting articles, and informative pieces we have read. When sharing, we are recalling and rephrasing ideas in our own words as we learn about new sources of ideas, new ways of thinking about the world, and new paths to discovery. Adults do this spontaneously, as do good young readers.

In a moment, we will turn to an explication of readers' workshop. Before doing so, turn to your dual entry diary and briefly review your entries. Then, with a partner, share your entries, using this exchange as the beginning point for a comprehensive discussion about the reading process. Share your own reading history and how it has served or disserved you in your own life. It is always fascinating to learn the varied histories of other readers. Spend time listening to these tales, as they are almost always instructive about how we do or do not become avid, capable lifelong readers. Remember now to return to the paired reading paired summaries activity.

READERS' WORKSHOP

Next, we will work through a readers' workshop experience. We use as our guide the exceptional work of Nancy Atwell (1987) and strongly encourage reading her excellent book *In the Middle.* Let's begin. To participate in readers' workshop, have available a book of your own choosing, as you will be reading for 20 minutes. Once you have selected your book, perform a quick evocation activity. Read anything written about the book or author on the dust jacket, the preview, any chapter headings, or the table of contents. Speculate for a minute about the text, what the text might be about, who the characters might include, how the text will unfold. After this evocation speculation, you will read your chosen book silently for 20 minutes. After reading, you will write a brief response. Be prepared for your response to be shared in small groups of three or four. To prepare, keep in mind several important ideas regarding your response:

1. Each response should be a personal reflection, not a retelling; it should interpret the reading meaningfully in terms of your own experiences and beliefs.

2. Consider your responses as the beginning of a dialogue.

3. Your responses should include some evaluative statements such as "I like this book because . . ." or "This article is effective because it clarified . . . for me" or "I do not think I agree with the author because. . . ."

Sample responses from students may serve as a guide.
Samantha (Grade 8) wrote the following:

This book was hard to put down because something was happening all the time. I could relate to the main character because she is a lot like me. What I liked most though is that all the characters are real to me. No one is too weird or has some super-power or something stupid like that. I could just get into all of the characters.

Bryan (Grade 6) wrote the following:

It was sad when the boy died in the story. I guess I knew he was going to die but still I did not want him to. I wanted someone to find a cure even though I knew it wouldn't happen. I think everyone did the best they could to help, even Michael Jackson. Ryan was brave—everyone should read this book.

Peter (Grade 7) wrote the following:

I do not quite understand how Steve and John got into so much trouble. I don't think the author did such a good job of explaining how that could happen. It kind of ruined the story for me because it just seemed stupid all the time that they were in trouble when they didn't need to be. I thought about reading the first part over to see if I missed something but then said no. Now, cause I am writing this I think I should read it again. That might help me like the book more or maybe make me just start a new one I'd like more.

Now, begin your first 20 minute reading. When finished reading, take about six to eight minutes to write your reading response. Then, form pairs or small groups of three or four and allow time for sharing. First, though, since this is the first readers' workshop sharing, your colleagues will likely be unfamiliar with the reading material being shared. Therefore, at this point in readers, workshop, each reader needs to provide a brief context for the reading, such as the title, author(s), and a few words about the topic or story line before sharing written responses. Later, sharing will build on this information so less background is required.

Quick Reflections

In keeping with our customary practice, take a few minutes now to think and share your thoughts on this reading experience so far. Think about the following:

- How you approached reading knowing you would be sharing your thoughts
- How you responded to the sustained reading time
- What you experienced in the sharing groups—how it went, what you learned, and how you felt, that is, what was the impact of sharing your own reading with others?

THE FOUR CORNERSTONES OF READERS' WORKSHOP

Let's now proceed with readers' workshop.
Readers' workshop is composed of four primary activities:

Mini-lesson   Reading   Conferencing   Responding

1. Mini-Lesson

While we want students to read as much as possible, there is much we want and need to share, then the mini-lessons are a mechanism by which much instruction is accomplished.

Mini-lessons are short, targeted lessons, addressing particular ideas or topics of which we want students to be aware. There are three categories of mini-lessons: procedural (describes how readers' workshop is conducted), content focused (addresses the elements of narrative and expository text), and process focused (the processes of reading, inferring, predicting, presentations about authors or writing techniques, and also may include reading aloud to the class).

Mini-lessons typically come at the beginning of the class and last from a few minutes to 10 or 15 minutes. The inspiration for mini-lessons comes from multiple sources. There are mini-lessons explaining readers' workshop procedures so students will know how to proceed, those that share important ideas about reading and writing that respond to students' interests, or topics that emerged from student-survey results or expressed interests or needs. Mini-lesson topics may relate to something the teacher has noticed about student-reading activities. For example, a teacher might observe students selecting only one genre. A mini-lesson about different genres and their structure and importance may be an appropriate response.

The list of possible mini-lesson topics is lengthy and may address something in particular students should look for as they read: the use of adjectives, whether a book is written in the first or third person, plot twists, character development, how to select books of interest, kinds of writers, discussion about a particular author, how to use the library, or Internet to access reading material. At the beginning of each instructional period, mini-lessons are quite frequent but become less frequent as the year progresses.

Usually, the school year begins with a mini-lesson describing how the class will be structured, the rules for readers' workshop, and expectations for students and the teacher. Evaluation procedures are discussed so students understand how their progress will be measured. It is common for teachers to survey their students about reading to learn their attitudes toward reading and what they know about books and authors.

Since readers' workshop sometimes involves writing about reading, a mini-lesson on writing responses to reading should be delivered early in the school year. Students unfamiliar with readers' workshop will not know what or how to write about their reading. Since they will begin to experience reading differently, their response will no longer be restating what the author said or presenting basic facts but rather writing about their own reactions to text; what they noticed about the writing, story line, or characters; what they liked about the book or author and why; or how the content relates to what they already know. To respond well, they will need examples of responses and some modeling.

2. Reading

The best way to promote active reading by students is to provide opportunities for sustained silent reading. Students come to value what their teachers value. They understand that time is valuable so what we chose to commit time to ought to be what we most value. When reading is an add-on activity or something to do later, students assign it less value. They begin to expect less from their reading experience and benefit less as a result. Readers' workshop incorporates dependable, predictable opportunities for sustained silent reading. Students are able to anticipate reading time, prepare for reading, and anticipate that reading is expected for the entire reading workshop time.

Fifteen minutes is usually long enough for reading in the beginning. As students grow accustomed to reading independently, this time is gradually increased to 30 minutes or more.

3. Conferencing

Reading conferences are conversations between teacher and student. A conference always includes discussion about the text the student is reading and the student's reactions to his or her reading. It may include reading part of the text orally to check difficulty level or to assess oral reading fluency. Through conferences, reading becomes social, as teachers demonstrate interest in student reading, provide encouragement, expand student awareness of literary elements, and provide opportunities to assess student reading comprehension by asking students to respond to what they have read.

Some suggested conference questions include the following:

- Why did you choose this book?
- Tell me about the book. What part do you like best? Why?
- Tell me more about it. Read the part that is most exciting.
- What parts are unclear?
- How did you feel when this happened?
- What did you think when this happened?
- How can you find out more about your topic?
- What have you learned from this book?
- What problems are you having? What problems did you have?
- Do you feel comfortable with the difficulty level of the writing?
- What questions would you like to ask me? How can I help you?
- What is the story problem of this book? How is it being solved?
- Do you know any other books by this author?
- Were there any words that were unfamiliar? How did you handle them?
- How do you like the subject matter? Is it an area of interest for you? Is this the first time reading about this topic, or are you already familiar with the topic?

Conferencing typically takes place during silent reading time. Each classroom handles conferencing differently according to the number of students and the physical arrangement of the classroom. Conferences usually last three to five minutes per student, allowing time to meet with three to five students during readers' workshop.

One method of managing readers' workshop is for the teacher to move about the classroom with a chair, randomly selecting students for conferencing. The chair keeps the teacher at eye level with students, establishing a more relaxed conference atmosphere. It is important that conferences avoid becoming mini-evaluations. It should remain a dialogue between two readers about reading, with the student doing as much talking as the teacher.

Another way to conference is to have students come one at a time to the teacher's desk or other designated location in the classroom. This may be less disruptive than the teacher moving about the classroom. If students come to the teacher's desk or a table in a corner of the room, students should sit beside the teacher rather than across from the teacher. This contributes to the relaxed nature of conferencing by maintaining the sense of partnership.

Tips for Successful Reading Conferencing

1. Conferences are designed to be relaxed and informal. Since the other students are reading, it is important to speak quietly. Interruptions during conference time are strongly discouraged. Students not conferencing are instructed to ask questions only during the brief breaks between conferences. The teacher-student relationship during conferencing is one of mentor and partner. Students are conferencing to build on what they know and understand about reading and the text they are reading at the time and to demonstrate their reading capabilities so jointly they can decide what is needed next to continue to grow as a reader.

2. Students must have reading material of interest and at an appropriate reading level. Interest can be generated by learning about your students' lives and inclinations and selecting books that connect to their world. Book talks introduce students to books they might never consider but would enjoy if exposed. Book talks also escalate the quality of literature children select by exposing them to the story lines of great books they might otherwise avoid.

3. During readers' workshop, the room must be quiet with no disruptions and no talking—only reading. Establish strict rules about this and enforce them.

4. Everyone in the class must read. Even the most reluctant readers will read if they have a book they have selected and enjoy and expectations for reading are clear. Even students who are resistant in the beginning begin to look forward to the reading and conference time.

   The most rewarding outcome of individual reading conferences is the warmth and understanding that develop between the teacher and students. Students' interests, reading needs, and beliefs about themselves as readers blossom through these interactions.

5. The dialogue between the teacher and the student depends on where the student is in his or her reading at the moment. When a student begins a new book, it is useful to have the student orally read a selection from the book to check for difficulty. Some students like to conference each time they read. Be flexible and schedule the conference times according to students' and teacher's interests and needs. Keeping track of conferences through careful notation on conference cards is a critical management tool. These notes serve as a helpful guide to subsequent conferences. Conference cards are short forms that document the content of the conferences, topics covered, student responses, reading selections, teacher observations, and anecdotal notes.

6. Use a section of the chalkboard to list those students who will have reading conferences that day. Schedule them on the basis of
   - interval between conferences,
   - book completion,

- student request, or
- teacher interest in a particular student's reading activities.

On another section of the chalkboard, list those students not scheduled but who wish to have a conference for their own reasons. After the scheduled conferences and as time permits, meet with students who have signed up. Any students who wanted a conference but did not have one because of time constraints can be scheduled the following day.

4. Responding

Just as students need time for reading, they need time to respond, time to integrate what they have read into what they already think and believe, and they need time to savor their literary experiences. This is understandable for literature study but perhaps less transparent for content study. But when reading is one of the primary means of changing student thinking or increasing knowledge, reader response is an essential part of the teaching-learning process. There are numerous ways students can respond to reading. Later in this chapter, two reader response approaches, Questioning the Author (Beck, McKeown, Hamilton, & Kucan, 1997) and Literature Circles (Short & Kaufman, 1995), are presented. However, first, we will look at reading class activities before examining content-area reading. Conferencing is one means of providing students with opportunities to reflect on and respond to reading. However, conferences are brief and often have multiple agendas, limiting opportunities for responding. Responding to reading is more fulfilling if it resembles more of a sustained dialogue, either oral or written, and occurs student-to-teacher, student-to-student, and within groups.

LITERARY LETTERS

Student-to-student response is critical and can occur on several levels. One way for students to dialogue is through literary letters. These are brief, thoughtful, personal responses to reading intended to stimulate dialogue between two readers. Students will often send letters to introduce friends to a new book or converse with others reading the same book, reading about the same topic, or reading another book by the same author.

Literary letters are often spontaneous, reflecting students' thoughts immediately after they read. They often contain spelling and grammatical errors, and because they constitute writing for thinking and are not intended for wider publication, spelling and grammatical errors are not considered important but simply a reflection of the early stage in the writing process.

BOOK TALKS

Another means of responding to reading is called book talks. Book talks are usually short explanations delivered by a student or teacher about a particular book. It usually involves speaking to the entire class and is a means of introducing a new book or author to the group. Book talks are frequently scheduled at the end of readers' workshop and take about 10 to 12 minutes. This allows time for one or more students to say something about their reading and time for members of the group to respond.

Book talks are an excellent way for students to hear about books their peers are reading and enjoying. They create excitement about reading and provide students with language to express what they understand, how they connect, and their own feelings about what they are reading. It also helps create a community of readers who understand, appreciate, and apply the reading process. It helps students understand that the reading process is not completed when the act of reading is finished; rather, it is completed only when readers have thought about their reading and expressed their thoughts in some form.

There are some important roles for students to understand when holding book talks. These roles are (1) the sharer and (2) the audience or listener. The sharer is the person who will provide the book talk, and the audience includes the sharer's classmates and the teacher.

The sharers should be prepared to

- tell the title and/or author,
- briefly tell about the book or story explaining what happens,
- pick important parts to share,
- choose a favorite part to read or share,
- tell why they chose the book, and
- tell why they like the book or a particular character, topic, line, quote, or idea from the book.

The audience or listeners should be prepared to

- listen,
- say the person's name, then
  - ○ tell what they liked about how and what the sharer talked about,
  - ○ ask what kind of book it is,
  - ○ ask why it was chosen,
  - ○ ask to hear more about it, and
  - ○ tell what it made them think of (some other book; something that has happened to you), and
- use "I like what you said . . ." or "What I found interesting. . . ."

Keeping Track of Reading

An important part of readers' workshop involves students monitoring their own reading activities and progress. Self-monitoring and self-evaluation are important steps for students to take as they become independent learners. They can become proficient, insightful, thoughtful, realistic appraisers of their own development if they are given the opportunity and the means for self-evaluation. This does not mean teachers forsake their responsibility for assessing student progress. In fact, providing honest feedback to students about their academic development is a crucial role for teachers.

Sample Self-Monitoring Goals

- Number of books read
- Frequency of book starts
- Number of books and number of chapters
- Number of book talks lead
- Frequency of literary letters

READERS' WORKSHOP RULES

There are rules that guide readers' workshop, which should be shared with students and posted in the classroom, so students will be clear about expectations. They include the following:

1. You must read the entire time.

2. You may not disturb anyone.

3. No bathroom breaks or drinks are permitted.

4. Choose a book or reading material before readers' workshop.

5. Listen during mini-lessons.

6. Be ready to share when asked.

7. Sit anywhere you are comfortable.

SUMMARY OF READERS' WORKSHOP

Good readers are thoughtful readers. Our goal for reading is beyond fluency to critical, thoughtful reading and to satisfying cases of interestedness, mild or severe. Reaching this goal requires immersing readers in the reading process so readers have opportunities to read in a thoughtful setting where they are exposed to a variety of reading materials for self-selection and have opportunities to correspond with those modeling a love of reading. We know when students take ownership of their reading, the rewards for reading become internalized. Readers' workshop orchestrates a process of shifting the motivation for reading and learning from an extrinsic to intrinsic locus of control, for in the final analysis, what we hope for our students is that they develop an internal drive to read and learn that carries them well beyond the classroom.

ANALYSIS OF READERS' WORKSHOP AND THE ERR FRAMEWORK

Now that you have reviewed the readers' workshop process, look at your journal entry. Think now about how readers' workshop and the ERR framework coincide. Share thoughts with a partner.

It is probably evident that the overall structure of readers' workshop closely parallels the ERR framework. At a global level, the mini-lesson to begin the workshop serves as an evocation process. Whether procedural or literary in nature, it prepares students for the reading process and sets purposes for the reading to come. The sustained silent reading time is coincidental with the realization of meaning phase, and responding to reading is a reflection-stage activity.

Beneath the global structure, there is much about the readers' workshop process that embodies the framework. Once students are actively engaged in readers' workshop, they are engaging continuously in the various stages of the framework. Sending literary letters to one another or completing their reading journals engages students in an ongoing walk through the three stages of the framework. Their discussions take the form of both reflections and evocations. Reflections of their recent reading are transformed through dialogue into evocations about future readings. At the dialogue level, their writing serves as the content, representing valued thoughts about their reading and is indicative of the realizations of meaning phase. Students' dialogue then becomes a mechanism for monitoring how well, how frequently, and how actively students are engaging in various phases of the reading process.

CONTENT READING AND READERS' WORKSHOP

Recent national and international assessments document the decline in American students' content or disciplinary reading abilities (Shanahan & Shanahan, 2008). Students, particularly in middle and upper grades, are failing to comprehend content texts. Even though students read the text, they appear to derive limited benefit from their reading, as the misconceptions, misunderstandings, and information gaps they held prior to their reading remain intact after reading. The absence of thoughtful reading of content text has reached the level of a national emergency. Shanahan and Shanahan offer this gloomy assessment. They write, "American high school students cannot read at the level necessary to compete in a global economy, and many are likely to have difficulty in taking care of their health needs (Berkman et al., 2004) or participating in civic life . . ." (p. 42).

Our most recent example of readers' workshop was intended for implementation in a literature or reading class. This was done intentionally as it is important for content teachers to understand how the workshop engages readers thoughtfully at all stages of the learning process. It is also intended to emphasize the role of time, ownership, and response in any reading exercise, so it is clear these elements should also be planned into content or disciplinary instruction. Furthermore, as recent investigations by Shanahan and Shanahan (2008) suggested, reading demands, the types of reading required, and the skills sets necessary for successful text comprehension vary by discipline. Consequently, no single set of strategies will meet all readers' needs across disciplines. Disciplinary literacy, then, requires composite approaches defined in part by the discipline itself and by instructor purposes and learner outcome expectations. Discipline-specific instruction, then, necessitates teachers knowing about various strategies and what they enable students to do, how they promote thinking, and what type of thinking they encourage. With this more in-depth knowledge of the tools of instruction, teachers can knowingly select the tools that will best lead students to the desired learning outcomes. In the following section, more specific applications of the reading process to content reading are presented to facilitate thoughtful study of content.

APPLYING THE READING PROCESS TO CONTENT AREAS

Consider now how you might apply readers' workshop to a content lesson. With a partner, pick a topic and text and consider how to apply readers' workshop to the lesson.

Reading in Content Areas—Setting the Stage

One of the most difficult aspects of planning for student reading of content text is determining the purpose for reading a selected text and the most important outcomes expected from student reading. Often, we let students guess what is most important or what the teacher expectations are. This works well for students who guess correctly, those who are self-motivated, or those who already have an interest in the topic. For others, this approach leaves them confused, unsure, or unmotivated. The first task we have as teachers is to prepare or set the stage for students to read content text. A few steps for accomplishing this include the following:

1. Having a well-articulated content-based purpose for reading text

2. Presenting *essential* vocabulary that may be unfamiliar

3. Determining how the text will be used to support instruction

4. Encouraging student predictions about content

5. Activating students' prior knowledge of related content

6. Stimulating content-related discussion

7. Considering the concepts required for understanding the objectives of the reading task and checking to see if students have sufficient prior knowledge to understand these concepts

8. Making connections through discussion and developing relations between this content and previous content

9. Explaining clearly expectations and learning objectives for the reading task

10. Developing a sense of questions to guide thinking to higher levels of thought and ultimately to judgments and applications

Reading in Content Areas—Questioning and Discussion

As we have discussed in previous chapters, questioning plays a central role in the thinking process. The kinds of questions students are asked influence the kinds of content-related thinking students perform. In *Reading and Learning in Content Areas*, Ryder and Graves (1994) offer a series of question categories to guide students' content reading. They suggest questions that accomplish the following:

1. Highlight lesson content. Use questions or guides to direct student attention to specific text-based information. Example:
   - In science—be sure you understand the process of homeostasis
   - In art—be sure you understand the differences among color, hue, and color saturation.

2. Integrate lesson content with previously learned material by using questions to connect previous content with new content material. Example:
   - In science—be sure you understand the effects of aging on homeostasis.
   - In art—be sure you understand why the various levels of saturation evoke different types of emotional reactions.

3. Structure higher-level understanding. Provide questions that lead students toward applications of the information to novel situations or contexts. Example:
   - In science—how can our knowledge of homeostasis help us understand the functioning of the circulatory system?
   - In art—what colors would you select for your opponents' pregame locker room?

4. Promote integrations of students' experiences, values, cultural backgrounds, and knowledge with the new learning experience. Ask questions and guide discussion that encourages students to build their own understandings of the text out of an acknowledged set of understandings. Example:
   - In science—be sure you understand the process of homeostasis.
   - In art—be sure you understand the differences among color, hue, and color saturation.

5. Integrate lesson content with previously learned material by using questions to connect previous content with new content material. Example:
   - In science—how is homeostasis influenced by geographic region, environment, and culture, and how does that relate to your life and life-style?
   - In art—certain cultures use different levels of color saturation in their clothes. What are the traditional ancestral colors of this region?

When promoting content-based discussion and asking guiding questions, it is good to keep a few things in mind. First, the conversation should stay focused. The teacher's task is to understand the main objectives of the lesson and what student outcomes are sought. Conversation should center on the main objectives. However, teachers must listen to their students to understand what is behind their thinking rather than considering only what is in their own minds. Too much teacher control will inhibit student thinking and prevent their thinking from coalescing around a topic. Students should be encouraged to engage in speculative thought. Second, discussion is intended to elicit multiple ideas and perspectives and should include as many students as possible. Connections between various student ideas should be emphasized. Third, adequate time should be allowed for students' questions and responses.

APPLYING READERS' WORKSHOP PROCESS TO SCIENCE

As a practical learning task using the following text on geology, let's look at how all this fits together. During the next 30 minutes or so, you will read and prepare a lesson applying the four components of readers' workshop (mini-lesson, reading, conferencing, and responding.) First, read the text and determine the objective of this lesson—that is, what you want your students to know and be able to do after they have read the text, not only now but, say, five years from now. To set purpose and objectives, divide into small groups at random and without regard to grade level or content area. As a group, determine objectives for the lesson, write them down, and use them to guide throughout the lesson. Read the following text (Wolfe et al., 1971) now.

Folds

You have learned how rocks crumble and decompose when exposed to air and water. The products of this weathering are transported by streams and other agents of erosion. Eventually, the fragments and solutions that result from weathering of old rocks are deposited as sediments. If these layers of loose materials are later cemented together, they become sedimentary rocks.

The best evidence of crustal movements is to be found in sedimentary rocks. Sediments are almost always deposited in horizontal layers. As a result, sedimentary rocks should be found in horizontal beds, or strata. Yet layers of sedimentary rocks are often found tilted far from the horizontal. What could happen to rock layers to produce a fold?

It seems obvious that the rocks must have moved in response to pressure. You can model this for yourself by pushing from both sides of a stack of paper. The paper will adjust to the pressure by bulging up into a fold. Similar results are achieved by using clay or other materials that make a more realistic model of rock layers. In clay models, breaks and fault movements are often seen among the folds. Such faults are commonly found in folded rock layers.

Over a large area of land, the layers are often crumpled into a series of folds. The layers rise and fall, much like a series of waves. The upfold is called anticline, the downfold, a syncline. A step-like fold is called a monocline.

You may be wondering how it is possible for a brittle solid, such as rock, to fold. You know from your own experience that you cannot squeeze rocks and change their shape. You have read, however, that rocks below the surface become warmer with depth. They are subjected to enormous pressure from the weight of overlying rocks. Under these conditions, solid rock may react plastically (like putty) to pressure. Most folding apparently occurs in sedimentary rocks that are not fully cemented. The entire process, however, by which various kinds of rocks fold is not clearly understood, and much research remains to be done.

Geologists once believed that folding was caused entirely by horizontal pressure, or compression. Recent experiments have shown, however, that all kinds of folds may develop in layered material around the edges of a rising mass as it pushes upward. When masses of heated rock below the surface expand and push up, overlying rock layers may fold and slip to the sides. Similar features form when masses of salt are pushed up to form salt domes. Salt is a very light mineral. Under pressure at depths, a horizontal layer of salt may bulge and be forced up through the rocks like a bubble rising in water.

Many of the mountain ranges of the world are made up of tremendous thicknesses of sedimentary rock. In some mountains, these rocks appear to have formed from a series of layers of sediments as much as 9 to 10 kilometers thick. Careful study of these rocks shows that the sediments must have been laid down in a large trough. Apparently, the bottom of the trough sank slowly at a rate of about 200 to 300 meters each million years. In most places, the water in the trough appears to have been less than 300 meters deep. Such troughs may be hundreds of kilometers long and tens of kilometers in width. The San Joaquin Valley (The Great Valley of California) is a modern example of such a trough. Such slowly sinking troughs are called geosynclines. Smaller folds are developed in the layers of a geosyncline as it sinks, dragging the rocks downward into the trough. (pp. 162–164)

PLAN

SHARE

Now that you have read the article, proceed to develop your plan. When they are complete, share with others. Your plan should address each of the four components.

- Mini-lesson
- Reading
- Conferencing
- Responding

So when developing the plan, attend carefully to the various ways the components are incorporated into a lesson. Only after you have completed your plan, review the following sample lesson using the "Folds" text.

Sample Lesson

As lesson objectives, students should know the following:

- How geology might influence where and how people live
- What sedimentary rock is and how it changes shape
- How pressure and heat cause rock to change shape to form different land masses
- How sedimentary layers are formed

Mini-Lesson

Share with the class the vocabulary words they will need to know to understand the text. This is often a difficult choice. Some teachers are inclined to choose the most difficult words or those specific to the content area—the technical terms. These words may in fact not be important to know at all. In the "Folds" passage, the vocabulary words most useful for the students to know before reading include the following:

folds	layers	trough	crustal movement	pressure

This selection of vocabulary words may seem surprising, but three thoughts have guided the decision process. First, consider what we want students to remember about this lesson five years from now. What knowledge is most relevant to them? Second, select words that are foundations for the important concepts we wish to develop. Third, examine the text and determine which terms are clearly defined within the text. In the "Folds" text, some might select sedimentary, anticline, syncline, monocline, and geosyncline. Yet all these terms are clearly defined within the text. Furthermore, these words are technical terms used by geologists. They are not terms people typically use to communicate their understanding about geology. For those who wish to become geologists, these terms are important and will become a routine part of their vocabulary later. For eighth graders, they are only tangential to long-term understanding. Yet by providing readers foundational vocabulary that facilitates understanding of the text, students are more apt to recall the technical terms as well, as they will have more cognitive resources available to attend to these terms.

Begin the mini-lesson by asking students what they think about when you speak of land formations. Following a few responses, begin a brief discussion about land formation and how they influence where and how people live. With this background now, share photographs of various kinds of land formations: mountains, canyons, fault lines, or other large geological formations. Center discussion on how these land masses were formed. Review and discuss what students have learned already about this and ask them to consider how the land formations represented in the photos might have come to look as they do.

Encourage students to generate questions of their own before they begin reading. These questions and the identified and defined vocabulary words should be put on the board with instructions for students to link the text to the conversation as they read. Students can now begin reading the text.

Reading and Conferencing

For this lesson, conferencing is handled differently from what is typical of readers' workshop. First, have students form small groups of four or five. As they read independently, move from group to group checking for understanding. Ask students in each group if they are having any difficulties with the text or if they have questions. One or more students might read a paragraph aloud to the group. The teacher should also begin to build on the model of crustal movement by asking about other ways the earth's motion causes land formations. Encourage students to think about various models that they could create to represent the formations discussed in the text. Since this kind of conferencing takes time and the text is short, students in the other groups should be instructed to begin responding to the text within their groups as soon as they are done reading.

Responding

Having been instructed how to proceed before beginning to read, students now discuss first their thoughts and speculations before they read the article and then discuss how their speculations coincided with or were contradicted by the text. They then should work together to develop a model on paper, which would demonstrate formation of one of the geological structures described in the text. Encourage students to respond in their content journal by writing responses to the lesson's objectives (provided at the beginning of the class) using the vocabulary terms identified. Responding in their content journal would end this lesson unless the results indicate confusion or misunderstanding. Reader responses can be extremely informative about student understandings. If confusion or misunderstanding exists or persists, then further discussion is warranted.

READING IN CONTENT AREAS—THE LINK TO MATH

Best practices in math instruction have moved beyond the notion that computational practice and drill are the heart of math instruction. Mathematicians now emphasize that computation, like knowing how to read, is only the beginning of the math process. Mathematics teachers appreciate the instructional value of presenting students with relevant, complex mathematical problems, for which the solutions resolve real problems in concrete ways. National math standards (see NCTM Principles and Standards for School Mathematics at http://standards.nctm.org) emphasize the study of relations between various mathematics concepts rather than merely being able to compute accurately.

MATHEMATICS IS MORE THAN A COLLECTION OF CONCEPTS AND SKILLS

The National Council of Teachers of Mathematics (NCTM) has proposed a series of standards for mathematics instruction based on reconsiderations of what mathematics is and how it should be conceptualized in the classroom. They offer several recommendations:

NCTM goals for all students include the following:

To learn to

- value mathematics,
- communicate mathematically, and
- reason mathematically.

To become

- confident in their ability to do mathematics, and
- mathematical problem solvers.

Mathematical experiences should foster

- the disposition to do mathematics,
- the confidence to learn mathematics independently,
- the development and application of mathematical language and symbolism,
- a view of mathematics as a study of patterns and relationships, and
- perspectives on the nature of mathematics through a historical and cultural approach.

Mathematical tasks should

- integrate mathematical thinking with mathematical concepts or skills,
- capture students' curiosity,
- invite students to speculate and pursue their hunches, and
- test skill development in the context of problem solving.

NCTM also proposes consideration of four basic assumptions about teaching mathematics:

1. The goal of teaching mathematics is to help all students develop mathematical power.
2. What students learn is fundamentally connected with how they learn it.
3. All students can learn to think mathematically.
4. Teaching is a complex practice and hence not reducible to recipes or prescriptions.

Finally, NCTM describes a revised computational model consistent with the ERR framework and the conceptualization of teaching and learning embodied here. NCTM promotes the following:

- Classrooms as mathematical communities
- Logical and mathematical evidence as verification

- Mathematical reasoning
- Conjecturing, inventing, and problem solving
- Connecting mathematics, its ideas, and its applications

CHAPTER REFLECTION

Central to this chapter is the idea that reading, whether narrative or content specific, must become its own reward if we are to successfully develop lifelong readers. There are paths to accomplishing this vital goal. Evidence suggests (Gambrell & Marinak, 2009) that one key to developing self-motivated, lifelong readers is by providing authentic literacy tasks. Another key is providing choice, and a third is providing proximal (reading-related and reading-valued) rewards for reading. Readers' workshop, whether delivered as a part of a literacy course or in content study, offers opportunities for all three "keys" to intrinsic reward.

Earlier, we cited Nell Duke's (2003) research on the prevalence of narrative text and the dearth of experience with informational text and other genres in early reading. She stated the belief that this was a "missed opportunity to better prepare children for later schooling" (p. 1). She suggested informational texts have to combat a reputation for being inherently boring. In this chapter, you experienced various approaches to reading intended to connect readers to reading content regardless of genre. In earlier chapters, you read a variety of texts, some informational and some narrative. With each reading, readers were drawn into the text. Remember how our tearful mother sea turtle laid her golf-ball-size eggs into a tiny hole in the sandy beach, not once but several times yearly, while the males hung out at sea. Recall in "The Sniper," the sights, sounds, and smells of war shattering the serenity of the Irish dawn. As Duke (2003) asserted, our kids are growing up in the information age, and most of it is fascinating, so let's go exploring.

In content-related pairs or small groups where possible, consider for a moment your present or future classroom content. Imagine this content and the various sources and resources available to you from narrative and informational text to electronic media. With all these resources in mind, outline a coherent study sequence, utilizing a blend of genre and media that guides readers through these various mediums while simultaneously guiding them through the three-phase learning framework (ERR). This will take some time to accomplish. Allow 20 to 30 minutes for this once materials are gathered. To make this activity useful and more purposeful, work from genuine content materials and resources.

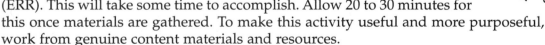

After you have completed your plans, share them with other content-area pairs or groups. Note how the various resources are integrated and check to see that the lesson is coherent and successfully falls under the ERR umbrella. Coincidental with this conversation, address as well the various strategies and methods presented in this chapter and how and where they fit within the ERR framework. Also, consider what types of questioning you might use to guide text exploration or discussion.

8

Learning to Write, Writing to Learn

Students need to tell each other and the world what they know—in order to find out what they know. Through the telling, they will learn. Through the telling, they will interpret the world as they see it to the rest of us.

—Judith Renyi

EVOCATION

This chapter will explore approaches to learning to write and will address writing in content or discipline areas. The approach to writing presented here is a process writing approach based primarily on Nancie Atwell's (1987, 1998) writer's workshop, Lucy Calkins and Shelley Harwayne's (1992) work with workshops and mini-lessons, and the work of James Moffet (1968). Recent reviews of research on writing and writing instruction (Coker & Lewis, 2008) support a process writing approach, especially when accompanied by well-orchestrated, professional development for all teachers, including discipline-specific teachers. We are especially supportive of this as we believe writing to be a powerful tool for learning in all content areas and believe it essential for content teachers to understand process writing and how to effectively incorporate writing as a tool for learning into content classroom instruction.

Before taking a closer look at writing, it will be helpful to take some time to examine your own recent writing experience. Throughout this text, you have been asked to engage in a variety of writing tasks across all phases of the ERR framework. For example, you have been keeping a journal, clustering, writing for cubing, and freewriting. Think for a moment about these writing experiences. Ask whether and how these writing activities have contributed to your own learning during this

STOP
THINK SHARE

professional development sequence. Ask if there are some writing strategies that have worked better for you and others less beneficial. Jot down a few notes in your journal; then share with a partner and finally with the larger group. Conclude with a general discussion about how writing has been incorporated into this text and whether the approach offered here is generalizable to other content-area teachers.

Once you have shared, we will look first at some issues related to writing in U.S. schools, the value of writing as a learning tool, and what recent research suggests are more effective ways of teaching writing and incorporating writing into content instruction. As you begin reading this portion of the text, recall your own experiences with writing, both in and out of school, as a tool for learning and thinking as well as your present use of writing for thinking and learning in your teaching. This thinking will be informative as we move to the final sections of this chapter, in which we present writer's workshop based on Nancie Atwell's (1987) model. This will provide a step-by-step model of process writing that can be applied immediately in your classroom and will be infused with your own insights into the writing process as you have experienced it.

OUTCOME EXPECTATIONS

At the conclusion of this chapter you should be able to do the following:

- understand that writing is best understood as a process, and this understanding is well supported by research on learning to write and writing to learn and understand, as well, the power of writing for thinking and learning;
- recognize that thorough knowledge and application of process writing for content learning is essential for students to benefit from writing-to-learn assignments in the disciplines;
- be prepared to implement writer's workshop or components of this model in your classroom, including those who are content or discipline specific teachers; and
- use the writing process, including prewriting strategies previously described, to support your personal writing.

WRITING RESURGENCE

Today, we are witness to a global resurgence in writing. Not too long ago, many were lamenting the loss of writing as an active form of day-to-day communication. Telephones and televisions moved oral and visual mediums to the forefront. This has all changed with high-speed, portable, Internet access and software to support texting, Twitter, wikis, Facebook, and blogging. Young people enthusiastically engage in writing, some documenting nearly every moment of their existence.

Some of this writing certainly lacks traditional conventions (texting) while some forms serve as platforms for a variety of writing genres (blogging, wikis, etc.). The volume of writing is staggering as instant communication has evolved to constant communication. Young people rarely speak on their mobile phones, as texting has become the preferred medium. To offer an example of the proliferation of writing, from 1999 to 2009 Wikipedia articles have grown from a few thousand to over 13,000,000 in 260 different languages with over 25,000 active editors at any given time.

The one place where writing remains a struggle and is less appreciated and more daunting is in school. In school, many students who text hundreds of times daily, often surreptitiously in class, are suddenly at a loss for words. Certainly, content and expectations differ, but people who gravitate naturally toward writing for day-to-day communication should not suddenly be tongue-tied by a writing assignment. Yet they are. The most recent National Assessment of Educational Progress (NAEP, 2007) report estimates 7 of 10 fourth, eighth, and twelfth graders are "low achieving" writers who fail to meet writing-proficiency goals. Of further concern, Coker and Lewis (2008) suggested writing was increasingly playing a gatekeeping role in the workplace. They reported as well that "U. S. corporations spend an estimated $3.1 billion annually to remediate their employees' writing skills" (p. 234). Compounding remediating student writing deficiencies are two significant writing gaps. One is the broad gap in writing achievement linked to socioeconomic status, gender, and ethnicity. The second is the gap in teacher knowledge about writing reflected in the broad differences between teacher preparation programs in emphasis and perspective on writing instruction.

The contrast between the world of writing outside school and in school may be quite unnecessary. Certainly, among young people, there is an inclination to write when there is perceived value and purpose for writing, an identified audience, or, in many instances, a vast social network, all of which seem more than ever to substantiate the core writing components of social engagement and authenticity.

Yet with all this writing, it is clear that skilled writing does not evolve naturally. As Coker and Lewis (2008) concluded,

> Research into the cognitive processes of expert writers has clearly demonstrated that effective and skilled writing is neither a natural consequence of language developmental nor an organic unfolding of natural developmental processes. Writing is a complicated activity that is dependent on a rich assortment of cognitive processes and on the social context of the writer. (p. 233)

But how do we move students from the comfort of texting, and other forms of more spontaneous electronic authorship, to academic writing? The transition should be easier today because students already understand the social dynamic involved and the power of purposeful written communication. The task of academic writing then should be to help students realize the joy that comes from what Garrison Keillor has often described in his radio program *Writer's Almanac* as the "act of discovery" when engaged in thoughtful writing. Students' nonacademic writing is typically brief and to the point. Academic writing allows students to explore in greater detail what they understand and believe or think about ideas, concepts, or events. These explorations offer genuine opportunities for self-discovery, which can be exhilarating. Too frequently, the joy is lost as otherwise glib and insightful young people clam up, their writing production suddenly plummeting reduced to formulaic prose and paragraph counting.

Where have we gone wrong? James Moffett (1968) informed us that writing in school should be practiced as it is out of school. Writers need real audiences, real topics, real purposes, and they need a process for writing that leads them from an idea to a finished piece of written work. Coker and Lewis (2008) drew the same conclusion from their research review, suggesting that writing is a complicated process, and for adolescent writers, best accomplished when combined with multiple approaches grounded within a process-writing model.

So what is process writing? In brief, the writing process involves a series of experiences and opportunities writers work through that takes them from an idea to a final written piece that communicates effectively with readers and typically includes the conventions of writing, as would a publishable piece of writing. Not all student writing progresses this far, but the writing process can take the writer to publication level when appropriate. The experiences and opportunities that typically define the writing process include immersion in a writing community, frequent and reliable opportunities to write, peer and teacher feedback, multiple draft development involving revisions of text, exposure to explicit writing instruction, editing for final drafts, conferencing, and real audiences to which authors might read their final draft or published works.

Relying on Graham and Perin's (2007) work, Coker and Lewis (2008) encourage teachers to view process writing as an umbrella strategy under which a number of more specialized instructional strategies are applied. Writing research seems to indicate that under a process-writing umbrella, several strategies have emerged as more effectively supporting developing writers. They include the following:

1. Self-Regulated Strategy Development (SRSD), which is itself a process writing strategy involving "explicit instruction in writing strategies and self-regulated methods, mastery learning, and one-on-one instruction" (Coker & Lewis, 2008, p. 237)

2. Collaborative writing, which involves group work at all stages of the writing process

3. Sentence combining or linking sentences together to present increasingly more complex thought

4. Inquiry activities targeted at building in a knowledge base for discipline-specific writing

5. Discipline-specific writing as a means to building content knowledge or for integrating knowledge across content areas

Here, we will present James Moffett's (1968) conception of the context of the writer, and then, in brief, we will explore Nancie Atwell's (1987) writer's workshop as the umbrella process-writing model.

WRITING DEFINED

James Moffett (1968) held that discourse was "a unity—somebody, talking to somebody about something" (p. 14). In Moffett's conception of written discourse, the writer is writing about something he or she has chosen to write about to an audience, which happens to be interested in what the writer has to say. Viewing writing as such a discourse helps understand the need to inform our students that when writing, they are engaged in a conversation. They are talking to somebody they can identify about something they care about and are interested in discussing. It is through this realization of engaged conversation that developing writers will begin to see the power of their own writing.

It may be helpful to view Moffett's (1968) conception of unity as a triangle (Figure 8.1).

Figure 8.1

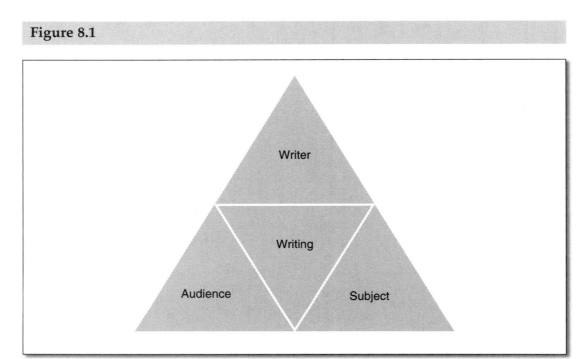

With this model, teachers can see the unity of the process and can serve their students well by emphasizing the elements of writer, audience, and subject when making writing assignments. It is helpful to discuss who the audience is for particular works. Often, the audience in a classroom is other students—either as individuals, in small group, or the entire class. Occasionally, it is the teacher. There is perhaps some value in identifying other intriguing audiences, such as a character from history.

In the case of writing for thinking, the audience may be oneself. The author writes to understand, to clarify, to remember, to organize, to sort out thoughts, to reflect, and to communicate understandings. Often, individual writing will be shared in pairs and then with the entire class. We have found that the conversation following writing to oneself to be rewarding, often filled with surprise at the diversity and development of ideas.

Three basic teaching principles guide the creation of classrooms where writing for thinking flourishes. First, writing for thinking is intended to facilitate thinking and is not graded. If writing is to produce a free flow of ideas, writers must write without concern for mechanics and without being judged for either content or form. Sometimes, students, accustomed to being graded, take some convincing before believing their teachers are truly interested in what they think. Of course, writing that has been through the writing process to final draft may be graded. Second, related to the first but important to distinguish, writers must feel free to take risks. They must believe they can express their thinking freely and that their thinking will be respected. Third, writers must be provided response to the content of their writing, which requires opportunities to share and discuss their writing with others in their writing community.

WRITER'S WORKSHOP

Getting Started

Before proceeding, stop for a moment to consider what might be the first obstacle you as a writer encounter when preparing to write. Think about that moment when you take pen in hand and stare down at a blank piece of paper or gaze into a blank document on your monitor. When you have in mind one or two obstacles you face, remember and read on. For many writers, unless a particular concrete assignment is provided, the initial obstacle is deciding just what to write about. Finding a topic is fraught with difficulty. Often, writers are stymied by their own filtering system. We eliminate potential topics before they have a chance to prove themselves worthy. "No, that's not exciting or interesting enough for a reader." or "Who wants to read about that?" or "I am not a good enough writer to write about that." All these and more haunt writers' topic selection process. And then there is the fear factor (see the following) that Stephen King (2000) refers to in his delightful book, *On Writing*.

The Initial Struggle

What to write about? Finding a topic, theme, or focus for writing is no simple matter. Many writers struggle to locate an entry point for writing; students surely wrestle with this. Even when assigned a topic, determining how to focus, how to narrow to a manageable degree, is challenging.

> Good writing is often about letting go of fear and affectation. Affectation itself, beginning with the need to define some sort of writing as "good" and other sorts of writing as "bad," is fearful behavior.
>
> —Stephen King (2000)

Often, what inhibits young writers is the belief that worthy writing is always about something grand and glorious or explores some wholly uncharted territory. This, of course, is not the case. What writers write about is what they know about. A 2009 interview in the *Bangor Daily News*, Bangor, Maine, with Pulitzer Prize–winning author Richard Russo exemplifies this truth. Speaking to the interviewer about his latest novel, *That Old Cape Magic*, "Russo revealed that both he and his main character were at the same intersection in their lives when he began writing the book" (Herber, 2009, p. D1). Also, Senator Barbara Boxer has written her second novel. Not surprising, her lead character is a female Senator. Nancie Atwell (1987) speaks to the reality of writing about what one knows about when discussing writers' need to establish their "writing territories" (p. 120). In presenting her own running list of topics, genres, and audiences as a model for her students, a list of territories she suggests "represents my self-portrait as a writer," she makes her list " . . . personal, specific, diverse, and unpretentious . . ." (p. 120). She then uses her list to stimulate students to generate their own list of writing territories. She does this in conversations with students about how items found their way to her list. They got there

because they represent real experiences, real memories, real interest, real imagination, and dreams. She then invites her young writers to recall out loud stories of their own.

Once writers begin to develop their own lists, it is useful to pair them so they can share their lists and learn from one another. Students then add to their territories lists throughout the school year.

What we typically do with our students, and what we would like you to do now, is to go through the initial steps of the workshop process as follows:

1. Begin developing your own writing territories. Think of topics that might be of interest to you, using some of the prompts shared by Nancie Atwell (1987). Think as well about the genres you are interested in writing in: poetry, letter, short story, essay, newspaper article, or other possibilities. Finally, consider your audiences: students, parents, community leaders, Wikipedia, blog readers, a relative. The list is endless. To help with the topic search think about the following:

   a. What hobbies you have and how you came to enjoy one of them
   b. A special time you spent with a grandparent or relative and what made it special
   c. Childhood memories of family events or gatherings
   d. A hair-raising experience
   e. A scene you witnessed that you will never forget
   f. A belief you hold strongly and are committed to
   g. A moment when you did something really well and are proud of your success
   h. A funny or embarrassing event that makes you laugh (at least now if not then)

2. Once you have your list, share with a partner. Each of you elaborate (one or two paragraphs) on one or two writing ideas that particularly appeal to you at this moment as potential writing topics. Listen to each brief description and provide feedback as to how the stories might be of interest to a reader.

3. Select a topic, genre, and audience for one of the pieces on which you elaborated and begin writing. Using the freewrite strategy, write for 15 minutes, being sure your writing is sufficiently well developed to be understandable when read to your partner, as you will share this writing.

4. After 15 minutes of writing, share your writing with your partner. As a reader, you are obligated to do two things. One, read what you have written. Do not paraphrase or skip anything. Two, read unapologetically. That is, do not do what so many authors do at this moment and begin with an apology. It is common to hear people begin reading their writing by announcing something like, "This is not so good" or "I couldn't really say what I wanted to" or worse. Here, what is beginning to form is a writing community. Everyone is in the same position, having begun with a freewrite, and has the same responsibility to support her or his fellow writers. All writing at this point is freewriting. It is rough and sketchy at best. That is how it is supposed to be. The role of the listener is extremely important in writer's workshop. The listener is to provide specific, useful, positive feedback to the author. Partners are active working partners, listening to story content, how it is being told,

and responding to the writer with informative comments regarding what works well in the piece of writing, what is of greatest interest to the reader, what a reader would want to learn more about, but also, what is distracting, unclear, or perhaps irrelevant. The respondent also speaks to genre and how well the message is conveyed. Commentary is always supportive and should serve as a positive force for writing growth.

5. With responses in hand, writers now return to writing. Take 20 minutes more to work on your writing piece. Since it is essential that writers always take full ownership of their writing, partner feedback is only advice and suggestion. Each author must decide what feedback to attend to and what to ignore. There is no imperative for writers to accept partner suggestions. For the next 20 minutes, you can extend your work, elaborate on what you have already written, or revise it in some way. Remember that the sharing process will continue within the writer's workshop, and for some, this work will proceed to a finished product to be read to the entire class.

Working through this process, you have participated in the beginnings of writer's workshop. It is only the beginning and in a writing class, likely, the only time everyone will be at the same place at the same time. From here, writers move in quite different directions along unique time lines. That is not to say the teacher sits back and watches as writing unfolds. Quite to the contrary, the teacher's role remains critical. The essential areas of teacher control when orchestrating a workshop include the following:

1. Providing the three cornerstones of writing: time, ownership, and response

2. Creating context

3. Delivering mini-lessons

4. Establishing expectations and setting rules

5. Keeping track

Three Cornerstones

As with readers, writers begin with three basic needs: time, ownership, and response. *Time* on task is necessary for writers to believe they are becoming writers, to sense the true job at hand and the joy of writing. The time committed must be reliable, predictable, and dedicated. Writers must be able to anticipate when and for how long they will be able to write without interruption. Writing is absorbing mental work. Flittering in and out of the task won't do. Furthermore, time is value. Failing to commit time communicates lack of value. What we do not have time for we do not value.

Writing is personal and involves risks. What we commit to paper or to electronic image is forever there. It represents us at a given point in time yet has a timeless presence. Unlike the spoken word, which can be retracted or rephrased, what we write is forever. Since the risks are taken exclusively by the author, ownership of the content must too belong to the author. Without ownership, the author is no longer the somebody speaking to someone but rather the servant to someone. The author's link to the message becomes diluted, and writing is no longer an act of discovery. For writers to sustain their energy and purpose, they must be responsible for the content and take full ownership of the method.

Literacy was borne from community and a commitment to caring (Degnin, 2009). Language represents accrued commonality and agreed realities between peoples. Its various forms of expression have consequence (*response*) as their intention. Writing in a vacuum renders writing meaningless. We could very well add to Moffett's (1968) description of writing as somebody talking to someone about something in anticipation of real consequence. Fundamental to writer's workshop is response. Responses come from the writer, from peers, from teachers, and from other accessible audiences.

Creating Context

Students are remarkably flexible. We ask them to write, and mostly, they do regardless of their surroundings. Yet we know that writing is a demanding task, requiring concentration, readily available resources, necessary equipment, and a relatively risk-free psychological environment. We also know that each writer is different, and each writer needs change from time to time. We recognize these writing realities, but rarely do we accommodate them. To truly facilitate student writing, attention must be paid to the writing climate. Today, students are quite facile writing on computers, though many still prefer paper and pencil. Computer access means access to resource support and boundless information but also access to immediate distractions. Many students cannot compose online without also multitasking, that is, twittering, posting to Facebook, or other distractions. So hard copy resources such as thesauruses and dictionaries and other supportive texts remain essential.

For many students, and more and more, we are learning that for boys in particular, an imposed organizational structure is critical to successful completion of assigned work. An organized workshop enables writers to keep track of their work and their teacher to successfully monitor and evaluate student writing. More important, it provides writers with clear structural support so they are not distracted by wondering how things get done and can attend to only what they must write. Whether you are a working to develop writers or assigning writing for learning, student writers need a supportive setting that enables them to write successfully.

Mini-Lessons

Mini-lessons are a big part of writer's workshop, which we will address briefly here. There is much written about mini-lessons with myriad examples of how to conduct mini-lessons. Calkins (1986) suggests that when done properly mini-lessons can "encourage wide-awakeness" (p. 45). For our purposes, we will speak to the basics of why and how. We mentioned that writing is complex and rarely comes naturally. Learning the conventions of writing, language usage, composition, and genres requires ongoing instruction and practice with plenty of feedback along the way. Writing begins with prewriting and early writing activities that lack conventions and are intended to elicit ideas. And much student writing stays at this level. However, some student writing will progress to more finished levels, displaying proper writing conventions, exhibiting knowledge of a specific content, and residing within a specific genre. Moving from rough draft to final draft demands specific skills that need to be taught and practiced. These skills are best taught within the context of authentic writing so students can apply newfound writing skills directly to their own compositions. As teachers observe student writing, more often topics for mini-lessons emerge from students' own writing and become a natural next step in their writing development.

A mini-lesson is so-called as it rarely lasts more than ten minutes, though some do take longer. They are highly focused and are intended to provide information about a single topic or area that students can then apply immediately to practice. They take several forms. Procedural mini-lessons explain how writer's workshop works. At the beginning of each year or in some cases the beginning of each term, a procedural mini-lesson is offered so students understand from the first class forward how writer's workshop is conducted. For discipline-specific courses, a procedural mini-lesson is just as essential and should include discussion of the role writing to learn plays in learning course content. It might also be a good time to point out that national assessment of content-area knowledge now includes writing samples as part of the testing procedure, so developing the capacity to express one's content knowledge in writing is an essential skill.

Another type of mini-lesson is related to writing conventions. These mini-lessons typically develop out of direct observation of student writing. You may observe students struggling with a particular verb usage or some other language usage issue. They may appear ready to try a new genre but need explicit information before proceeding. Capitalization and spelling issues may need to be addressed or the use of adverbs. Students may not be clear about how to revise a piece they want to move forward to final draft. Mini-lessons can also address content. Students may be expressing some confusion about historical events or need some additional information to understand why an event is important now, though at the time, it did not seem so significant; for instance, the battle in 451 between Attila the Hun and a coalition of Romans and Visigoths (Man, 2005). The Romans and Visigoths were normally enemies but united to stop Attila near what is now Orleans in the heart of France (Gaul). Attila was stopped on the plain there, though allowed to escape with his army partially intact. If not stopped there, Attila would have gone on to take all of Gaul and precipitate the collapse of Rome. All of Europe and the role of Christianity would have changed forever had that battle resolved otherwise.

What makes mini-lessons an essential part of writer's workshop is that the content is usually derived from identifiable student needs when engaged in authentic writing activities. They are intended to take students from where they are and move them forward in their own writing while providing an atmosphere that values writers and the writing process and writing as a tool for learning. Like readers' workshop mini-lessons, writer's workshop mini-lessons afford teachers an opportunity to speak directly with their students about issues central to their daily work. Often, a mini-lesson is delivered to the entire class, but just as often, it is offered to a small group of students taken aside, while the rest of the class is writing, to work on specific needs of those particular writers. When done, in the latter forum, they take on the cast of a conference. Conferencing, as we know from readers' workshop, involves individuals or small groups and usually addresses quite personal needs, issues or levels and/or rates of progress for those readers or writers.

Establishing Expectations and Setting Rules

Writer's workshop works because it is well organized and operates according to specific rules and expectations, and because the rules are adhered to by teacher and students alike. Beginning with the opening procedural mini-lessons, clarifying expectations and setting parameters create a sense of purpose and value for writing that builds respect for the writing process and for each other as writers. It is not enough to state expectations at the outset. Students need the rules restated and enforced in order to develop an appreciation for them. Workshop rules should be few and simple. Be quiet, people are writing; always be writing, revising, sharing your writing with a partner, researching, conferencing, self-monitoring your writing progress, or participating in mini-lessons; always have what you need for writing with you; always provide positive support for the writing of others. We believe in student-developed rules as well. As writing workshop progresses, a mini-lesson may focus on establishing additional rules students believe may further facilitate their own writing work.

Keeping Track

Writer's workshop is a process with many parts. Making it all work for both students and teachers requires a fair amount of record keeping by both students and teachers. In our discussion, we spoke of how essential ownership is to writers. This extends to taking responsibility for maintaining some record of writing activities. In most cases, record keeping is a shared responsibility, as teachers must also hold writers to account for their writing growth, their willingness to be adventurous, and their indulgence in the writing process. Students keep track of their topic search ideas, the pieces they have written, where they are in the development of various pieces of writing, the types of writing they have engaged in, the types of writing they would like to undertake, how long their various writings have been, what they have learned from mini-lessons and conferences, and how it appears in their writing. They may also be responsible for specific documents such as an editing worksheet developed as a reminder of the conventions most often forgotten or something specific to a particular writer. The teacher too maintains records on these same issues in documents shared with the student. In writer's workshop, assessment and monitoring are combined and are conducted as a partnership. To provide specific feedback, teachers also maintain records of conference conversations, goals for each student's writing, including targeted expectations for student development.

Content-Area Writing and Writer's Workshop

Earlier, we promised that content-area teachers would not have to become writing teachers. You don't. However, knowledge of process writing will make content-area writing-to-learn assignments more valuable. Whether writers write for writing class or history class, the process is the same. Writers need a supportive environment (community), opportunity to write, productive feedback throughout the process, clear rules and expectations, opportunities to think first in text and meet conventions later through revisions and editing, and chances to listen and share.

> To steep ourselves in a subject matter, we have first to plunge into it. When we are only passive to a scene, it overwhelms us and, for lack of answering activity, we do not perceive what bears us down: We must summon energy and pitch it at a responsive key in order to take it in.
>
> —John Dewey

Take time now to discuss writer's workshop and what it suggests for how you will incorporate writing into your content instruction. Spend time discussing with a partner or in small groups. If writing is not already part of your content instruction, think as well about how it might serve your content and your students. When this discussion nears an end, say, 15 or 20 minutes, in a small group, add one last dimension. Consider how process writing and the ERR framework might merge. There are some obvious links when we think of moving from a topic search through early writing and conferencing and/or sharing to final draft. There are other, perhaps more subtle, parallels and applications as we contemplate content-area writing to learn. While discussing various application possibilities, keep track of the ideas in your journal. Then on your own, or with a content-area partner, develop a lesson using your own content and applying a writing-for-thinking component embedded within the ERR framework.

Role, Audience, Format, and Topic (RAFT)

RAFT is a writing-to-learn strategy developed by Carol Santa (1988) and her colleagues through the Creating Independence through Student-owned Strategies (CRISS) program. It is a cross-content writing strategy based on prompts for student writing.

RAFT is an acronym for the following:

R—Role (Who are you as a writer?)

A—Audience (To whom is the writer writing?)

F—Format (What form of writing will the author select?)

T—Topic (What will the writing be about?)

RAFT is perhaps best used in the reflection phase as a culminating experience. One important element of this strategy is that teachers can offer a somewhat limited selection of, say, topics but give students choices over the other elements of RAFT. This satisfies the teacher's wish for students to use writing for thinking on a particularly important area of study yet respect the importance of ownership in the writing process through choice. Applying RAFT is relatively easy once students understand some fundamental elements of writing.

R. For example, one critical element related to role that students must understand is that all writing reflects perspective or point of view, and that no writing is without bias. This idea is of course evolutionary in that students awaken to the implications of this idea over time as they mature and realize the significance of perspective in chronicling historical events or writing newspaper reports or political discussions. Students will need familiarity with the different hats they can wear as writers.

A. Audience can be one of the most playful and intriguing elements of writing. Students can learn some critical lessons about writing as a medium for communication by writing on similar topics but to varying audiences. Or students might be assigned a topic and a single audience to address and then compare their writing to see how each approached that particular audience. Another possibility is to present a topic and ask if writing varies according to audience and format.

How might students present an issue if they were texting a friend, twittering or blogging, or writing a formal letter to their senator or the queen of England, their teacher or parents?

F. Conversations about audience, as we have seen, also precipitate deliberations about format. As students learn and become practiced with various writing formats, they are placing more writing tools in their communications toolbox. Students are often eager to learn various formats for writing and seek alternatives to basic narrative writing. Varying format offers opportunities for creative writing and avenues for expression that might not surface if students are limited to basic essay writing.

T. Selection of writing topic often presents the greatest struggle in content-area writing. Teachers usually have in mind some specific essential questions for students to address. When considering topics, it is useful to think in terms of the overarching questions students should address; then consider the conceptual ways in which that essential point can be approached. This can yield differing topic prompts. As is true with any discipline, there is always far more to explore than there is time for in an academic year. Consider the broad array of essential questions and which ones students might be able to extrapolate to from what is presented through the course and make topics available in these areas. Finally, there are always lots of ways to approach any topic. Giving writers the opportunity to think through specific writing prompts, they might like to pursue is an effective way to engage them in writing about central issues for class.

As we have suggested, for RAFT to succeed, students require knowledge of perspectives, audience, and format. These are excellent topics for mini-lessons in writer's workshop. Here, students can be asked to write pieces with particular perspectives that have been discussed and modeled—the same of course for format, role, and audience. Once students are experienced, then RAFT can be quite an effective content area writing strategy.

To implement RAFT, do the following:

1. Be sure students have the skills necessary to apply to the various possibilities RAFT offers.

2. Provide writing prompts and, when needed, sample leads for assorted role, audience, and format options.

3. Ask students to make RAFT choices according to how you would like the assignment to impact both individual writers' needs as writers and the class as a whole. It may be useful at times to have a class diversify choices so, when sharing, students will be exposed to multiple perspectives or formats on a particular topic.

4. Provide students with time to write and the opportunity for feedback. Students should be encouraged over time to vary RAFT selections. Sometimes, students get stuck. It is fine to set expectations for some writing diversity.

Here is one example of RAFT writing choices related to one of our earlier example writing topics. You will recall the discussion regarding land use choices in

Maine and their environmental implications. One RAFT writing choice might look like the following:

R—Environmentalist

A—State of Maine Land Use Regulatory Commission

F—Letter

T—Control of land use along state waterways

Another might include the following:

R—Middle-income all-terrain-vehicle or snowmobile enthusiast

A—Newspaper readership

F—Letter to the editor

T—Accessing land for recreational use

One adaptation to RAFT we are familiar with adds a new dimension to the writing piece. Some are adding an "S" to make the acronym RAFT(S). The "S" refers to "**S**trong verb" and suggests prompting students to reflect on how strongly they feel about a particular topic, whether they are disturbed, angry, curious, confused, quizzical, dumbfounded, enraged, gratified, or relieved, for example. There are times when student sentiment about a topic may be important to the presentation. There are times when this might be less relevant. It is an interesting adaptation to consider. One suggestion to assist students with making choices is to have students keep a chart of their own writing history with various RAFT options that have been presented to them either in general discussion or mini-lessons or they have direct experience with as writers. They can keep this chart in their journal as can you.

Self-Regulated Strategy Development (SRSD)

We mentioned SRSD earlier as one of the process-writing strategies to receive research support for enhancing student writing. SRSD was developed over 20 years ago to support the writing efforts of struggling learners. As we know, writing is a complicated process. Writers need to work hard to develop a message. This requires knowledge of content, organization skills, goal directed activity—both for self-management and as a feature of composition—understanding of audience and perspective, and then the application of formal writing mechanics. Even for skilled writers, these complex processes pose serious challenges. The research on SRSD has demonstrated efficacy of the strategy first for struggling learners and subsequently for all school-aged developing writers. The areas of evident growth for writers using SRSD are in quality of their writing, understanding of writing processes, and their overall approach to writing. Process writing improvements have been demonstrated in draft revision skills, evidence of content knowledge, writing conventions, and the capacity to plan and organize for writing.

Basically, SRSD focuses first on deliberate discussion and elaboration of self-regulatory behaviors essential for most writers to be successful. These include setting purpose and outcome goals; establishing steps or strategies or procedures as self-instructions to achieve goals; monitoring progress, including monitoring goal oriented behaviors; and providing self-reinforcements for achievements. Along with these self-regulatory functions, six phases of prewriting and writing performance are proposed. They include the following:

1. Activating background knowledge and schema for both process and content

2. Determining which strategies to apply, including subsequent outcomes for strategies considered

3. Engaging in cognitive evocation of the application of the selected strategy to the piece of writing being composed

4. Committing the process or strategy to memory so its application is fully realized and then sticking with it

5. Determining in advance available support

6. Engaging independently in the writing process employing the selected strategy

This strategy can be elaborated at multiple levels. More advanced writers write with an awareness of the process, applying it as needed. Less advanced writers can be led with some deliberation through the process until its application becomes more automatic or routinized. What we appreciate about the strategy is that it engages students at both content and process levels. In so doing, it emphasizes the primacy of content while acknowledging the essential role of process knowledge in putting the writing tool to work effectively for learning and communication. This strategy also begins with evocation activities for both process and content, grounding the student before proceeding. It then guides students through a multitiered realization phase that relies on original evocations and is goal oriented, involving writers cognitively and metacognitively. Finally, it leads writers to finished pieces and concludes with orchestrated reader-response activities that facilitate self-reflection on the piece and the process.

CHAPTER REFLECTION

Writing can be a joyful process, a process of illumination and self-discovery. Students do not often feel this way about writing in school. There is much we can do to create an environment for writing that provides students the tools for writing while encouraging them to become lifelong writers. Writing, though, is not simply a subject to be taught. It is also a powerful tool for thinking and learning that can facilitate content-area learning. Certainly, content-area teachers do not wish to become writing teachers, yet the contribution to content-area learning constructive writing activities makes it difficult to ignore. The goal for content-area teachers is to determine how best to incorporate writing into content-area instruction to maximize student learning while remaining focused on essential content. Several strategies are offered here to support content-area writing. It will be useful at this time to gather in small groups to discuss how you will incorporate writing and elements of writer's workshop in your content-area studies. Think about the three cornerstones of writing and the various strategies discussed, and propose ways writing can be introduced in support of content learning. Think as well about the ERR framework. Consider how writing can be incorporated in the various phases and how writing purpose might change as it is incorporated into each of the phases.

9

Reflection

What we achieve inwardly will change outer reality.

—Plutarch

EVOCATION

Before we engage in a discussion about two issues central to our thinking, truth and transformative learning, it makes sense for you to engage in some independent thinking to bring to an awareness level your own views. So we would like you to begin to think about "truth." Truth is a powerful concept about which we all have some thoughts. The pursuit of truth has been, both explicitly and implicitly, a recurring theme throughout the text. When we speak about students engaging in the construction of meaning, truth takes on new dimensions with interesting implications for teachers and students. Discussions about curriculum and what the big ideas and issues are for our lessons take on new significance and lead us in interesting directions. Take five minutes and complete a freewrite on the topic of "truth." Use the freewrite to express your own thoughts on the nature of truth, how you define truth, how you arrive at truth, how you know it when you see it, or how your understanding of truth might impact your teaching. When you are finished, share with a partner, looking for ways differing definitions of truth might have consequences for teaching. Keep these thoughts in mind as you read the rest of this chapter and consider how your present understanding of truth compares with ours.

LEARNING CENTERED

In drawing this professional development sequence to a close, we think it might be useful to offer a summary of the root ideas that have underscored our work together. This discussion represents an attempt on our part to end as we began, with full disclosure. The fundamentals of our beliefs have emerged throughout the text. In

Chapter 3, we discussed Dewey's (1987) ideas of the reciprocal process of learning, and we will go into greater depth below. Throughout the text, we have also referred to the work of the cognitive and motivational psychologist Mihalyi Csikszentmihalyi (1997). His work on *flow* and how people become fully engaged learners also informs our thinking about instruction. We will speak primarily about two basic ideas: transformative educational experiences and truth. You will see that our conception of these two ideas, borrowed from many others, is that they are the result of interplay between what might appear to be opposites but are in reality two complementary elements of a relationship in positive tension. You may recall this idea of joining opposites to bring about a third, more unified idea was first addressed in the introduction. You have likely noticed that in our instructional model, we invite students and teachers to engage one another in a dialogue about ideas and content, and to wrestle with these ideas in a genuine give-and-take. We ask students to step forward and take responsibility for their learning, but we also propose a central role for the teacher. We encourage students to construct meaning from their experiences but also to listen to others and be open to the thoughts and insights of both peers and their teachers. Finally, we encourage teachers to provide instruction that leads to genuine lasting student learning. This requires learning experiences that truly result in permanent change in students. This Professional Development Sequence (PDS) has asked you to become different as an outcome of your involvement. You have been encouraged to become a different teacher from the one you were when you started. Change is hard, so we have not asked this of you without some grounding in theories about learning that make sense to us. We want to review briefly some of that grounding. We also want you to engage in some final thoughts about your involvement in this professional development experience and to consider where you would like to go from here.

We will first speak to the grounding ideas for our belief system regarding thinking and learning and then engage you in some additional reflections. We confess; the discussion of some of our foundational beliefs gets a bit philosophical. It is important to understand how our ideas have coalesced, but sometimes the language gets complicated. Please bear with us, as we hope the discussion to follow opens a window to our thinking that will resonate with you or give ground for a healthy discourse about what it means to learn and what truth looks like. Then, please engage in the final reflections. They constitute an essential reflection on the process you have undergone.

TRANSFORMATIVE EXPERIENCES

As you have worked through this experience, you may have noticed that we are not entirely constructivists. Though there is much that is constructivist in our method, we do not support entirely the student-centered approach. We believe more strongly in the significance of the teacher and of the educative value of both a self-driven, student-controlled approach and an open, reflective, receptive model. David Wong (2007), in his discussion of Dewey's concept of the aesthetic in education, explained the importance of both engaging and engaged students taking responsibility for their learning and, at the same time, bringing to students ideas, interpretations, and experiences apart from their own initiative that invite them to be open and receptive in order to advance their own self-directed learning. For an experience to be educative, he suggests, it must be transformative. That is, it must result in real change. There must be outcomes of the educative experience, and these must be manifest in "new thoughts, feelings, and actions, and also as the world reveals itself and acts on us in new ways" (p. 6). But how do we engage in and orchestrate transformative experiences? For Dewey (1987), transformative experience occurs when we are engaged in a process whereby there is action followed by reflection on the consequences of those actions. In other words, learners have an experience and see that there are consequences to that experience and take time then to be open (receptive) to those consequences and to consider them in meaningful terms that result in real change to the learner. All the better is when these experiences and their consequent reflections occur in cyclical fashion, building on one another toward sophisticated understandings of the consequences of complex experience. He refers to this as a process of *active doing* and *receptive undergoing*. Wong (2007) elaborates,

> The degree that any activity is aesthetic and educative . . . is related to the degree that an active doing and receptive undergoing are joined in perception. We do something, we undergo its consequences, we do something in response, we undergo again. And so on. The experience becomes educative as we grasp the relationship between doing [action] and undergoing [reception]. (p. 6)

How this differs from the purely constructivist ideal is perhaps less clear. Again, Wong (2007) clarifies,

> The ideal relationship between person and world is often embodied in the constructivist vision of student-directed learning. In this view, students control their interactions with the environment and give meaning to what emerges. They are intentional and reflective throughout the whole experience. On the other hand, we are also aware that aesthetic experiences are not "willed" into existence. In fact an excess of conscious control and self-awareness is more likely to obstruct rather than facilitate the having of transformative experiences. (p. 6)

The idea of undergoing requires some broader understanding. It stands in contrast to active doing, so it is receptive in nature. For Dewey receptive undergoing is what enables us to absorb meaningfully our experiences. He writes, "There is . . . an element of undergoing, of suffering in its larger sense, in every experience. Otherwise, there would be no taking in of what preceded" (Wong, 2007, p. 6). For Dewey, learning comes in the evolving interaction between active doing and receptive undergoing, which he refers to as a kind of suffering. This suffering, though, is one that comes with change or transformation. Change can be painful for certain, but at times, it can also be exquisite pain. This suffering refers to the sort of suffering we all experience as we lose part of who we are in order to become someone other as learning and growth occur. If we are to have transformative experiences, then we are necessarily becoming something other than who we were before those experiences. There is a certain mourning for the loss, as in a loss of innocence, but it is temporary and should be a change that in its outcome brings about potential for flourishing.

As we elaborated this professional development experience and the instructional practices it proposes, we considered how to orchestrate experiences that created cycles of active doing and receptive undergoing. In conceptualizing this PDS as a means of engaging in this transformative process, we took Dewey's idea to heart that the " . . . perception of relationship between what is done and what is undergone constitutes the work of intelligence" (Wong, 2007, p. 7).

TRUTH

Complementary to Dewey's transformative paradigm is a notion of truth described by Degnin (2009) to which we subscribe and from which we derive some inspiration for the interactive, learning-centered, educative experience we describe in this text. Without becoming overly obscure, we simply view the seeking of truths as an encompassing goal for our students. For this to make sense, we have to spend a few minutes considering just what truth means and how we come by it. Take a few moments now to review your own thoughts from your earlier freewrite on what truth means for you and how you define truth. Now, read on with these thoughts in mind.

We consider the idea of truth to be a compelling one for educators because, in the words of Francis Dominic Degnin (2009), " . . . the measure of truth of a belief is its success in integrating the whole of experiences in ways which support human flourishing" (p. 6). Certainly, the end point for education is human flourishing. This seems so at the individual as well as the community level. It is why we care about education at all. So how does truth lead to human flourishing? Degnin, in his articles "Truth, Faith and Intelligent Designs: A Pedagogical Essay" and "Talking With Students About Truth: Using Heidegger to Loosen the Grip on Absolutes" provides a guide. Basically, Degnin suggests there is an interactive relationship between an object and our perception of it. He asks how it is we know, for example, that a flag is red. Does the truth of this lie in the flag or in our perception of the flag? He offers that, in essence, " . . . the only way to measure the truth of our perception is by knowing the truth of its object, while the only way to know the truth of our objects is if we know the accuracy of our perceptions" (p. 6). Or more briefly put, truth is found in "the relationship between an idea and its object" (p. 6). "This suggests that truth functions not as an absolutely correct correspondence between our ideas and reality but as a creative means for organizing our experiences in ways which serve our basic needs" (p. 7).

If our aim as educators is to bring students to some form of truth that is transformative and has as its outcome the possibility to flourish, then our task is to guide students through two important relationships. The one relationship is between active doing and receptive undergoing, that is, relations between students' willful exploration and their openness to the consequences derived from that exploration in a reciprocal and ongoing process. The other is the relationship between object and perception, or for our purposes, between content and concept, in an interactive and reciprocal hermeneutic circle that, again, likely describes " . . . how we actually live our lives" (p. 6). So when we create opportunities for reciprocal engagement and reflection in a context of openness (receptively), where teacher and students each play vital roles in negotiating the correspondence between ideas and reality, we set the stage for transformative educative experiences. The ERR framework in its variations offers teachers and students a means whereby they can negotiate these two relations simultaneously. We see the reciprocal and ongoing unfolding of the ERR framework as an instructional framework, which enables teachers to lead students in a quest for truths that, when revealed, enable students to find the experience transformative.

FINAL REFLECTION

We have nearly come to a stopping point. You have worked hard to get here. We hope this path has led to much sharing with your peers and a great deal of discussion about teaching and learning and how best to accomplish both. It will not come as any surprise to you that before this process comes to a close, we would like you to engage in some reflection. Of course, we want you to reflect on multiple levels. This time, we ask that you reflect on the usual two levels of content and process. We also encourage you to look back at the opening quote to this chapter by Plutarch. Plutarch speaks to the change within as the starting point for all other change. We believe ultimately that lasting change

> Education either functions as an instrument which is used to facilitate integration of the younger generation into the logic of the present system and bring about conformity, or it becomes the practice of freedom, the means by which men and women deal critically and creatively with reality and discover how to participate in the transformation of their world.
>
> —Paulo Friere

occurs only when individuals believe and live with new realities, with clear knowledge of new possibilities, and with the intention to realize those possibilities. So begin your reflection by asking yourself if you have experienced change personally through your work with this PDS. If so, how do you know, what does change look like? Has your experience led you to see any new possibilities for your own practice? What are your intentions with respect to these possibilities? How will you realize them? After you have thought about this, do some writing and then share your thoughts with a partner.

Once that discussion has wound down, turn to some reflections on specific content. What has struck you as particularly significant, useful, or intriguing? What do you think might have the greatest impact on your teaching? Are there some strategies you think might be particularly helpful in your teaching? Again, jot down your thoughts and then share with a partner or in a small group. If you have access to a small group, this would be the ideal group to share your thoughts with here.

As you are now accustomed to doing, next, reflect on the process. How well did this professional development experience play out for you? Were you engaged in the activities? Did participation bring you to a fuller understanding of the content and how you might implement the instructional pieces in your own classroom? Think back to your experiences as you proceeded through the PDS and then share your preliminary thoughts with a partner and with a small group.

Finally, using your journal as a resource, take 15 to 20 minutes to write out your reflections from these prompts in a more complete

reflection of your experiences with the PDS and its impact. When finished, first share with a partner and then in a small group. As you share, begin to develop a list of strategies attempted in classrooms of what worked and what was less successful. Return to your ERR chart. Make sure you have it up to date, and then, use it as a guide for discussing implementation.

WHAT TO DO NOW?

Consistent with the ERR framework, we see this professional development experience as embodying the framework. That is, it is structured to provide an ERR experience within an umbrella ERR sequence. But professional development is always ongoing; consequently, completion of this PDS should serve as an evocation for what is to come next in your own professional development. Discuss with your group or think on your own about what should come next for you, for your group.

We would also like you to be aware that in completing this process, you have joined a large, actually huge, family of teachers from around the world with whom we have had the privilege to work. Beginning in the United States, then extending to educators in an enormous number of countries around the world, educators have learned to teach using the ERR framework. They have gone on to develop an extensive list of strategies to complement implementation. Several journals have been spawned in a number of languages enabling teachers to share their work with other teachers, implementing the framework in their classrooms. What has consistently occurred is that teachers who have gone through this experience together have remained in contact to continue their dialogue on teaching and learning and to support one another as implementation proceeds. Many set a series of monthly meetings to be sure to stay in contact, and many set a particular agenda so there are expectations for participants going forward in terms of implementation and sharing successes and struggles. Each group is different. Your group should discuss what makes sense for you and make plans for your continued work. We wish you great success and many transformative experiences that will lead to your flourishing along with your students.

Appendix A

SEA TURTLES AROUND THE WORLD

Sea turtles roam the temperate seas throughout the world. These oddly graceful creatures inhabit the coastal waters of North and South America, the Mediterranean Sea, Africa and India, and the shores of the South China Sea. Many adults live in shallow estuaries and bays or in coastal waters along vast tracks of shoreline. Some even venture up rivers where they are snagged by fishing lines. Of course, they are caught only briefly before snapping the line of some excited fisherman and meandering on their way.

There are six different kinds of sea turtles: Green, Black, Loggerhead, Ridley, Hawksbill, and Flatback. Green sea turtles typically roam from nesting to feeding grounds along the coast. However, some wander across the Atlantic Ocean from the Ascension Islands to Brazil, a journey of over 2,094 kilometers (1,300 miles). Leatherbacks are the champions of long distance migration with some Leatherbacks found as much as 5000 kilometers (3,000 miles) from their nesting beach. One variety of Ridley called an Olive Ridley may be seen traveling in large groups throughout the eastern Pacific and Indian Oceans.

Unlike land turtles, sea turtles cannot retract their limbs, called flippers, or their head into their protective shell. Rather they depend on their size and their hard shell for protection. How big do they get? The Leatherback is the heavy-weight of all sea turtles. An adult can reach 1.9 meters (six feet) in length and weigh up to 500 kilos (1,200 pounds). The record weight for a Leatherback is over 900 kilos or about 2,000 pounds. The smallest is Kemp's Ridley at only 55 to 65 centimeters (22–30 inches) and 30 to 50 kilos (63–100 pounds).

Young turtles are hatched from eggs that have been laid in sand pits on beaches, usually where the mother turtle was born. Female Leatherbacks can lay up to nine clutches of eggs in a season; other sea turtle varieties lay two to three clutches in a season. Typically, the female lumbers ashore at night and lays her eggs in shallow pits she digs with her hind flippers. Once the pit is prepared, the mother will lay from 50 to 200 leathery, mucous covered eggs—each about the size of a ping-pong or golf ball. When the egg-laying process begins, females are unperturbed by their surroundings. They go about the business of laying their eggs as tears stream from their eyes. Some say this is to prevent sand from getting in their eyes. Once the eggs are laid, the females crawl back to the sea and leave their little ones to fend for themselves. The male turtle, though offshore during the egg laying process, never returns to land.

Being a sea turtle hatchling is risky business. Most (90%) do not survive their first hour. As they emerge from the nest, these tiny creatures face almost certain death from fishes, seabirds, raccoons, dogs, and other predators.

Sea turtles are generally solitary creatures. From the time they first enter the water, sea turtles are inclined to spend most of their time alone floating on the surface, taking in the sun's energy. Flatbacks can be seen floating motionless on the ocean surface with a bird perched on their backs. This behavior changes somewhat during nesting season. At this time, usually the warmest time of the year, Olive Ridleys can be found gathering in large numbers in front of their nesting beaches.

Sea turtles' diets vary by species. Loggerheads and Ridleys dine on assorted vegetation, including seaweed and grasses as well as crabs, mollusks, jellyfish, and shrimps. Hawksbills feed in and around coral reefs and prefer sponges, squid, and shrimp. Adult Green and Black sea turtles are the only herbivorous sea turtles, but they are not dedicated vegans, as they will survive as carnivores in captivity without much convincing.

Giant sharks and killer whales are a threat to sea turtles. However, the biggest threat to sea turtles is humans. Besides eating turtles and turtle eggs, long-line fishing practices are deadly for sea turtles. It is estimated long-line fishing kills 4.4 million sea turtles, bullfish, sharks, marine mammals, and sea birds annually. Shoreline development encroaches on sea turtle nesting grounds, limiting population development. Leatherback populations have declined by 95% since 1980 and could disappear in just a few years.

Appendix B

Liam O'Flaherty, born in 1897, certainly may be ranked as one of the outstanding Irish literacy figures of modern times. Some of his works, such as *The Assassin* (1928), *Famine* (1937), and *Land* (1946), have been translated into several languages. Collections of his stories best known in the United States are *The Mountain Tavern and Other Stories* (1929), *Spring Sowing* (1924), and *Two Lovely Beasts* (1948). His numerous works include also verse, plays, biographies, a travel sketch based on a trip to Russia, novels, a tourist's guide to Ireland, and two autobiographical accounts, *Two Years* (1930) and *Shame the Devil* (1934). One of his most famous stories is "The Informer" (1925), which in 1935 was made into a movie that has since become a classic. In 1949, a one-act play version of the story was prepared, and it has been performed with considerable success. The civil war in Ireland that flared during the second decade of this century made a deep impression on O'Flaherty. Many of his best-known writings reflect his experiences during that period of terror and bitterness.

THE SNIPER

The long June twilight faded into night. Dublin lay enveloped in darkness but for the dim light of the moon that shone through fleecy clouds, casting a pale light as of approaching dawn over the street and the dark water of the Liffey. Around the beleaguered Four Courts, the heavy guns roared. Here and there through the city, machine guns and rifles broke the silence of the night, spasmodically, like dogs barking on lone farms. Republicans and Free Staters were waging civil war.

FIRST STOP

On a rooftop near O'Connell Bridge, a Republican sniper lay watching. Beside him lay his rifle, and over his shoulders were slung a pair of field glasses. His face was the face of a student, thin and ascetic, but his eyes had the cold gleam of the fanatic. They were deep and thoughtful, the eyes of a man who is used to looking at death.

He was eating a sandwich hungrily. He had eaten nothing since morning. He had been too excited to eat. He finished the sandwich, and, taking a flask of whiskey from his pocket, he took a short draught. Then he returned the flask of whiskey from his pocket. He paused for a moment, considering whether he should risk a smoke. It was dangerous. The flash might be seen in the darkness, and there were enemies watching. He decided to take the risk.

Placing a cigarette between his lips, he struck a match, inhaled the smoke hurriedly, and put out the light. Almost immediately, a bullet flattened itself against the

149

parapet of the roof. The sniper took another whiff and put out the cigarette. Then, he swore softly and crawled to the left.

He rolled over the roof to a chimney stack in the rear and slowly drew himself up behind it until his eyes were level with the top of the parapet. There was nothing to be seen—just the dim outline of the opposite housetop against the blue sky. His enemy was under cover.

Just then, an armored car came across the bridge and advanced slowly up the street. It stopped on the opposite side of the street, fifty yards ahead. The sniper could hear the dull panting of the motor. His heart beat faster. It was an enemy car. He wanted to fire, but he knew it was useless. His bullets would never pierce the steel that covered the gray monster.

Then around the corner of a side street came an old woman, her head covered by a tattered shawl. She began to talk to the man in the turret of the car. She was pointing to the roof where the sniper lay. An informer.

The turret opened. A man's head and shoulders appeared, looking toward the sniper. The sniper raised his rifle and fired. The head fell heavily on the turret wall. The woman darted toward the side street. The sniper fired again. The woman whirled around and fell with a shriek into the gutter.

Suddenly, from the opposite roof, a shot rang out, and the sniper dropped his rifle with a curse. The rifle clattered to the roof. The sniper thought the noise would wake the dead. He stopped to pick the rifle up. He couldn't lift it. His forearm was dead. "I'm hit," he muttered.

Dropping flat onto the roof, he crawled back to the parapet. With his left hand, he felt the injured right forearm. The blood was oozing through the sleeve of his coat. There was no pain—just a deadened sensation, as if the arm had been cut off.

Quickly, he drew his knife from his pocket, opened it on the breastwork of the parapet, and ripped open the sleeve. There was a small hole where the bullet had entered. On the other side, there was no hole. The bullet had lodged in the bone. It must have fractured it. He bent the arm below the wound. The arm bent back easily. He ground his teeth to overcome the pain.

Then, taking out his field dressing, he ripped open the packet with his knife. He broke the neck of the iodine bottle and let the bitter fluid drip into the wound. A paroxysm of pain swept through him. He placed the cotton wadding over the wound and wrapped the dressing over it. He tied the ends with his teeth.

Then, he lay still against the parapet and closing his eyes, he made an effort of will to overcome the pain.

In the street beneath, all was still; the armored car had retired speedily over the bridge with the machine gunner's head hanging lifeless over the turret. The woman's corpse lay still in the gutter.

SECOND STOP

The sniper lay still for long time, nursing his wounded arm and planning escape. Morning must not find him wounded on the roof. The enemy on the opposite roof covered his escape. He must kill that enemy, and he could not use his rifle. He had only a revolver to do it. Then he thought of a plan.

Taking off his cap, he placed it over the muzzle of his rifle. Then he pushed the rifle slowly upward over the parapet, until the cap was visible from the opposite side of the street. Almost immediately, there was a report, and a bullet pierced the center of the cap. The sniper slanted the rifle forward. The cap slipped down into the street.

Then, catching the rifle in the middle, the sniper dropped his left hand over the roof and let it hang, lifelessly. After a few moments, he let the rifle drop to the street. Then he sank to the roof, dragging his hand with him.

Crawling quickly to the left, he peered up at the corner of the roof. His ruse had succeeded. The other sniper, seeing the cap and rifle fall, thought that he had killed his man. He was now standing before a row of chimney pots, looking across, with his head clearly silhouetted against the western sky.

The Republican sniper smiled and lifted his revolver above the edge of the parapet. The distance was about fifty yards—a hard shot in the dim light, and his right arm was paining like a thousand devils. He took a steady aim. His hand trembled with eagerness. Pressing his lips together, he took a deep breath through his nostrils and fired. He was almost deafened with the report and his arm shook with the recoil.

Then, when the smoke cleared, he peered across and uttered a cry of joy. His enemy had been hit. He was reeling over the parapet in his death agony. He struggled to keep his feet, but he was slowly falling forward, as if in a dream. The rifle fell from his grasp, hit the parapet, fell over, bounded off the pole of a barber's shop beneath and then clattered on the pavement.

Then, the dying man on the roof crumpled up and fell forward. The body turned over and over in space and hit the ground with a dull thud. Then, it lay still.

The sniper looked at his enemy falling, and he shuddered. The lust of battle died in him. He became bitten by remorse. The sweat stood out in beads on his forehead. Weakened by his wound and the long summer day of fasting and watching on the roof, he revolted from the sight of the shattered mass of his dead enemy. His teeth chattered; he began to gibber to himself, cursing the war, cursing himself, cursing everybody.

He looked at the smoking revolver in his hand, and with an oath, he hurled it to the roof at his feet. The revolver went off with the concussion and the bullet whizzed past the sniper's head. He was frightened back to his senses by the shock. His nerves steadied. The cloud of fear scattered from his mind, and he laughed.

THIRD STOP

Taking the whiskey flask from his pocket, he emptied it at a draught. He felt reckless under the influence of the spirit. He decided to leave the roof now and look for his company commander to report. Everywhere around was quiet. There was not much danger in going through the streets. He picked up his revolver and put it in his pocket. Then he crawled down through the skylight to the house underneath.

When the sniper reached the laneway on the street level, he felt a sudden curiosity as to the identity of the enemy sniper whom he had killed. He decided that he was a good shot, whoever he was. He wondered did he know him. Perhaps he had been in his own company before the split of the army. He decided to risk going over to have a look at him. He peered around the corner into O'Connell Street. In the upper part of the street there was heavy firing, but around here all was quiet.

The sniper darted across the street. A machine gun tore up the ground around him with a hail of bullets, but he escaped. He threw himself face downward beside the corpse. The machine gun stopped.

Then the sniper turned over the dead body and looked into his brother's face.

Source: "The Sniper" by Liam O'Flaherty from *Spring Sowing* (© Liam O'Flaherty [1924]) is reproduced by permission of PFD (www.pfd.co.uk) on behalf of the estate of Liam O'Flaherty.

Appendix C

HALLOWEEN THOUGHT: BATS ARE BEAUTIFUL AND DO GOOD DEEDS

Ken Wells

Section 1

Bats are creepy. Bats are ugly. Bats get tangled in your hair. Bats spread lots of diseases. Turn your back and bats will suck your blood.

"People think those things," says Merlin D. Tuttle. "But bats are probably the most misunderstood creatures on the face of the earth."

Mr. Tuttle, among a few dozen of the world's scientists who seriously study bat biology, should know. He has traveled the globe investigating bats. He has braced nights in jungles, scaled mountains, climbed trees, and wandered deep into caves just to get to know bats better.

Bats, Mr. Tuttle concludes, not only have enormous scientific value—current bat research holds promise for improving birth control, fighting cancer, and treating speech defects—but also are often highly intelligent and easily trained. Some large, fruit-eating bats, raised as pets, have shown the affection and loyalty usually associated with the family dog.

Experts in Sonar

The 41-year-old Mr. Tuttle, who earned a doctoral degree studying the winged mammals, adds, "Bats have mastered the night sky like dolphins have mastered the sea." The bat's sonar navigation system, known as echolocation, is so advanced, in fact, that it goes beyond current scientific understanding.

But new, intriguing knowledge that casts more favorable light on the shy, nocturnal creature hasn't seemed to help the bat's rather gloomy public reputation. "Because of fear and ignorance, millions of bats all over the world are being needlessly destroyed," Mr. Tuttle says. "A few species already are extinct, and several more are on the endangered list," he adds.

But Mr. Tuttle and other friends of the bat are striking back. They formed Bat Conservation International, a group that intends to boost bats globally. The organization recently helped set aside a preserve for Britain's endangered horseshoe bats; it began ambitious efforts to preserve bat-cave habitats in the United States, and it is lobbying for increased private and public spending on bat research.

Section 2

But a large part of Bat Conservation International's mission will be to handle the bat's public relations.

"An important part of our job is to rehabilitate the image of the bat," says Stephen Kern, the organization's sole employee.

Currently, Bat Conservation International, based at the Milwaukee Public Museum where Mr. Tuttle is the curator of mammals, is rich in aspirations if not in money or members. But the group already has struck on the pro-bat propaganda front, publishing a pamphlet that obviously reflects Mr. Tuttle's attitude toward bats.

The following are among the pamphlet's bat stats:

- Bats, for their size, are the world's longest-lived mammals, with some species surviving 30 years or more. ("If humans could duplicate bat physiology, we'd all live to be as old as Methuselah," Mr. Tuttle says.)
- About 1,000 bat species exist. They account for about one-fourth of the world's mammal species. An estimated 70 million bats living in a series of caves near San Antonio, Texas, are probably the largest concentration of vertebrates on the planet.
- The world's smallest mammal happens to be a variety of bat the size of a bumblebee. It lives in Thailand.
- One species of bat almost single-handedly pollinates a $90 million fruit crop in Asia. Bats may be the most important seed-dispersing animals in some tropical rain forests.
- Bats eat bugs by billions. A single gray bat, an American species considered endangered, eats about 3,000 insects a night. A 20-million-member colony of Mexican free-tail bats in Texas eats about 250,000 pounds of bugs in a single feeding cycle.
- Bat guano mined from caves is a major source of fertilizer in numerous developing countries. It helps grow about one-third of the world's black pepper.
- Bats are considered quite edible in Asia and Africa and throughout the Pacific. A good bat dinner in a nice restaurant on the island of Guam will cost you $25.

Section 3

Mr. Tuttle doesn't eat bats, but he thinks the fact that others do shows that bats have a usefulness not usually ascribed to them, particularly in Western culture, where bat phobia is most rampant. "Bats in America, Europe and Latin America," he adds, "suffer persecution more than bats in other parts of the world, principally for two reasons: the Dracula-vampire syndrome and overblown fears that they spread disease, particularly rabies."

"Dracula," says Bat Conservation's Mr. Kern, "is all literary and movie hype. The 14th-century Romanian nobleman upon whom the legend is based seems to deserve a bad reputation, considering his penchant for impaling unruly peasants on long wooden stakes. But the bat seems to have just got dragged haplessly into the tale, since there were and are no bloody-sucking bats in all of Europe," Mr. Kern says.

Still, the legend was so persistent that Spanish conquistadors got to the New World expecting to find a blood-sucking bat. When they did, they named it the "vampire," after its fictitious Transylvanian cousin.

The Blood Suckers

Of the three species of blood-sucking bats found in Central and South America, only one is prevalent enough to be considered a dangerous pest. But "it's just a little fellow—about three to four inches long" and clearly prefers cattle to people.

"To judge all bats by the vampire is the same way people used to shoot every hawk they saw because one hawk stole the chicken. Most people treat hawks better than that now, but today all bats suffer because of the vampire's bad reputation," Mr. Tuttle says.

Rabies is a more serious problem, Mr. Tuttle concedes, but even the rabies threat in bats is slight compared with other wild animals such as skunks, raccoons, and foxes in particular—and even compared with household dogs and cats. Of 28 confirmed rabies cases in the United States since 1963, only five have been traced to bats (dogs were the main culprit). And even some of these bat cases are "suspect as to origin," says Denny Constantine, a veterinarian for California's public health service. "In Asia, where rabies control is poorer, only a single case of human rabies has been linked to a bat bite since records have been kept. But 15,000 cases have been linked to dogs," Mr. Tuttle says.

Moreover, Mr. Constantine says, "Bats don't go through the aggressive stage of rabies," meaning they don't usually attack people or other animals unless harassed or touched. So to avoid problem, Mr. Constantine suggests staying away from sick or injured bats or those acting peculiarly.

Section 4

The Ugliness Issue

But on a clear, warm California morning, Philip Leitner has his hands all over bats. Mr. Leitner, a professor of biology at St. Mary's college near San Francisco, is an avid bat hobbyist. He has driven out to a barn in California's wine country to collect a few so-called pallid bats for an upcoming science exhibition.

These tiny, page-brown bats, like most bats, are insect eaters by night and sleepers by day. After climbing into the darkened loft where the bats roost, Mr. Leitner deftly shakes a few into a net and brings them down into the light of day, where an essential question of the bat debate is being discussed: Are bats really ugly?

Whimsical as the question is, Mr. Leitner doesn't mind offering an opinion. An elemental requirement of a bat fancier, he says, is to be someone who "doesn't take himself too serious." Mr. Leitner, whose fascination with bats goes back to his childhood, thinks these bats "are kind of cute."

Actually, they are. On close inspection, pallid bats have endearingly large ears and a kind of friendly, canine face. "The pallid bat," Mr. Leitner says, "is an ordinary-looking bat." He once saw a rare spotted bat that even the most grudging bat-baiter might agree is "spectacular," he says.

Beauty and the Bat

Ask Mr. Tuttle about bat beauty and you get an earful. A crested bat has colors rivaling a peacock's, an African singing bat sports colors so striking that he calls it a "gorgeous little beast."

"Most people," Mr. Tuttle says, "don't get to see bats in all their beauty. In zoos, bats are usually displayed under unflattering infrared lights to simulate their cave environment, although many bats can tolerate a little daylight," according to Mr. Tuttle. "So one campaign of Bat Conservation International will be to persuade zoo keepers to get bats out of the spooky glare of infrared and into the more flattering light of day," Mr. Tuttle says.

"Bat beauty," Mr. Tuttle says, "is more than skin deep." Though he has studied bats since he was a teenager, he says he continued until recently to underestimate the bat's intelligence. But a certain Panamanian frog-eating bat helped change his mind.

The bat, Mr. Tuttle recalls, was a captive that quickly adapted itself to researchers by learning to take frogs from their hands. That done, Mr. Tuttle then hoped to coax the bat to begin swooping on frogs placed in a mock pond, where its tactics could be studied more closely. But the bat, by then, "already was too clever for that," preferring instead to "beg frogs from the researchers," Mr. Tuttle says.

So Mr. Tuttle released the bat and marched a couple of miles through the jungle contemplating how to capture another.

And who should follow? "Our bat flying out of the jungle, trying to land on our hands, " Mr. Tuttle says.

Source: *The Wall Street Journal* (1983, October 27). Reprinted with permission.

(Please note: This article has been subdivided for demonstration purposes. It is not necessary to reproduce the text when applying the various methods to text in your textbooks. Simply orally identify breakpoints so students will be clear what parts they are to read.)

Appendix D

THE HEART BEAT

Robert I. Macey

Section 1, Part A

1. Like any muscle, the heart can be stimulated, and it will conduct action potentials. In many ways, it behaves like a skeletal muscle, but there are some exceptions. Skeletal muscles contract only if they receive some external stimulus. Ordinarily, the stimulus is a nerve impulse leading to the muscle. This is not true of the heart muscle, which seems to be capable of exciting itself. Even if we cut all the nerves leading to the heart, it will continue to beat. This capacity for self-excitation is common to all heart tissue.

2. If we remove the heart of a cold-blooded animal (a frog, say) place it in a dish, and cover it with Ringer's solution, the heart continues to beat—even when it is completely disconnected from the body. If we now cut the heart into pieces, even the pieces continue to beat. However, some pieces beat faster than others. Those from the upper parts of the heart (the *atrium*) beat faster than those from further down (the *ventricle*).

Section 1, Part B

3. We do not know what causes this built-in rhythm of the heart. In a normal heart, the various parts do not beat at different times and with independent rhythms. This is because there is an excellent conduction system in the heart. The first piece of tissue that becomes excited generates an action potential. The action potential is then quickly transmitted to all parts of the heart, exciting the entire tissue. As a result, the entire heart beat is coordinated, pumping with maximum force, and sending the blood surging into arteries.

4. Figure D.1 shows the heart in more detail. In addition to being divided into a right and left side, each side is subdivided into two chambers—the atrium and the ventricle. At the rest, the atrium serves as a storage depot for blood returning from veins toward the heart. When the heart begins its beat, the atrium contracts first. Although it may help fill the ventricles with blood, it plays a very minor role in the pumping of blood. A moment later, the ventricles contribute most of the pumping action in the heart. The right ventricle is responsible for pumping blood through the lungs; the left ventricle is responsible for pumping blood through the rest of the body.

156

Section 2, Part A

One-Way Flow

5. When the heart muscles contract, why isn't blood squirted backward into the veins as well as forward into the arteries? And when the heart relaxes, why doesn't blood flow into it from the veins and arteries?

6. Imagine that the heart is transparent and that we can watch the action of blood flowing in and out of it (Figure D.1). First, we see the heart at rest and notice valve flaps between the atrium and ventricle (A-V valves) on each side of the heart. Blood is pushing down on them from above. Below the flap there is very little pressure because the heart is relaxed. This means that the pressure of the blood from above pushes the flaps open and fills the ventricle.

Section 2, Part B

7. Now, the muscles in the walls of the heart start pumping. They begin contracting and squeezing the blood in the ventricles. This is the last time when we might expect blood to flow back into the veins through which it entered, but as we watch, we notice something happening to the valve flaps. The pressure below the flaps is now much greater than the above. This forces the flaps of the valve toward one another until they close up tight. Blood cannot push its way back into the atria. Instead, it is forced into the arteries. The opening into the arteries is guarded by two other sets of valves, located between the ventricles and their arteries. When the heart was at rest, these valves were closed tight. The pressure in the arteries was greater than the pressure in the ventricles; this kept the valves shut and prevented blood backing up from the arteries into the ventricles. (Notice that the flaps of these valves do not hang down into the ventricle like A-V valves. Instead, they point upward into the arteries.) When the heart makes its pumping stroke, the high pressure of the blood in the ventricle pushes on the flaps of the valves, guarding the arteries and forces them open. Blood now flows through the open valves because the pressure of blood in the ventricle is now greater than the pressure in the artery. Each time the valves open and close, they produce a sound. If you listen closely to your heart beat, you hear two distinct sounds: "lub-dup." The first sound corresponds to closure of the A-V valves, the second to snapping shut of the valves between the ventricles and arteries. When these valves are damaged, the sounds change. For example, damaged valves between the left ventricle and aorta convert the sound to "lub-shh."

Section 3, Part A

Cardiac Output

8. The amount of blood pumped by the heart is staggering. When you are at complete rest, your heart pumps enough blood to fill four automobile gasoline tanks each hour. Let's break this down into more precise figures. During rest, the heart beats about 70 times per minute. During each beat, each side of the heart pumps roughly 70 ml of blood. The amount of blood pumped during each minute would then equal 70 ml per beat × 70 beats per minute, or 4,900 ml per minute (almost five liters, or 5.25 quarts, per minute).

Figure D.1   Blood flows into the heart from the veins when the heart is at rest. When the heart contracts, blood is forced into the arteries. Valves in the heart prevent blood from flowing in the reverse direction.

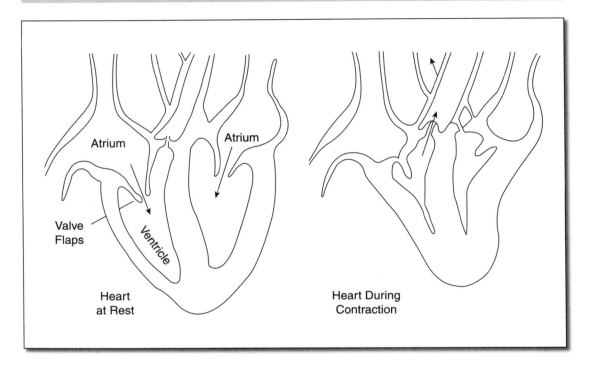

9. The amount of blood pumped by each side of the heart during each minute is called the cardiac output. During activity, the cardiac output changes. When you exercise strenuously, your cardiac output may rise to as much as 25 liters per minute. When a trained athlete exercises, his output may go as high as 40 liters per minute.

Section 3, Part B

10. The cardiac output is controlled in part by nerves of the autonomic nervous system. Impulses carried by sympathetic nerves to the heart tend to increase cardiac output by increasing both the rate of the heart beat and the strength of each beat. Impulses carried by the parasympathetic nerves to the heart tend to decrease cardiac output by slowing the rate of heart beat.

Section 4, Part A

Coronary Circulation

11. Blood leaving the heart enters the aorta en route to the organs of the body. The heart itself is one of these organs, and its thick muscular walls must be supplied with fresh blood. This is accomplished through the coronary circulation. You can see from Figure D.2 that coronary arteries arise from the base of the aorta and send blood back into the walls of the heart. These vessels branch into smaller arteries and capillaries that are imbedded in the heart muscle and, finally, blood is conveyed into the right atrium primarily through a large vein called the *coronary sinus.*

Figure D.2 The Coronary Arteries

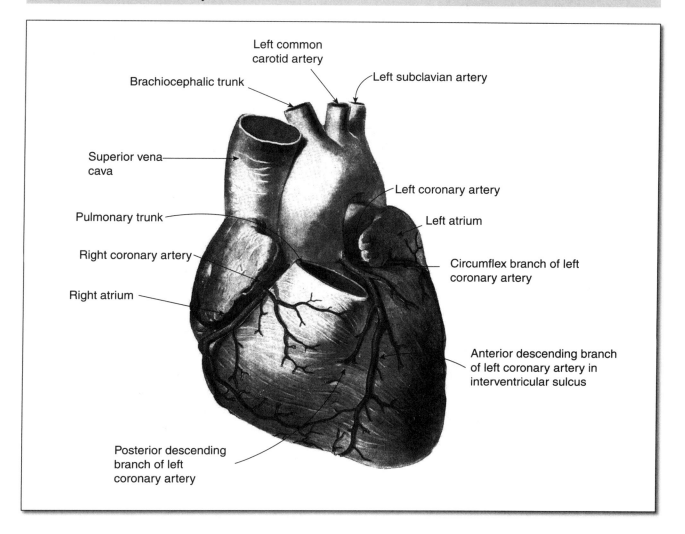

12. When one of the coronary vessels becomes occluded, the portion of the heart supplied by that vessel is deprived of oxygen and energy sources, and it stops contracting. This is what we call a heart attack. When a large portion of the heart is involved, it will no longer pump enough blood for survival. Coronary occlusion is responsible for about 30% of all deaths.

Section 4, Part B

13. Coronary occlusion often results from a disease called *atherosclerosis* in which fatty substances containing large amounts of cholesterol are deposited in the walls of arteries. In later stages of *arteriosclerosis*, fibrous tissue and calcium compounds intermingle with the fatty deposit so that the vessel walls become more rigid; this is called *arteriosclerosis* (hardening of the arteries).

If the fatty deposits break through the inside lining of a blood vessel, they form a surface on which the blood can clot. The vessel may become occluded at the site where the clot has formed, or the clot may break loose only to occlude another vessel downstream. Death occurs if a coronary occlusion is severe. If only a small coronary vessel is involved, the heart is weakened but may improve with time as connections with neighboring blood vessel enlarge to supply new blood.

(Please note: This article has been subdivided for demonstration purposes. It is not necessary to reproduce the text when applying the various methods to text in your textbooks. Simply orally identify breakpoints so students will be clear what parts they are to read.)

Appendix E

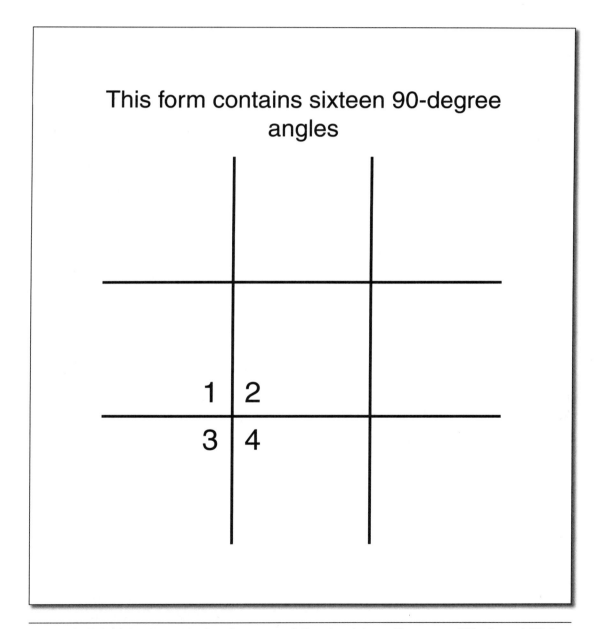

This form contains sixteen 90-degree angles

1 | 2
3 | 4

Appendix F

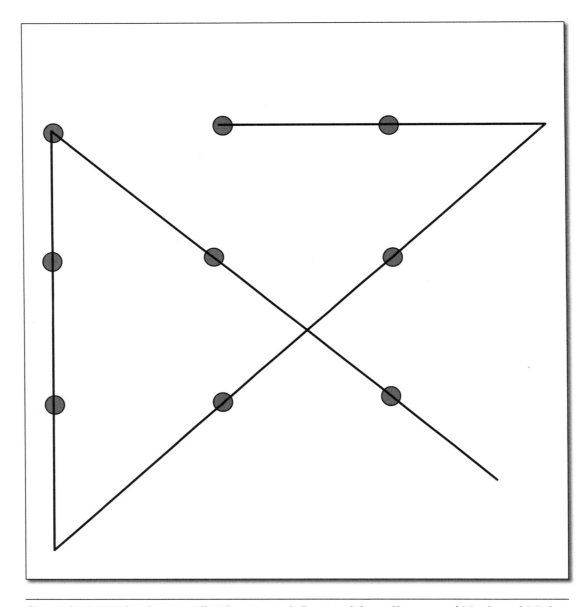

References

Anders, P., & Bos, C. (1986). Semantic feature analysis: An interactive strategy for vocabulary development and text comprehension. *Journal of Reading, 29*(7), 610–616.

Atkin, J. M., & Karplus, R. (1962). Discovery or invention? *Science Teacher, 29*(5), 45–47.

Atwell, N. (1998). *In the middle: New understandings about writing, reading, and learning.* Portsmouth, NH: Boynton/Cook.

Atwell, N. (1991). *Side by side: Essays on teaching to learn.* Portsmouth, NH: Heinemann.

Atwell, N. (1987). *In the middle: Writing, reading, and learning with adolescents.* Portsmouth, NH: Boynton/Cook, Heinemann.

Baloche, L. (1998). *The cooperative classroom.* Upper Saddle River, NJ: Prentice-Hall.

Barr, C. & Harbison, C. (2009). Book title output and average prices: 2004–2008. *Library and Book Trade Almanac, 54,* 504–512.

Beck, I. L., & Dole, J. A. (1992). Reading and thinking with history and science text. In C. Collins & J. N. Mangieri (Eds.), *Teaching thinking: An agenda for the 21st century.* Hillsdale, NJ: Erlbaum.

Beck, I. L., McKeown, M. G., & Gromoll, E. W. (1989). Learning from social studies texts. *Cognition & Instruction, 6*(2), 99–158.

Beck, I. L., McKeown, M. G., Hamilton, R. L., & Kucan, L. (1997). *Questioning the author: An approach for enhancing student engagement with text.* Newark, DE: International Reading Association.

Bloom, B. (Ed.). (1956). *Taxonomy of educational objectives: Handbook I. The cognitive domain.* New York: David McKay.

Boorstin, D. (1983). *The discoverers.* New York: Random House.

Brown, A., Palincsar, A., & Armbruster, B. (1984). Instructing comprehension-fostering activities in interactive learning situations. In H. Mandl (Ed.), *Learning and comprehension of text.* Hillsdale, NJ: Erlbaum.

Bybee, R. W., Powell, J. C., & Trowbridge, L. W. (2008). *Teaching secondary school science: Strategies for developing scientific literacy* (9th ed.). Upper Saddle River, NJ: Pearson.

Cai, M. (2002). *Multicultural literature for children and young adults: Reflections on critical issues.* Westport, CT: Greenwood Press.

Calkins, L. (1986). *The art of teaching writing.* Portsmouth, NH: Heinemann.

Calkins, L. M., & Harwayne, S. (1992). *Living between the lines.* Portsmouth, NH: Heinemann.

Coker, D., & Lewis, W. E. (2008). Beyond writing next: A discussion of writing research and instructional uncertainty. *Harvard Educational Review, 78*(1), 231–251.

Costa, A. L. (1992). An environment for thinking. In C. Collins & J. N. Mangieri (Eds.), *Teaching thinking: An agenda for the 21st century* (pp. 169–181). Hillsdale, NJ: Erlbaum.

Cotton, K. (2003). *Principals and student achievement: What the research says.* Alexandria, VA: Association for Supervision and Curriculum Development.

Cowan, E., & Cowan, G. (1980). *Writing.* New York: Wiley.

Csikszentmihalyi, M. (1997). *Finding flow: The psychology of engagement with everyday life.* New York: Basic Books.

Csikszentmihalyi, M. (1975). *Beyond boredom and anxiety.* San Francisco: Jossey-Bass.

Cukier, K. (27, February 2010). Data, data everywhere. A special report on managing data. *The Economist, 394*(8671), 3–18.

Dansereau, D. F., & Johnson, D. W. (1994). Cooperative learning. In D. Druckman & R. A. Bjork (Eds.), *Learning, remembering, believing: Enhancing human performance* (pp. 83–111; references pp. 319–327). Washington, DC: National Academy Press.

Darling-Hammond, L., & Bransford, J. (Eds.). (2005). *Preparing teachers for a changing world: What teachers should learn and be able to do.* San Francisco: Wiley & Sons.

Degnin, F. D. (2009). Truth, faith, and intelligent design: A pedagogical essay. *Universitas: The University of Northern Iowa Journal of Research, Scholarship, and Creative Activity, 5*(1), 1.42–3.42.

Dewey, J. (1987). My pedagogic creed. *The School Journal, 54*(3), 77–80.

Dillon, J. T. (1983). *Teaching and the art of questioning.* Bloomington, IN: Phi Delta Kappa.

Duke, N. K. (2003). Reading to learn from the very beginning: Information books in early childhood. *Young Children, 58*(2), 14–20.

Eisner, E. (2002). *The educational imagination: On design and evaluation of school programs.* Upper Saddle River, NJ: Merrill/Prentice Hall.

Elbow, P. (1982). *Writing without teachers.* New York: Oxford University Press.

Francis Dominic Degnin. (2009, Spring) Truth, faith, and intelligent design: A pedagogical essay. *Universitas: The University of Northern Iowa Journal of Research, Scholarship, and Creative Activity, 5*(1).

Freire, P. (1970). *The pedagogy of the oppressed.* New York: Seabury.

Friedman, T. L. (2005). *The world is flat: A brief history of the twenty-first century.* New York: Farrar, Straus and Giroux.

Gambrell, L. B. (1980). Think time: Implications for reading instruction. *The Reading Teacher, 34*, 143–146.

Gambrell, L., & Marinak, B. (2009). Nurturing the motivation to read. *Reading Rockets.* Retrieved December 10, 2008, from http://readingrockets.org/article/29624

Gardner, H. (1999). *The disciplined mind: What all students should understand.* New York: Simon & Schuster.

Gillet, J. W., & Temple, C. (1995). *Understanding reading problems: Assessment & instruction* (4th ed.). White Plains, NY: Longman.

Goddard, Y. L., Goddard, R. D., & Tschanner-Moran, M. (2007). A theoretical and empirical investigation of teacher collaboration for school improvement and student achievement in public elementary schools. *Teachers College Record Volume, 109*(4), 877–896. Retrieved April 10, 2009, from http://www.tcrecord.org/content.asp?contentid=12871

Graham, S., & Perin, D. (2007). *Writing next: Effective strategies to improve writing of adolescents in middle and high school.* Washington DC : Alliance for Excellent Education.

Greene, M. (1994). Difference, inclusion, and the ethical community: Moving beyond relativism. In C. K. Kinzer & D. J. Leu (eds.), *Multidimensional aspects of literacy research: Theory and practice. Forty-third yearbook of the National Reading Conference* (pp. 28–29). Chicago, IL: National Reading Conference.

Gunning, T. (2007). *Creating literacy for all students.* Boston: Allyn & Bacon.

Herber, H. (1970). *Teaching reading in content areas.* Englewood Cliffs, NJ: Prentice Hall.

Herbert, R. (2009, August 3). Author Richard Russo draws from his own experiences for new novel "That Old Cape Magic." *Bangor Daily News,* Bangor, Maine, p. D1.

Hotovsky, P. (2008). Coconut. *In bending the notes* (pp. 3–4). Charlotte, NC: Main Street Rag.

Johnson, D., & Johnson, R. (1989). *Cooperation and competition.* Edina, MN: Interaction.

Johnson, D. W., Johnson, R. T., & Bartlett, J. K. (1990). *My mediation notebook.* Edina, MN: Interaction Books.

Johnson, D., Johnson, R., & Holubec, E. (1993). *Circles of learning cooperation in the classroom.* Edina, MN: Interaction.

Kagan, S. (1992). *Cooperative learning.* San Juan Capistrano, CA: Kagan Cooperative Learning.

King, S. (2000). *On writing: A memoir of the craft.* New York: Scribner.

Kleitzen, S. B., & Dreher, M. J. (2003). *Informational text in K–3 classrooms: Helping children read and write.* Newark, DE: International Reading Association.

Klooster, D. J. (2001). What is critical thinking? *Thinking classroom, 2*(4), 36–40.

Klooster, D. J., Steele, J. L., & Bloem, P. L. (Eds.). (2002). *Ideas without boundaries: International education reform through reading and writing for critical thinking.* Newark, DE: International Reading Association.

Kostalova, H. (2003, January). Jeannie Steele thinks about how ERR was developed and many other ideas. An interview. *N.O.T.E.S., Orava Association for Democratic Education, 4,* 3–4.

Langer, J. A., & Applebee, A. N. (2007). *How writing shapes thinking: A study of teaching and learning.* WAC Clearinghouse Landmark Publications in Writing Studies. Available at http://wac.colostate.edu/books/langer_applebee/

Man, J. (2005). *Attila: The barbarian king who challenged Rome.* New York: Thomas Dunne Books.

Manzo, A. (1969). The ReQuest procedure. *Journal of Reading, 31*(11), 123–126.

McArthur, J. W., & Sachs, J. (2009). Needed: A new generation of problem solvers. *Chronicle of Higher Education, 55*(40), 64.

McLuhan, M. (1964). *Understanding media: The extensions of man.* New York: McGraw Hill.

McKeown, M. G., Beck, I. L., & Sandora, C. A. (1996). Questioning the author: An approach to reading meaningful classroom discourse. In M. Graves, P. Van den Broek, & B. M. Taylor, (Eds.), *The first r: Every child's right to read.* New York: Teachers College Press.

Meredith, K. S. (2002). Freedom, responsibility, and democratic schools. *Thinking Classroom, 3*(2), 39–43.

Meredith, K. S. (2001). The political and historical context for education reform in Central and Eastern Europe and Central Asia. In D. J. Klooster, J. L. Steele, & P. L. Bloem (Eds.) *Ideas without boundaries: International reform through reading and writing for critical thinking* (pp. 22–37). Newark, DE: International Reading Association.

Meredith, K. S., & Steele, J. L. (1997). Learning for understanding. In Z. Kollarikova, P. Gavora, J. Steele, & K. Meredith (Eds.), *Critical thinking II.* Bratislava, Slovakia: State Pedagogical Institute of Slovakia.

Meredith, K. S., & Steele, J. L. (1996). Questioning for critical thinking. In P. Gavora, J. L. Steele, K. S. Meredith, & Z. Kolláriková (Eds.), *Pedagogical Spectrum, 4*(11–12), 15–36. Bratislava, Slovakia: State Pedagogical Institute of Slovakia.

Meredith, K., Steele, J., & Kikusova, S. (2001). Critical issues: Democracy, community, self, literacy, and the values of global conversation. *Journal of Literacy Research, 33,* 169–202.

Meredith, K., Steele, J., & Temple, C. (1998). *Creating thoughtful readers.* Newark, DE: International Reading Association.

Moffett, J. (1968). *Teaching the universe of discourse.* Boston: Houghton Mifflin.

Morrow, J. B. (2008). Book trade research and statistics. Prices of U.S. and foreign published materials; American book production 2004–2007. *Bowker Annual Library and Book Trade Almanac, 53,* 505–566.

National Assessment of Educational Progress. (2007). Available at http://nationsreportcard.gov/writing_2007

National Council of Teachers of Mathematics. (1989). *Curriculum and evaluation standards for school mathematics.* Reston, VA: Author.

National Endowment for the Arts. (2004). *Reading at risk: A survey of literacy reading in America.* Washington, DC: Author.

Nelson, G., & Ockenga, E. (1997). *Democratic practices in math in elementary school.* Bratislava, Slovakia: Orava Foundation for Democratic Education.

O'Flaherty, L. (1924, January 12). The sniper. *The New Leader.*

Ogle, D. M. (1992). Developing problem solving through language arts instruction. In C. Collins & J. Mangieri (Eds.) *Teaching thinking: An agenda for the 21st century* (pp. 25–40). Hillsdale, NJ: Lawrence Erlbaum Associates.

Ogle, D. (1986). K-W-L: A teaching model that develops active reading of expository text. *The Reading Teacher, 39,* 564–570.

Palincsar, A. S., & Brown, A. L. (1989). Instruction for self-regulated reading. In L. B. Resnick & L. E. Klopfer (Eds.), *Toward the thinking curriculum: Current cognitive research* (pp. 19–39). Alexandria, VA: Association for Supervision and Curriculum Development.

Palincsar, A. S., & Brown, A. L. (1984). Reciprocal teaching of comprehension-fostering and comprehension-monitoring activities. *Cognition and Instruction, 2,* 117–175.

Palmer, P. J. (1998). *The courage to teach: Exploring the inner landscape of a teacher's life.* San Francisco: Jossey-Bass, Inc., Publishers.

Paul, R., Elder, L., & Nosich, G. (1995). *Critical thinking: How to prepare students for a rapidly changing world.* Cotati, CA: Foundation for Critical Thinking.

Pearson, P. D., & Fielding, L. (1996). Comprehension instruction. In R. Barr, M. L. Kamil, P. Mosenthal, & P. D. Pearson (Eds.), *Handbook of reading research* (vol. 2). White Plains, NY: Longman.

Pearson, P. D., Hansen, J., & Gordon, C. (1979). The effects of background knowledge on young children's comprehension of explicit and implicit information. *Journal of Reading Behavior, 11,* 201–209.

Pittelman, S. D., Heimlich, J. E., Berglund, R. L., & French, M. P. (1991). *Semantic feature analysis: Classroom applications.* Newark, DE: International Reading Association.

Pressley, M. (2002). Comprehension strategy instruction. In J. Osborn & F. Lehr (Eds.), *Literacy for all: Issues in teaching and learning.* New York: Guilford.

Rényi, J. (1993). *Going public: Schooling for a diverse democracy.* New York: The New Press.

Richardson, J. (1996, Dec.–1997, Jan.). Leading the way to the cooperative school. *School Team Innovator,* 2–6.

Rico, G. (2000). *Writing the natural way,* (2nd ed.). Boston: Houghton Mifflin.

Rosenblatt, L. (1978). *The reader, the text, the poem: The transactional theory of the literary work.* Carbondale, IL: Southern Illinois University.

Roth, K. J. (1990). Developing meaningful conceptual understanding in science. In B. F. Jones & L. Idol (Eds.), *Dimensions of thinking and cognitive instruction* (pp. 139–175). Hillsdale, NJ: Erlbaum.

Rumelhart, D. E. (1982). Schemata: The building blocks of cognition. In J. Guthrie (Ed.), *Comprehension and teaching: Research and reviews* (pp. 3–26). Newark, DE: International Reading Association.

Ryder, R. J., & Graves, M. F. (1994). *Reading and learning in content areas.* New York: Macmillan.

Saletan, W. (2007, Sept. 23). The double thinker. *New York Times Book Review.*

Sanders, N. M. (1969). *Classroom questions: What kinds?* New York: Harper & Row.

Santa, C. (1988). *Content writing, including study systems.* Dubuque, IA: Kendall/Hunt.

Shannon, P. (2007). *Reading against democracy: The broken promises of reading instruction.* Portsmouth NH: Heinemann.

Shannon, P. (1989). *Broken promises: Reading instruction in twentieth-century America.* Granby, MA: Bergin & Garvey.

Shanahan, T., & Shanahan, C. (2008). Teaching disciplinary literacy to adolescents: Rethinking content-area literacy. *Harvard Education Review, 78*(1), 40–59.

Short, C., Harste, J., & Burke, C. (1996). *Creating classrooms for authors and inquirers.* Portsmouth, NH: Heinemann.

Short, K., & Kauffman, G. (1995). "So what do I do?" The role of the teacher in literature circles. In N. Roser & M. Martinez (Eds.), *Book talk and beyond: Children and teachers respond to literature* (pp. 140–149). Newark, DE: International Reading Association.

Sill-Briegel, T. & Camp, D. (2000, May). Using literature to explore social issues. *The Social Studies, 91*(3), 116.

Slavin, R. (1986). Learning together. *American Educator, 10*(2), 6–11.

Stahl, S. (1999, March). Bringing old ideas to new times: Learning principles of Kurt Lewin applied to distance education. *The Technology Source.* Available online at http://ts.mivu .org/default.asp?show=article&id=38

Steele, J. L. (2001). The reading and writing for critical thinking project: A framework for school change. In D. Klooster, J. L. Steele, & P. L. Bloem (Eds.), *Ideas without boundaries: International reform through reading and writing for critical thinking.* Newark, DE: International Reading Association.

Steele, J. L., & Meredith, K. S. (1995). *Democratic pedagogy national staff development manual.* Bratislava, Slovakia: Orava Foundation for Democratic Education.

Steele, J. L., & Meredith, K. S. (1991). *Working together—Growing together: Constructive evaluation of language learning.* Moline, IL: Moline Public Schools District 40.

Steele, J. L., & Steele, P. (1991). The thinking-writing connection: Using clustering to help students write persuasively. *Reading Horizons, 32,* 41–50.

Szasz, T. (1974). *Childhood: The second sin.* London: Routledge & Kegan-Paul.

Tatum, A. W. (2005). *Teaching reading to black adolescent males: Closing the achievement gap.* Portland, ME: Stenhouse Publishers.

Temple, C., & Gillet, J. (1996). *Language and literacy: A lively approach.* New York: HarperCollins.

Temple, F. (1997). *Tonight by sea.* New York: HarperCollins.

Tierney, R. J., Readence, J. E., & Dishner, E. K. (1985). *Reading strategies and practices.* Boston: Allyn & Bacon.

Vacca, R. T., & Vacca, J. L. (2008). *Content area reading: Literacy and learning across the curriculum* (9th ed.). White Plains, NY: Longman.

Vaughan, J. L., & Estes, T. H. (1986). *Corn or maize: What good is it? Reading and reasoning beyond the primary grades.* Boston: Allyn & Bacon.

Voss, J. (1992). Introduction to chapter 1. In C. Collins & J. N. Mangieri (Eds.), *Teaching thinking: An agenda for the 21st century.* Hillsdale, NJ: Erlbaum.

Vygotsky, L. (1962). *Thought and language.* Cambridge, MA: MIT.

Warnock, J. (2001, Jan–Feb). Brief reviews of major works of James Moffett. *The Voice, 6*(1), 14–15.

Wells, K. (1983, October 27). Halloween thought: Bats are beautiful and do good deeds. *The Wall Street Journal.*

Whitehead, A. N. (1957). *The aims of education and other essays.* New York: Macmillan.

Wolfe, C. W., McCombs, L. W., Skornik, H., Battan, L. J., Fleming, R. H., & Hawkins, G. S. (1971). *Earth and space science* (2nd ed.). Lexington, MA: D. C. Heath & Co.

Wong, D. (2007). Beyond control and rationality: Dewey, aesthetics, motivation, and educative experiences. *Teachers College Record, 109*(1), 192–220. Retrieved January 23, 2009, from http://www.tcrecord.org

Yangchen, P. (2009). *Teacher learning in a Tibetan school in exile: A community of practice perspective.* (Unpublished doctoral dissertation.) University of Northern Iowa, Cedar Falls.

Yopp, R. H., & Yopp, H. K. (2000, February). Sharing informational text with young children. *The Reading Teacher, 53*(5), 410.

Zelina, M. (1994). *Strategie a metody rozvoja osobnosti dietata.* Bratislava, Solvakia: IRIS.

Zelina, M., & Zelinova, M. (1990). *Rozvoj tvorivosti deity a Maltese.* Bratislava, Slovakia: Slovenske Pedagogicke Nakladatelstvo.

Index